DICTIONARY OF
LITERATURE IN
ENGLISH

WITHDRAWN

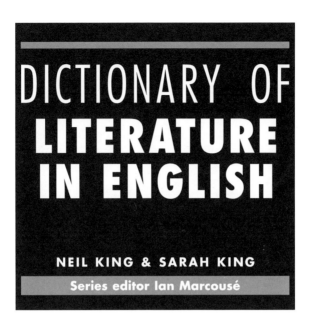

DICTIONARY OF
LITERATURE
IN ENGLISH

NEIL KING & SARAH KING

Series editor Ian Marcousé

FITZROY DEARBORN PUBLISHERS
LONDON · CHICAGO

Copyright © 2001, 2002 Neil King and Sarah King

This edition based on *The Complete A-Z English Literature Handbook*, first published in the United Kingdom by Hodder and Stoughton Educational, 2001

Published in the United States of America by
Fitzroy Dearborn Publishers
919 North Michigan Avenue
Chicago, Illinois 60611
USA

A Cataloging-in-Publication Record is available from the Library of Congress

ISBN 1-57958-381-4

First published in the USA 2002

Typeset by GreenGate Publishing Services, Tonbridge, England and Alacrity, Banwell Castle, Weston-super-Mare, England

Printed in the USA by Edwards Brothers, Ann Arbor, Michigan

PREFACE

It is not intended that this book should cover every technical term, concept, and writer in English. The aim is to focus upon those that a high school or college student might encounter, adding a few extra useful terms and writers in order to achieve a reasonable level of completeness. Each entry begins with a straightforward definition, followed by some selected detail. In the interest of clarity there is a good deal of simplification.

One of the most important uses of this book is as a cross-referencing tool. Cross-referenced entries are in *italics*, and they have been constructed so that a web of entries interrelate in order to give an overall picture of areas of interest: for instance, *literary theory* will lead on to entries such as *structuralism* and *postmodernism*, and then into related areas such as the traditional *Leavisite* views on *practical criticism*.

A major purpose of this book is to provide a quick overview on writers who may crop up in classroom discussion or in reading related to course assignments. Each writer is defined by type, significant preoccupation and/or style, and a selection of notable works. Sometimes collections and selections of a writer's work are listed that, while strictly speaking are not "notable" works, may help direct you to useful publications. This book covers literature in English, not just English literature, and hence writers using English outside the United States and Great Britain are also included. There are a few selected entries devoted to writers in a foreign language who have had a major influence on literature in English.

This book is a companion, to be dipped into as the need arises to enhance your overall grasp of literature written in English, which in turn will give you the confidence to lift your work to the highest level of which you are capable.

Neil King, Sarah King

ACKNOWLEDGMENTS

We would like to thank Philippa King for her help with background research on various authors; Professor Angus Ross, Liz Whittome, and other readers for their helpful suggestions while the work was in progress; Greig Aitken of Hodder for his sensitive editorial assistance; and Neil's English Literature students, who kept asking questions that have helped us to clarify what we wanted to write.

abridged: this term indicates when passages of a book have been omitted in order to produce a shortened version of the original.

Abse, Dannie (b.1923): Welsh poet, playwright, novelist, and autobiographer. Much of his writing is firmly rooted in his own experience as a Jewish, Welsh doctor. Notable works include ASH ON A YOUNG MAN'S SLEEVE (1954), FUNLAND AND OTHER POEMS (1973), WHITE COAT, PURPLE COAT: COLLECTED POEMS 1948–1988 (1989), A POET IN THE FAMILY (1974), THE VIEW FROM ROW C (1990).

abstract can refer to:

- a summary or outline of a piece of writing
- ideas (rather than "things," which are concrete).

An example of abstract language is "Hope springs eternal in the human breast" (*Pope*). See *concrete language, concrete poetry*.

absurd, theater and literature of the, focus upon a notion that human existence is essentially absurd and meaningless, and that humans are isolated individuals in an alien universe. The theater of the absurd came to prominence in the 1950s, combining *existentialism* with *farce* to provide a type of *black comedy*. Notable among absurd *dramatists* are *Beckett* (especially WAITING FOR GODOT and ENDGAME), Eugene Ionesco (1909–94), *Pinter*, N.F. Simpson (b.1919). See *surrealism*.

accent: another word for *stress*, particularly in a line of *verse*.

Achebe, Chinua (b.1930): Nigerian novelist and poet. His themes concern such matters as European attitudes toward and impact upon Africa, and African social and political problems. As a critic he argues that the African *novel* must be concerned with local issues and avoid a contrived universality, but at the same time he defends writing in English rather than his native Ibo because he accepts the reality that he must gain as wide an audience as possible for his ideas. Notable works include THINGS FALL APART (1958), NO LONGER AT EASE (1960), ARROW OF GOD (1964), A MAN OF THE PEOPLE (1966), ANTHILLS OF THE SAVANNAH (1987), HOME AND EXILE (2001).

Ackroyd, Peter (b.1949): English novelist, biographer, poet, and critic. Most of his *novels* are a mingling of *genres* that explore the relationship between the past and present in a kind of *faction*, and are often located in London. Notable works include EZRA POUND AND HIS WORLD (1980), HAWKSMOOR (1985), CHATTERTON (1987), FIRST LIGHT (1989), DICKENS (1990), DAN LENO AND THE LIMEHOUSE GOLEM (1994), LONDON: THE BIOGRAPHY (2000).

act: a section of a play. *Elizabethan* and other traditional *drama* is made up of five acts, which divide very roughly as follows:

- act I – *exposition*
- act II – *rising action* or complication
- act III – *crisis/ climax/ turning point*
- act IV – *falling action*
- act V – *catastrophe, dénouement,* and *resolution.*

The German critic Gustav Freytag (1816–95) saw this sequence as pyramid-shaped, act III being the point of the pyramid. Over the past 200 years the number of acts in a play has gradually diminished; nowadays, two acts with one interval is the norm.

action may mean:
- the unfolding of a series of events in a *story* or play
- the *plot* as a whole.

actual reader: see *implied reader*.

adaptation: any reworking of one medium into another. The most popular kind is the translation of *novels* into films or television scripts, e.g. *Austen*'s SENSE AND SENSIBILITY into a film, or *Waugh*'s BRIDESHEAD REVISITED into a television drama serial. The art of such adaptation can be creative in itself, and if successful can have a stimulating effect upon the sales of the original book. The study of "*text* into pictures" has become a popular subject in both schools and universities.

Adcock, Fleur (b.1934): New Zealand-born British poet. Her *poetry* has been noted for its sensitive yet shrewd observation of contemporary society, unsentimental treatment of relationships, psychological insights, and classical *themes*. Notable works include SELECTED POEMS (1983), THE VIRGIN AND THE NIGHTINGALE (1983, translation of medieval Latin *poems*), LOOKING BACK (1997).

Addison, Joseph (1672–1719): English essayist, journalist, poet, and playwright. Associated with *Steele* and *Jonathan Swift*. He founded THE SPECTATOR magazine, which is still published, his many public and political posts influencing his writing. He is best known for his journalism, written in refined, accessible *prose* known as "middle style," which was acclaimed by *Johnson*. Other notable works include THE CAMPAIGN (1705) and CATO (1713).

Admiral's Men, The: a company of Elizabethan actors managed by *Henslowe*, and rivals to The Lord Chamberlain's Men (later *The King's Men*). *Shakespeare* wrote for both companies at various times.

aesthetic distance: see *distance*.

aestheticism was a late 19th century European movement, originating principally in France, which advocated the appreciation of "art for art's sake," reacting among other things to Victorian materialism and *utilitarianism*. *Ruskin*, *Swinburne*, and *Wilde* were among the foremost proponents of the movement in England. The *poetry* of the *Pre-Raphaelites* is characteristically aesthetic in its sensuousness and striving for musical effect rather than sense; in America *Poe* advocated the importance of "the poem for the poem's sake." Eventually followers of the movement began to dress, speak, and behave in an affected manner, becoming increasingly eccentric in their views and sliding into what became known as *decadence*. See *aesthetics*.

aesthetics is the appreciation and study of beauty, and is linked to notions of good taste in the arts. See *aestheticism*.

affectation, in a literary sense, is the use of a pretentious *style* of writing that is unsuited to the *form* or subject matter.

affective fallacy: the idea that it is inappropriate to judge a *poem* by its emotional or other impact upon the reader, and that *poetry* should be judged by *objective criticism*. *Reader-response theory* is a reaction to this idea. See *intentional fallacy, new critics*.

age of reason: see *Enlightenment*.

age of sensibility (or **age of Johnson):** generally considered to cover *literature* written in England between approximately 1745 and 1780.

age of transcendentalism: a term sometimes used to cover types of American *literature* written in New England during the *American renaissance*. See *transcendentalism*.

Agee, James (1909–55): American novelist, poet, screenwriter, and film critic who often brought an objective reporter's eye to his writing. Notable works include LET US NOW PRAISE FAMOUS MEN (1941, a touching account of the plight of Alabama sharecroppers during the 1930s Depression years), AFRICAN QUEEN (1951, film script with John Huston), and the semiautobiographical A DEATH IN THE FAMILY (1957).

agitprop is nowadays used to describe leftwing writing that is overtly political in its aims. The word is a conflation of "agitation" and "propaganda" from the Russian word "Agitpropbyuro," or "Office of Agitation and Propaganda," which was founded by the Communist Party of Russia in 1920 to make sure that all arts were in line with communist doctrine. *Brecht* and, to a lesser extent, *Fugard* are among *dramatist*s whose plays may be described as agitprop. See *documentary theater*.

agrarians: an early 20th century movement of American writers who favored the idea of "back to nature" or "back to grass roots."

Aidoo, Ama Ata (b.1942): Ghanaian playwright, novelist, poet, *short story*, and children's writer. Her plays offer constructive but uncompromising criticism of Ghanaian society and are often concerned with the position of women in African society as a whole. Notable works include THE DILEMMA OF A GHOST (1964), CHANGES (1991).

Albee, Edward Franklin (b.1928): American playwright. Influenced by the *theater of the absurd*, his plays often express disillusionment with the values of middle-class America. He claims that his intention as a *dramatist* has always been "to offend – as well as to entertain and amuse." Notable works include THE ZOO STORY (1959), THE AMERICAN DREAM (1961), WHO'S AFRAID OF VIRGINIA WOOLF? (1962), A DELICATE BALANCE (1966).

Alcott, Louisa May (1832–88): American novelist and *short story* writer, best known for her domestic *novel* LITTLE WOMEN (1868–69), written for young girls but enjoyed by a wide adult readership. Alcott's tale of four sisters growing up in a close-knit New England family proved hugely popular, and a series of books known as the "Little Women Series" followed. Other notable works include AN OLD-FASHIONED GIRL (1870), EIGHT COUSINS (1875), JACK AND JILL (1880), A MODERN MEPHISTOPHELES (1889).

aleatory writing refers to *poetry* and other arts where the elements (words, in the case of *literature*) have apparently been put together as if by the throw of a dice. In fact there is nearly always some *method* behind such apparent randomness. Among others *Ashbery* and *William Burroughs* have been described as employing aleatory *technique*s. Jackson Pollock (1912–56) is regarded as having used such techniques in painting, and there are many examples in the field of music.

alexandrine: a type of metrical line, also known as iambic hexameter. *Pope* considered the line to be clumsy, illustrating it in his ESSAY ON CRITICISM thus:

> A needless Alexandrine ends the song
> That like a wounded snake drags its slow length along

The alexandrine after the pentameter makes the point, but Pope cheats a little by using monosyllabic words, which often create a slowing effect, in the alexandrine. *Spenser* in THE FAERIE QUEENE and *Keats* in "The Eve of St. Agnes" both use alexandrines to good effect. See *meter, Spenserian stanza.*

alienation effect: this term refers to stage presentation by means of which, through *devices* such as *songs* that preview or review the *action*, and *heroes* and *heroines* with unattractive *character* traits, the audience is alienated, and thus, unlike in more *naturalistic* or realistic *drama*, is prevented from becoming emotionally involved, and helped to employ reason rather than emotions and to maintain an objective critical *viewpoint* of the play's subject matter. This device was evolved by *Brecht* through the work of his Berliner Ensemble. See *Brechtian, distance, epic theater.*

allegory is something that can be read with two *meanings* – an obvious literal meaning and a "below the surface" meaning. Often there is a point-by-point parallel between the literal and the symbolic meanings. Allegories are a way of conveying comment upon people, moral or religious ideas, historical and/or political events, and/or theories. In medieval times a popular *device* was the dream vision whereby the *narrator* supposes that s/he falls asleep and has an allegorical dream, e.g. *Dante*'s DIVINE COMEDY, *Langland*'s PIERS PLOWMAN, *Chaucer*'s HOUSE OF FAME. *Bunyan*'s PILGRIM'S PROGRESS is one of the best known of allegories: it is about a man called Christian and his journey to the Heavenly City, but it represents anyone's struggle through life. Allegories may be of any length from brief *poems* (e.g. those of *Blake*) to a whole book (e.g. *Spenser*'s THE FAERIE QUEENE or *Orwell*'s ANIMAL FARM). It is closely related to *fable* and parable.

alliteration: the use of repeated consonants in neighboring words, most often at the beginning of those words, e.g. in *Percy Shelley*'s "O wild west wind." It is a fundamental *device* in the alliterative *verse* of Old English such as BEOWULF (8th century), THE WANDERER and THE SEAFARER, and medieval *poetry* such as SIR GAWAIN AND THE GREEN KNIGHT and *Langland*'s PIERS PLOWMAN (both 14th century). It can create a strong effect by introducing pattern into the language. See *assonance, consonance.*

allusion: a reference, sometimes implicit, to any aspect of another piece of *literature*, art, or life in general. *T.S. Eliot*'s THE WASTE LAND is full of allusions, some of which he explains in his notes to the *poem*. Allusiveness can enrich a *text* for a reader who recognizes the allusions. See *intertextuality.*

alternate rhyme or **alternate rhyming couplets** is the rhyming of alternate lines of *verse* (abab). See *rhyme, rhyming couplets.*

alternative literature is a term applied to any writing that at the time seems to be outside the mainstream, such as *underground literature*. Such writing as has any merit invariably becomes a part of the mainstream, e.g. significant elements of the *Beat movement*. See also *subversion.*

Alvarez, A. (b.1929): English poet, critic, and novelist. Influenced by *Donne* and *Empson*, he rejected *the Movement*, preferring the work of various American poets. His *poetry* is marked by economy of language and tight *verse form*. Notable works include THE SHAPING SPIRIT (1958), THE SCHOOL OF DONNE (1961), THE NEW POETRY (1962).

ambience is another word for *atmosphere*. See also *mood, tone*.

ambiguity, thoroughly explored by *Empson* in his SEVEN TYPES OF AMBIGUITY, is the ability of words and sentences to have more than one *meaning*, deliberately or unintentionally. Sometimes ambiguity is the result of *connotations* of which the individual reader is aware but the writer is unaware. See also *pun*.

ambivalence occurs when the reader has mixed feelings or opposing views toward an event or object, e.g. perhaps toward Lear in the first two *acts* of KING LEAR. An ambivalent attitude can be built up by a writer presenting the *narrative* from more than one *viewpoint* (see *narrator/narrative voice*), e.g. in *Faulkner*'s AS I LAY DYING or *Graham Swift*'s LAST ORDERS.

American renaissance: a term sometimes used to cover American *literature* written between the period 1828–65.

Amis, Kingsley (1922–95): English novelist and poet. Associated with *the Movement* and the *angry young men*, his *novels* are often comic and mildly *satirical*, with his later works taking on a darker *tone*. Notable works include LUCKY JIM (1954), TAKE A GIRL LIKE YOU (1960), THE ALTERATION (1976), JAKE'S THING (1978), THE OLD DEVILS (1986).

Amis, Martin (b.1949): English novelist, *short story* writer, essayist, and journalist. Son of *Kingsley Amis*, he is *witty*, cynical, and fiercely *satirical*, and one of the most stylistically inventive of modern *prose* writers. Notable works include MONEY (1984), EINSTEIN'S MONSTERS (1987), LONDON FIELDS (1989), TIME'S ARROW (1991), NIGHT TRAIN (1997).

amplification is a *rhetorical device* in which language is used to emphasize, magnify, or extend. *Dickens* often used the device, most famously in his opening to BLEAK HOUSE to create an *atmosphere* of fog, literal and *metaphorical*. See *palilogy, repetition*.

anabasis is the building toward the *climax* of the *action*.

anachorism: any aspect of an *action*, *character*, or *scene* that is out of sequence, usually as a deliberate part of the *structure*. See *analepsis, flashback, in media res, prolepsis*.

anachronism: anything that is too early or too late for a given time period. It may be a mistake, but more often it is a deliberate ploy in *literature* or dramatic productions to stress the timelessness of the universe. For instance, *Shakespeare*'s reference to a clock in JULIUS CAESAR; or the setting of his HENRY V within the *context* of the Falklands War (as by the English Shakespeare Company in 1987) might give a sense of the play having a contemporary meaning.

anagnorisis means "recognition," and is the moment when one or more *characters*, often the *protagonist*, recognize the truth. The word can apply to *tragedy* or *comedy*, but is most often applied to the former, e.g. when in *Shakespeare*'s OTHELLO the Moor realizes that Iago has practiced against him, or in KING LEAR when the king faces the fact that he is "a very foolish, fond old man." See *Aristotle, peripeteia*.

analepsis is another term for *flashback*. See also *anachorism, flashforward, in media res*.

analogues are *stories* that have parallels in other cultures, languages, and/or *literatures*. For instance, in medieval literature there are many analogous stories of knights or other *heroes* slaying dragons or monsters.

Anand, Mulk Raj (b.1905): Indian novelist and *short story* writer. Much influenced by time spent in England, he tries to blend indigenous language *rhythms* and story-telling *methods* with contemporary literary *techniques*. He is known for his concern for human rights and realistic and sympathetic portrayal of the Indian poor. Notable works include UNTOUCHABLE (1935), COOLIE (1936), THE VILLAGE (1939), THE SWORD AND THE SICKLE (1942), THE BIG HEART (1945).

anapest: a single anapestic foot. See *meter*.

anapestic: see *meter*.

anaphora: a *rhetorical device* where a word or group of words is repeated in successive clauses. It can be found in many literary *forms* including *songs*, *ballads*, psalms, and *prose*. A famous nonliterary example is British prime minister Winston Churchill's (1874–1965) "We shall not flag or fail. We shall go on to the end... We shall fight them on the beaches... We shall never surrender." See *incremental repetition*, *rhetoric*.

anastrophe: a more extensive changing around of word order than *hyperbaton* by which whole phrases are altered from their normal order for emphatic effect. Used in both *prose* and *poetry*, it has an impact upon the reader that involves confusion as much as enlightenment.

anatomy: a thorough examination of a subject, sometimes partly *satirical*, e.g. *Lyly*'s EUPHUES: OR, THE ANATOMY OF WIT, Robert Burton's (1577–1640) ANATOMY OF MELANCHOLY (1621). Sometimes *fiction* can be part anatomy, as in *Melville*'s MOBY-DICK which is in parts a whaling handbook.

Anderson, Sherwood (1876–1941): American novelist, *short story* writer, and playwright. His most widely known work is WINESBURG, OHIO (1919), a *collection* of *tales* (called "*grotesques*" by the *author*) about a small-town community in the American midwest. Other notable works include the *story collections* HORSES AND MEN (1923) and DEATH IN THE WOODS (1933), and the autobiographical A STORY-TELLER'S STORY (1924).

androcentric means "man-centered," and is used as an alternative term for phallocentric. See also *phallocentric literature*.

anecdote: a short *tale* relating to a single incident told for amusement or gossip, often an entertaining element in *biographies*.

Angelou, Maya (b.1928): American poet, playwright, and autobiographer who has also written television documentaries and for the screen. She has been a political activist and is a powerful communicator on African-American culture. Notable works include I KNOW WHY THE CAGED BIRD SINGS (1970) and other autobiographical writings.

Anglo-Saxon period: see *Old English period*.

angry young men: a term invented in the 1950s for a group of English writers, musicians and artists, including *Kingsley Amis, Braine, Sillitoe* and, notably, *Osborne* (in whose play LOOK BACK IN ANGER the *antihero* Jimmy Porter is the prototypical angry young man). They resented the upper-class lifestyle and superior attitude of the establishment, and their works express their scorn for the hypocrisy of society in post-war Britain where, despite promises and aspirations, working or middle-class educated people were unable to break into influential areas. Their writing was often powerful, sometimes bitter and angry, often humorous, and much of it received critical acclaim.

angst is a constant state of anguish caused by the dread of being responsible for making one's own decisions and choices in life. See *absurd, theater and literature of the, existentialism.*

anisometric: a term describing a *stanza* containing lines of unequal length, e.g.

> O sweet spontaneous
> earth how often have
> the
> doting

> (the opening stanza of *e.e.cummings*'s "O Sweet Spontaneous," 1923)

antagonist: the *character* in a *drama* who is the main opponent of the *hero* or *protagonist*, e.g. Claudius in HAMLET.

antanaclasis is a figurative *device* (see *figurative language*) whereby a word is repeated in two or more of its senses, e.g. when in *Shakespeare*'s play Othello says:

> Put out the light, and then put out the light   (act V, scene 2)

The first "light" refers to the candle, the second is a *metaphor* for Desdemona's life.

anthology: a *selection* in a single volume of work by different writers (often erroneously used for a selection from the work of a single writer). Sometimes the volume will be of a particular *genre*, e.g. *postcolonial literature, science fiction,* or *poetry;* or dedicated to a particular period, e.g. *metaphysical* poetry or the American *short story.* See also *collection.*

Anthony, Michael (b.1932): Trinidadian novelist and *short story* writer. He is a sympathetic but acute observer of ordinary people, sometimes focusing upon children. Notable works include THE YEAR IN SAN FERNANDO (1965), GREEN DAYS BY THE RIVER (1967).

anthropomorphism is when nonhumans are given human abilities to think and, often, speak. Works from all eras, from Aesop's FABLES through WINNIE THE POOH by A.A. Milne (1882–1956) to *Ted Hughes*'s CROW, have made use of this *device.*

anticlimax refers to any kind of letdown when an anticipated *climax* is not achieved. It might apply to the *plot* of a *story* or play, but is most often applied to intentional *bathos* in a sentence or in *poetry. Johnson* described it as "A sentence in which the last part expresses something lower than the first." A good example of anticlimax in poetry comes in *Pope*'s THE RAPE OF THE LOCK when it describes Hampton Court Palace:

> Here Britain's statesmen oft the fall foredoom
> Of foreign tyrants, and of nymphs at home;

> Here thou, Great Anna! whom three realms obey
> Dost sometimes council take – and sometimes tea.
>> [the final word pronounced "tay" in the 18th century]

Anticlimax is often used in *mock heroic* writing.

antihero: a *protagonist* who displays generally unheroic traits, such as Jimmy Porter in *Osborne*'s LOOK BACK IN ANGER.

antimasque: devised by *Jonson* in 1609, a brief spectacle before or during the *masque* proper, often a *grotesque burlesque* of it.

antinovel: an experimental type of *fiction* that deliberately defies the *conventions* of the traditional *novel*. Some possible aspects include alternative beginnings and endings; lack of clear *plot* or *character* development; diffuse or disconnected *episodes*; unconventional vocabulary, punctuation, and/or syntax; nonsequential use of time; and, at the most extreme, pages that are colored, blank, detachable, shufflable into different sequences, and/or contain *signs*, *symbols*, drawings, or collages. *Sterne*'s TRISTRAM SHANDY is sometimes regarded as the forerunner of the antinovel. Modern writers who have experimented with aspects of the *genre* include *Joyce, Woolf, Beckett.* See also *avant-garde, fabulation*.

antiphonal describes a *poem*, hymn, or prayer that is divided into two parts, one responding to or echoing the other, e.g. *Marvell*'s "Dialogue Between the Soil and the Body" (1681).

antiphrasis is an ironical, even sarcastic, *figure of speech* wherein a word is used in a sense opposite to its real *meaning*, e.g. calling somebody "clever" who has done something stupid. The *device* is sometimes used in *litotes*.

antiplay/antitheater: *drama* that deliberately flouts or distorts dramatic *convention*, as often in *theater of the absurd*.

antistrophe is the changing around of word order to create an emphasis, e.g.

> This hour her Vigil, and her Eve, since this
> Both the year's, and the day's deep midnight is.

(from Donne's "A Noctural Upon St. Lucy's Day, Being the Shortest Day," 1633)

antithesis is:

- a *rhetorical* term denoting the balancing of two contrasting statements, e.g. "To err is human; to forgive, divine" (*Pope*); or when Brutus in *Shakespeare*'s JULIUS CAESAR says "not that I loved Caesar less, but that I loved Rome more."

- an argument set up in opposition to a *thesis* (as in a political debate or a court of law).

See also *oxymoron, paradox, parallelism*.

Anyidoho, Kofi (b.1947): Ghanaian poet. A professor of English at the University of Ghana, he is interested in *comparative literature* and bilingualism, writing in both English and Ewe, his first language. Notable works include A HARVEST OF OUR DREAMS (1984).

aphorism: a brief, pithy, sometimes *witty* saying, close in meaning to *maxim* or *proverb*, but usually more serious than an *epigram*. A good *collection* of aphorisms is THE OXFORD BOOK OF APHORISMS (1983) edited by John Gross.

apocryphal, derived from the biblical APOCRYPHA, is a term used to refer to a work of disputed or unknown origin or authorship, e.g. certain works such as THE TWO NOBLE KINSMEN (?1613, see *Fletcher*) or EDWARD III (1596) attributed by some to *Shakespeare*.

aporia is nowadays a key term in *deconstruction* theory, used to define the point where contradictory meanings in a *text* cause it to "deconstruct" so that no clear *meaning* can be certain.

aposiopesis: an intentional break in a speech leaving it unfinished. This can have a powerful and threatening effect, e.g. "if you do that I'll..."; or as in KING LEAR where Lear rails against his daughters Regan and Goneril

> I will have such revenges on you both,
> That all the world shall – I will do such things –   (act II, scene 4)

apostrophe is a *figure of speech* addressing an object, e.g. in *Dunn*'s "Ode to a Paper Clip"; or a person, e.g. in *Wordsworth*'s "Sonnet to Milton"; or an idea, e.g. in *Milton*'s "L'Allegro": "Hence loathed Melancholy!" as if Melancholy existed and could understand. See also *invocation*.

apothegm is the technical word for an *epigram* in *prose*.

archaisms, in a literary sense, are old or obsolete words or syntax that are deliberately used for effect. In THE FAERIE QUEENE *Spenser*, an admirer of *Chaucer*, used archaisms to create a bygone world of courtly *romance*. Thereafter *Milton, Chatterton, Keats, Tennyson,* and others from time to time used archaisms to evoke another age. In order to give dignity to their writings, the translators of the authorized version of the BIBLE (1611) and others employed archaisms. Their use has always been associated with a notion of *poetic diction*, and such archaic words as "thee" and "thou" were accepted usage in *poetry* until well into the 20th century.

Arden, John (b.1930): English playwright. Always concerned by social injustice, his *themes* often involve a clash between rigid authority and anarchic *subversion*. His recent plays have been more forcefully *polemic* and less intellectually balanced than his much admired earlier ones. Notable works include SERGEANT MUSGRAVE'S DANCE (1959), THE WORKHOUSE DONKEY (1963), ARMSTRONG'S LAST GOODNIGHT (1964).

argument may mean:

- a line of reasoning
- a summary of a *plot*, e.g. that which *Coleridge* provided for "The Rime of the Ancient Mariner"
- a declaration of purpose at the beginning of an *epic*.

Aristotle (384–322BC): ancient Greek philosopher and writer whose book POETICS is a good introduction to the nature of *literature*, and who introduced many terms, useful especially in discussing *drama*, such as *anagnorisis, catharsis, peripeteia*.

Armah, Ayi Kwei (b.1938): Ghanaian novelist. His writings tend to reflect continuing African suffering and disillusion with independence, often employing *imagery* of decay and disease. Notable works include THE BEAUTIFUL ONES ARE NOT YET BORN (1968).

Armitage, Simon (b.1963): English poet. Sharply observant, *witty*, and popular, he uses, among other things, his experiences as a probation officer and his native West Yorkshire *settings* and manner of speech. Notable works include ZOOM (1989), KID (1992), BOOK OF MATCHES (1993), THE DEAD SEA POEMS (1995), CLOUDCUCKOOLAND (1997), LITTLE GREEN MAN (2001), SELECTED POEMS (2001).

Arnold, Matthew (1822–88): English poet and critic. His works are considered by some to be among the best of the *Victorian age*. The *elegy* "Dover Beach" (1867) is probably his most acclaimed *poem* in which he uses the ebbing of the tide as a *metaphor* for the diminishing of religious faith in society. His *collection* of *essays* CULTURE AND ANARCHY (1869) contains many of his central critical *arguments*.

Arthurian legend: many versions exist of the semihistorical legend of King Arthur and the Knights of the Round Table. *Malory* collected many of the *stories* into his MORTE D'ARTHUR, a tale of *courtly love* and chivalric behavior that was printed by *William Caxton*, the first English printer.

Ashbery, John (b.1927): American poet. A leading member of the New York school of poets, he had an interest in art that generated strong visual *imagery* in his *poetry*. Notable works include SELF-PORTRAIT IN A CONVEX MIRROR (1975).

aside: a theatrical *convention*, often leading to *dramatic irony*, whereby a *character* in a play speaks to one side so that the audience may hear (sometimes by being directly addressed) but, it is supposed, so the other characters on stage do not hear. Nowadays this *device* is used more in *farce* and pantomime than in other kinds of *drama*. See also *soliloquy*.

association: the mental connection between objects and ideas. *Coleridge* writes of this idea in BIOGRAPHIA LITERARIA, and he and *Wordsworth* wrote many conversational *poems* (see *conversation piece/poem*) and other writings in which the poet's *mood* and surroundings lead to an association, often between the past and the present, and through a natural and freely structured progression of thought. Coleridge's "Frost at Midnight" and Wordsworth's "Tintern Abbey" are good examples. An interest in rendering into words this freewheeling process of thought led to the development in the 20th century of the *stream of consciousness technique*. See *connotation*.

assonance, sometimes known as rhyming of vowels, is used to create a melodious effect, more often in *poetry* than *prose*, when similar vowel sounds are repeated, e.g. "wide" and "time." The *device* only occasionally results in the rhyming of words. It is the vocalic equivalent of *alliteration*, and is far more powerful in creating poetic effects than the more often noted alliteration. See also *consonance, half rhyme*.

asyndeton: a *rhetorical device* whereby small words such as articles, conjunctions, and possibly prepositions and pronouns, are omitted in order to create a particular effect, often of speed and concision. The *technique* is popular among many modern poets such as *Berryman, Auden, Robert Lowell,* and *MacNeice,* as in his

> World is crazier and more of it than we think,
> Incorrigibly plural. (from "Snow," 1935)

The opposite is *polysyndeton*.

atmosphere is the feeling or *mood* evoked by a part or whole of a work of art. For instance, it may be argued that the opening lines of *Shakespeare*'s HAMLET create an atmosphere of chill and suspenseful apprehension; or the description of Miss Havisham's house in *Dickens*'s GREAT EXPECTATIONS one of gloom, decay, and foreboding. See *ambience, tone*.

attitude: see *authorial intention*.

Atwood, Margaret (b.1939): Canadian novelist, poet, and *short story* writer. In her writing there are elements of social *realism* and *satire*, and she tends to adopt a feminist slant. She has spoken of the importance in her work of an individual refusing to be a victim. She sometimes focuses upon the Canadian landscape, for instance in SURFACING (1972), and has an ability to create a strong sense of place. Other notable works include THE HANDMAID'S TALE (1985), CAT'S EYE (1989, remarkable in its depiction of aspects of the behavior of young girls), and THE BLIND ASSASSIN (2000), for which she won Britain's Booker Prize in 2000.

Auden, W.H. (1907–73): English poet, playwright, critic, and editor. Influenced, among others, by *Yeats*, Karl Marx (1811–83), and Sigmund Freud (1856–1939), and friend and collaborator of *MacNeice, Spender, Day Lewis*, and *Isherwood*, he wrote *poetry* varied in *theme* and *style*, from the leftwing social comment of his early poetry to the interest in religion and Christian *viewpoint* of later writing. He was skilled in using contemporary language within traditional *verse forms*, and he had considerable influence upon poets who followed him. Notable works include THE DOG BENEATH THE SKIN (1935), THE ASCENT OF F6 (1936), LETTERS FROM ICELAND (1937), NONES (1951), THE SHIELD OF ACHILLES (1955), HOMAGE TO CLIO (1960), COLLECTED SHORTER POEMS (1966), COLLECTED LONGER POEMS (1968).

Augustan refers in English *literature* to writers active during the English *Augustan period* who admired and imitated the *wit*, elegance, and *style* of the classical writers, e.g. *Addison, Pope, Steele, Jonathan Swift*. From the stylistic point of view, some critics would include *Dryden*, who wrote before 1700, and *Goldsmith* and *Johnson*, who continued writing into the later 18th century. The term originally referred to such classical writers as Horace (65–8BC), Ovid (43BC–AD18), and Virgil (70–19BC), active during the reign of the Roman Emperor Augustus (27BC–AD14).

Augustan period (or the Age of Pope): generally considered to cover *literature* written in England between approximately 1700 and 1745, although *Goldsmith* confined the period to those works written during the reign of Queen Anne (1702–14).

Austen, Jane (1775–1817): often considered England's finest woman novelist. She wrote with great *wit, humor, irony*, and a keen interest in human nature, creating a precise picture of aspects of her age with *characters* such as the engaging Elizabeth Bennett, the obsequious Mr. Collins, and the obnoxiously haughty aristocrat Lady Catherine de Burgh in PRIDE AND PREJUDICE (1813). Her books all deal with ideas of position, etiquette, and *traditions* intrinsic to English society. Other notable works include NORTHANGER ABBEY (written 1798, published 1818), SENSE AND SENSIBILITY (1811), MANSFIELD PARK (1814), EMMA (1816), PERSUASION (1818).

Auster, Paul (b.1947): American novelist, poet, and essayist. Often his writing is experimental, the *setting* of his *stories* is New York, and his main subject the process of writing itself. Notable works include IN THE COUNTRY OF LAST THINGS (1987).

author: anyone who produces any kind of written material. *Literary theory* has increasingly questioned the author's place in the appreciation and understanding of *literature*. See also *death of the author, deconstruction, Marxist criticism, new critics, poststructuralism, structuralism.*

authorial attitude: see *authorial intention.*

authorial intention/authorial attitude: phrases used to signify what the *author* meant when s/he wrote a *text*. Many modern critics believe that what the author may or may not have intended is irrelevant, that there is no fixed *meaning* in a text, and that an individual reader's interpretation is all-important. They argue that an author may be ambiguous in her or his intentions, and that it is not "incorrect" if a reader's interpretation was not anticipated by the author. The *new critics* W.K. Wimsatt and Monroe C. Beardsley commented that the *poem* "is detached from the author at birth and goes about the world beyond his power to intend about it or control it." The same is applied to a playwright or theater director's intentions and what the reader/audience read into a play/production. See *death of the author, intentional fallacy.*

authorial voice: see *voice.*

autobiographical memoir: a book dealing with events in the *author*'s life, but not a comprehensive *autobiography*, e.g. *Malan*'s MY TRAITOR'S HEART.

autobiography: a *memoir* of a person's life written by herself or himself. Classical writers such as Herodotus (*c.*480–425BC) wrote works that may be considered autobiographical. Bede (673–735) wrote a short account of his life in his ECCLESIASTICAL HISTORY (731). By the 17th century *diaries* had become popular. In works from the 18th century a link between the *novel* and the autobiography can be found in *Defoe*'s ROBINSON CRUSOE. In the 19th century *Wordsworth* spent much of his time writing and rewriting THE PRELUDE, an autobiography in *poetry* of his early years. Among notable autobiographies are *Twain*'s LIFE ON THE MISSISSIPPI (1883), *Wilde*'s DE PROFUNDIS (1905), *Gosse*'s FATHER AND SON, *Brittain*'s TESTAMENT OF YOUTH. From the 1950s the writing of autobiographies escalated and nowadays anyone who has achieved fame, whether a sports personality, popstar, politician, scientist, explorer, or military leader, will write (or more likely have ghost written) his or her autobiography, often of scant literary merit. See *biography.*

autoclesis is a *rhetorical device* whereby an idea is mentioned negatively or dismissively in order to arouse interest in the listener, e.g. Mark Antony's treatment of Caesar's will in *Shakespeare*'s JULIUS CAESAR (1599).

avant-garde is a term used to describe works that are at the cutting edge, or "ahead of their time," deliberately setting out to be innovative, and even to shock; and in which the writer (or artist) experiments with new *techniques, forms,* and *themes.* The phrase is a French military term meaning "advance guard" and was initially used by and of certain 19th century French writers and artists.

Awoonor, Kofi (b.1935): Ghanaian poet and novelist who writes in both English and Ewe. Influenced by *Pound* and *Dylan Thomas,* he utilizes the oral *poetry* of the Ewes to try to blend European and precolonial cultures in order to explore the modern African psyche. Notable works include REDISCOVERY (1964), THIS EARTH, MY BROTHER (1970), NIGHT OF MY BLOOD (1971).

Ayckbourn, Alan (b.1939): prolific English playwright in the *comedy of manners tradition*. He explores a multiplicity of aspects of middle-class anxieties and neuroses, writing for his provincial theater in Scarborough, Yorkshire, and usually transferring his plays to London. He is innovative in his stagecraft and handling of his subject matter, unusual in one so popular and commercially successful. He is the most performed English playwright apart from *Shakespeare*. Notable works include RELATIVELY SPEAKING (1965), HOW THE OTHER HALF LOVES (1969), ABSURD PERSON SINGULAR (1972), THE NORMAN CONQUESTS (1973, trilogy), BEDROOM FARCE (1975), JOKING APART (1978), SISTERLY FEELINGS (1979), WAY UPSTREAM (1981), A CHORUS OF DISAPPROVAL (1984), A SMALL FAMILY BUSINESS (1987), THE THINGS WE DO FOR LOVE (1997). Most of his plays are *farces*, but some later work has developed increasingly dark *tones*.

B

Bacon, Francis (1561–1626): English philosopher and essayist, best known for his
ESSAYS (1597–1625), a *collection* of brief, pithy pieces on various topics which he
reworked as life taught him different lessons and modified his thinking. In act I,
scene 5 of *Shakespeare*'s play, Hamlet notes down an important observation on life in
his "tables," much as Bacon would have done. A scientist and a polymath, he also
held high government office. It was once fashionable to suggest that he was the true
writer of Shakespeare's plays (spurring a debate known as the Baconian Controversy)
on the assumption that one from Shakespeare's ordinary background could not have
written plays of genius. This theory is today discounted.

Baldwin, James (1924–87): American novelist, playwright, and essayist. He grew up
in Harlem, and his work centers on racial and sexual politics from the point of view
of African-American experience. Notable works include GO TELL IT ON THE
MOUNTAIN (1953), GIOVANNI'S ROOM (1956), ANOTHER COUNTRY (1962), JUST ABOVE
MY HEAD (1979).

ballad: a *poem* that tells a *story*, usually in the form of four-line *stanza*s or *quatrain*s
with lines 1 and 3 in unrhymed *iambic tetrameter*s, lines 2 and 4 in iambic *trimeter*s.
Thus the opening of arguably the most famous English literary ballad, *Coleridge*'s
"The Rime of the Ancient Mariner," runs:

> It is an ancient mariner
> And he stoppeth one in three
> – "By thy long grey beard and glittering hand
> Now wherefore stopp'st thou me?"

Sometimes all lines are tetrameters; sometimes the *rhyme scheme* is abcd, abab, or
aabb. Narrative folk ballads are passed on by word of mouth from generation to
generation, especially in rural areas, a traditional *form* of storytelling that still thrives
in remote parts of the world. A typical ballad has a swift opening, uses everyday
language, and often tells a story of disasters, battles, and conflicts in *dialog* and *action*,
sometimes with a *chorus*. Examples are the legends of the rebel Robin Hood, and the
Border Ballads telling of skirmishes and bloodshed on the England/Scotland
borders. Urban communities have created their own ballads, sometimes referred to
as street or broadside ballads. Notable literary ballads include *Keats*'s LA BELLE DAME
SANS MERCI (1819) and *Wilde*'s THE BALLAD OF READING GAOL (1898). See *lyric, song*.

Banks, Iain M. (b.1954): Scottish novelist. As well as his *science fiction novel*s, he has
also produced highly imaginative writings, sometimes controversially violent, which
explore modern culture. Notable works include THE WASP FACTORY (1984), WALKING
ON GLASS (1985), THE BRIDGE (1986), COMPLICITY (1993), AGAINST A DARK
BACKGROUND (1993).

Bankside: an area of Elizabethan London to the south side of the River Thames,
opposite the City and outside its limits and jurisdiction. There in Elizabethan times
thrived theaters, taverns, and brothels, all prohibited or disapproved of by the
controlling hand of the Puritans within the City. See *Globe Theatre, Rose Theatre*.

Barker, Howard (b.1946): English playwright. For a time he acquired something of a cult following, his postmodernist plays challenging social and political conventions, and questioning those in power. Notable works include THE HANG OF THE GAOL (1978), NO END OF BLAME (1981), VICTORY (1983), SCENES FROM AN EXECUTION (1984), THE CASTLE (1985).

Barker, Pat (b.1943): English novelist. Both her earlier work, which concentrates on the struggles of working-class women, and her more recent writing, which focuses on psychological issues, have a strong historical basis. Notable works include THE MAN WHO WASN'T THERE (1988), REGENERATION (1991), THE GHOST ROAD (1995), BORDER CROSSING (2001).

Barnes, Julian (b.1946): English novelist. In his books he often employs *faction*, combining *comedy* with psychological insight in a *witty style*. Notable works include METROLAND (1981), FLAUBERT'S PARROT (1984), A HISTORY OF THE WORLD IN 10½ CHAPTERS (1989), ENGLAND, ENGLAND (1998).

baroque: a term used to describe a style of architecture, art, and music, but it can be used appropriately for writing with similar 17th century features – that is, florid, exuberant, and dramatic. *Metaphysical* writing of the 17th century is sometimes so described.

bathos is when a writer, intending to be *pathetic*, overreaches and descends to the ridiculous. *Pope* established this term in OF THE ART OF SINKING IN POETRY (1727), and gives as an example:

> Ye Gods! Annihilate but Space and Time
> And make two lovers happy.

THE STUFFED OWL (1930), edited by Wyndham Lewis and Charles Lee, is a good *collection* of pompous bathetic *verse*. Some consider that bathos can cover intentionally absurd effects of this kind, but this is more properly one of the meanings of *anticlimax*.

Baxter, James K. (1926–72): New Zealand poet, dramatist, and critic. His largely religious writings cover a wide range of personal experiences. Notable works include BEYOND THE PALISADE (1944), PIG ISLAND LETTERS (1966), THE BAND ROTUNDA (1967), JERSUALEM SONNETS (1970), AUTUMN TESTAMENT (1972).

Beat movement: a 1950s looseknit group of American antiestablishment writers sometimes known as the Beat generation. Downbeat, offbeat, down-and-out, free-wheeling, unconventional, and sometimes anarchic in both writing and permissive lifestyle, they deliberately shocked middle-class Americans (whom they called "squares"). Influenced among other things by jazz and Zen Buddhism, its writers include *Kerouac* (who is credited with inventing the term "beat"), *William Burroughs, Ginsberg, Corso, Ferlinghetti*. The movement as such was short-lived, but influenced many who followed, such as *performance poets*. See also *alternative literature, underground literature*.

Beaumont, Francis (1584–1616): English playwright. Much admired by *Dryden*, he was reputed to be a shrewd judge of what worked well on the stage, *Jonson* relying upon his advice and judgment in reviewing and correcting his own work. Notable works include THE KNIGHT OF THE BURNING PESTLE (?1607), PHILASTER (1609), and THE MAID'S TRAGEDY (?1611), the latter two in collaboration with *Fletcher*.

Beckett, Samuel (1906–89): Irish playwright, novelist, *prose* writer, and essayist. He was friendly with and influenced by his fellow countryman *Joyce*. He has become associated with the *theater of the absurd*, his best-known work being WAITING FOR GODOT (1955, originally written in French) where, typical of his plays, stage trappings are *minimalist*, the focus being upon individuals within a stark predicament. He had considerable influence on, among others, *Pinter, Stoppard*, and *Fugard*. Other notable works include ALL THAT FALL (1957), ENDGAME (1958), KRAPP'S LAST TAPE (1958), HAPPY DAYS (1961), NOT I (1973).

Beckford, William (1759–1844): English novelist. A wealthy man, he enjoyed an extravagant lifestyle that was matched by his highly imaginative writing, his best-known work being the *gothic novel* VATHEK (1787). Other notable works include DREAMS, WAKING THOUGHTS, AND INCIDENTS (1784), AZEMIA (1797).

bedlam: a madhouse or lunatic asylum, named after St. Bethlehem's Hospital in London. At one time begging bedlamites released into the community would have been a common sight, e.g. "Mad Tom" in *Shakespeare*'s KING LEAR.

Beer, Patricia (1919–99): English poet. Incorporating many references to England's "West Country" and focusing on mundane scenarios, she creates an individual *style* that is both *witty* and serious. Notable works include LOSS OF THE MAGYAR (1959), MRS. BEER'S HOUSE (1968), MOON'S OTTERY (1978).

Behn, Aphra (1640–89): English playwright, novelist, poet, and translator. She took material from earlier writers, creating plays that explore with *wit* social issues of the time. She lived an adventurous life, and is credited with being the first Englishwoman to earn her living as a writer. Her *comedy* THE EMPEROR OF THE MOON (1687) uses elements of *commedia dell'arte*, introducing harlequinade and thus possibly the beginnings of pantomime to England. Other notable works include THE TOWN FOP (1676), THE ROVER (1677), OROONOKO (1688).

Bell, Gertrude (1868–1926): English travel writer. Her archaeological pursuits are noted in her writings, which frequently develop an interest in Arabic history. Notable works include THE DESERT AND THE SOWN (1907), AMURATH TO AMURATH (1911).

Belloc, Hilaire (1870–1953): French-born British poet, essayist, journalist, novelist, biographer, and travel writer. After turning his back on politics he befriended *Chesterton*, whose interests and Roman Catholic religion he shared. Prolific and skilled over a range of material and *forms*, he is best remembered for his humorous *verse*. Notable works include THE PATH TO ROME (1902), CAUTIONARY TALES FOR CHILDREN (1907), PONGO AND THE BULL (1910), EUROPE AND FAITH (1920), SONNETS AND VERSE (1923), BELINDA (1928).

Bellow, Saul (b.1915): American novelist. He writes with richness and humor as his philosophical interests lead him to explore the human soul in various social situations. Notable works include THE ADVENTURES OF AUGIE MARCH (1953), HERZOG (1964), MR. SAMMLER'S PLANET (1970).

Bennett, Alan (b.1934): English playwright, television and radio writer, and essayist. He is known for his sensitive, often melancholy portrayal of people, and his work frequently has a *satirical* edge. He does not see himself a committed political playwright like some of his contemporaries, but as "political" in its widest sense. He sometimes draws upon his north of England roots. Notable works include FORTY YEARS ON (1968), HABEAS CORPUS (1973), TALKING HEADS (1989), THE MADNESS OF KING GEORGE (1990).

Berryman, John (1914–72): American poet. His unique voice is heard through *poems* of personal and emotional exploration, which eventually led to his suicide in 1972. Notable works include THE DISPOSSESSED (1948), HOMAGE TO MISTRESS BRADSTREET (1956), THE DREAM SONGS (1969), DELUSIONS, ETC. (1972).

bestiaries: *tales* with a *moral* about real or imaginary animals. *Collections* of such tales, sometimes derived from Aesop's *fables*, were popular in *prose* or *verse form* in the Middle Ages, and writers such as *Chaucer* drew on them, e.g. in THE NUN'S PRIEST'S TALE in THE CANTERBURY TALES, with its cunning fox and vain cockerel.

Betjeman, John (1906–84): English poet, architecture critic, journalist, and broadcaster. His *poems* take a lighthearted and sometimes melancholic look at middle-class society. They are *traditional* in *style* and at first seem simple, but Betjeman's *technique* includes excellent *rhyme* and *rhythm*. English landscape and architecture were his passion. He was *poet laureate* from 1972–84. Notable works include COLLECTED POEMS (1958, revised 1962) and the autobiographical SUMMONED BY BELLS (1960).

Bible: term referring to the sacred *texts* of Judaism and Christianity. The Old Testament, the oldest surviving Hebrew text, contains the Holy Scriptures of Judaism; the Old Testament together with the New Testament, manuscripts in Greek, form the sacred book of Christianity. It was once said that an essential requisite for studying Western *literature* was a working knowledge of the Bible, and it is very valuable in order to appreciate and evaluate the *contexts* within which much English literature is written and understood.

bibliography: a list of books, articles, *essays*, and other written material that is available on a particular *author* or subject.

Bierce, Ambrose (1842–*c.*1914): American *short story* writer and journalist. Much of his writing is based on the bitterness he felt from his experiences in the Civil War. Notable works include TALES OF SOLDIERS AND CIVILIANS (1891).

biography: an account of a person's life and personality by another person, e.g. *Boswell*'s THE LIFE OF SAMUEL JOHNSON (1791), EMINENT VICTORIANS (1918) by Lytton Strachey (1880–1932), JOHN KEATS (1968) by Robert Gittings (1911–92). See *autobiography, diary, memoir.*

Bird, Isabella (1831–1904): English travel writer. Her adventurous spirit comes over in her writings, which inspired the women of her time who were mainly used to a narrow domestic existence. The playwright *Churchill* characterizes her in TOP GIRLS (1982). Notable works include A LADY'S LIFE IN THE ROCKY MOUNTAINS (1879).

Bishop, Elizabeth (1911–79): American poet. Much of her work is influenced by her time in South America and this adds to the strong sense of place in her work. Notable works include NORTH AND SOUTH/A COLD SPRING (1955), QUESTIONS OF TRAVEL (1965), GEOGRAPHY III (1977).

black comedy is a term used to describe *drama* where potentially horrific situations are treated with amusement and ridicule by both the *characters* and the audience, as is *Beckett*'s WAITING FOR GODOT. *Pinter, Albee,* and *Orton* are among other notable English playwrights of black comedy, whose antecedents go back to *Shakespeare*'s THE MERCHANT OF VENICE (?1596) and MEASURE FOR MEASURE (?1604), and beyond. The term is also extended to other kinds of *literature* such as *novels,* e.g. *Heller*'s CATCH-22 or *A.N.Wilson*'s THE HEALING ART. See also *graveyard school.*

Blake, William (1757–1827): English poet, engraver, and artist. His radical politics led him to befriend like-minded people such as *Godwin* and Thomas Paine (1735–1809). He admired *Milton* as a great national poet, but in THE MARRIAGE OF HEAVEN AND HELL (1790–93) he attacks Milton's PARADISE LOST and displays his unorthodox aversion to Christianity and all organized religions. He illustrated most of his writings with engravings, and much of this work was not discovered until after his death. In some ways a *Romantic* idealist in times of industrial revolution and political unrest, he demonstrates great depth and range in his work, from energetic, scathing attacks to lyrical tenderness. His brand of *Romanticism* is perhaps best summed up in his belief that "every thing that lives is holy." Notable works include THE FRENCH REVOLUTION (1791), VISIONS OF THE DAUGHTERS OF ALBION (1793), SONGS OF INNOCENCE AND OF EXPERIENCE (1794).

blank verse is unrhymed *iambic pentameter* (a common mistake is to describe any unrhymed *verse* as "blank"). It is the most common metrical pattern in English verse, notable users including *Milton* and *Wordsworth. Marlowe* and *Shakespeare* did much to make blank verse a flexible and powerful dramatic medium. See *meter.*

Blixen, Karen: see *Dinesen.*

Bloom, Harold (b.1930): American scholar and critic. He is known for his highly individual and often controversial *literary theories,* most famously about the influence of literary *tradition* on writers (THE ANXIETY OF INFLUENCE, 1973) and more recently about the origin of certain biblical *texts* (THE BOOK OF J, 1990). Other notable works include A MAP OF MISREADING (1975), FIGURES OF CAPABLE IMAGINATION (1976).

Bloomsbury group: the name given to a group of writers, intellectuals, and artists who between about 1907 and 1939 met in Bloomsbury, London to discuss their mutual views on the arts. Much opposed to the artistic and social constraints of the era, their influence on art and philosophy during and after World War I was extensive. Often regarded as elitist and dilettante, the group included *Forster,* Lytton Strachey (1880–1932), *Woolf.*

Blunden, Edmund (1896–1974): English poet, critic, and biographer. His writing includes some of the best of World War I *poetry.* Notable works include UNDERTONES OF WAR (1928).

blurb: publisher's comments printed on the cover of a book, often including an enthusiastic, brief summary of the contents and designed to entice the reader.

Boccaccio, Giovanni (1313–75): Italian writer who influenced many subsequent European writers. For instance, *narrative* and other aspects of *Chaucer*'s CANTERBURY TALES owe much to Boccaccio's *story cycle* THE DECAMERON (1349–51), in which ten people each tell one story a day over ten days. Writers whom he influenced include *Lydgate, Shakespeare, Dryden, Keats, Longfellow, Tennyson.* Among his output are *prose romances,* and some of his writing in Latin was widely read in England. Other notable works include FILOCOLO, FILOSTRATO, TESEIDA. The dates of most of his writing are uncertain.

Boland, Eavan (b.1944): Irish poet whose writing tends to be preoccupied with contemporary Irish troubles. Notable works include NEW TERRITORY (1967), THE WAR HORSE (1975), IN HER OWN IMAGE (1980), OUTSIDE HISTORY (1990), IN A TIME OF VIOLENCE (1994).

Bolt, Robert (1924–95): English playwright and screenwriter, best known for his historical plays. Notable works include A MAN FOR ALL SEASONS (1960).

bombast is pompous, overblown language. Polonius in *Shakespeare*'s HAMLET often speaks bombastically, and when giving his advice to the players Hamlet criticizes old-fashioned bombastic actors.

Bond, Edward (b.1934): English playwright. He is a controversial writer whose plays often deal with alienation from society and violence. Several of his works were initially banned. He highlights contemporary issues, the world's injustices, and the struggle of good for survival. He uses historical *character*s and *setting*s, and the writings of people such as *Clare* and *Shakespeare* (both in his writings and as a person). In the 1970s he said that "we need an active philosophy – time is running out." Notable works include SAVED (1966), THE NARROW ROAD TO THE DEEP NORTH (1968), EARLY MORNING (1968), LEAR (1971), THE SEA (1973), BINGO (1972), THE WAR PLAYS (1985).

book of hours: an illustrated prayer book. One of the most exquisite is the Duc de Berry's TRÈS RICHES HEURES (15th century).

Booker McConnell Prize for Fiction: an annual *literature* prize awarded in England since 1969, commonly known as the Booker Prize. Former winners include *Farrell* in 1973 for THE SEIGE OF KRISHNAPUR, *Golding* in 1980 for RITES OF PASSAGE, *Rushdie* in 1981 for MIDNIGHT'S CHILDREN, *Keneally* in 1982 for SCHINDLER'S ARK, *Coetzee* in 1983 for LIFE AND TIMES OF MICHAEL K, *Ishiguro* in 1989 for THE REMAINS OF THE DAY, *Margaret Atwood* in 2000 for THE BLIND ASSASSIN.

Boswell, James (1740–95): Scottish biographer and *journal* writer. He left Scotland for London to pursue an ambitious political life where he successfully published several anonymous *pamphlet*s and *verse*s. He then traveled widely, but remained in close contact with the London literary scene including *Johnson* and *Goldsmith*, publishing many works under the name "Hypochondriack." His many letters reveal his ambitiousness, countless affairs, and fits of depression. His writing is largely entertaining and readable, telling much of his life and times. Notable works include DORANDO (1767), AN ACCOUNT OF CORSICA (1768), THE JOURNAL OF A TOUR TO THE HEBRIDES (1785), THE LIFE OF SAMUEL JOHNSON (1791).

Bradbury, Malcolm (1932–2000): English novelist and critic. Admiring of modern experimental writers, his first three *novel*s were *campus novel*s. His favored *satirical style* of work centers on political and modern cultural opinions, which he questions through his frequent use of academic *character*s. Notable works include WHAT IS A NOVEL? (1969), THE HISTORY MAN (1975), DOCTOR CRIMINALE (1982), RATES OF EXCHANGE (1983), TO THE HERMITAGE (2000).

Bradley, A.C. (1851–1935): English critic and renowned Shakespearian scholar. Many of his opinions have been superseded by later scholarship; but his *criticism* is very readable, and still influential is his SHAKESPEARIAN TRAGEDY (1904), a *collection* of lectures in which he advances his theory of the *tragic flaw* in each of the *protagonists* in *Shakespeare's* major tragedies: in Hamlet it is indecision; King Lear, vanity; Macbeth, ambition; Othello, jealousy.

Bradstreet, Anne (?1612–72): American poet. After emigrating from England at the age of 16, her first work, THE TENTH MUSE LATELY SPRUNG UP IN AMERICA (1650), was published without her knowledge, then republished in 1678 with her corrections under the title SEVERAL POEMS COMPILED WITH A GREAT VARIETY OF WIT AND LEARNING. Influenced by Elizabethans such as *Spenser* and *Sidney*, her earlier *poems* tend to be longer historical works, the later progressing toward a more individual *style* and *form* exploring personal, domestic subjects, such as her family.

Bragg, Melvyn (b.1939): English novelist, journalist, and playwright. Much of his work is set in his native Cumbria, and he often uses a sense of place as a key to an exploration of social issues. Notable works include FOR WANT OF A NAIL (1965), THE MAID OF BUTTERMERE (1987), CRYSTAL ROOMS (1992), THE SOLDIER'S RETURN (2000).

Braine, John (1922–86): English novelist. He was born out of a working-class background and established himself as one of the *angry young men* of the 1950s. At this time his extreme leftwing views, from which his later writing veers away, criticized capitalist opportunism. Notable works include ROOM AT THE TOP (1957), LIFE AT THE TOP (1962), THE CRYING GAME (1964), THE JEALOUS GOD (1964), THE TWO OF US (1984).

Brand, Dionne (b.1953): Trinidadian poet and *short story* writer. Having spent much of her life in Canada, she has produced writing based on personal experiences of immigration expressed through *imagery* of the past and present. Notable works include FORE DAY MORNING (1978), SANS SOUCI AND OTHER TALES (1988), NO BURDEN TO CARRY (1992).

Brathwaite, Edward Kamau (b.1930): Barbadian poet, historian, and literary critic who draws upon African roots in order to develop the Caribbean culture. Notable works include RIGHTS OF PASSAGE (1967), MASKS (1968), ISLANDS (1969) – published as the trilogy THE ARRIVANTS – and OTHER EXILES (1975), X-SELF (1987).

Brecht, Bertolt (1898–1956): German dramatist and poet. Influenced by *expressionism*, he in turn had a major influence upon theater, breaking free from dramatic *conventions* with his desire to strip the stage of theatrical illusions, aiming to leave the audience feeling as if they had learned something. Notable works include MAN IS MAN (1927), THE THREEPENNY OPERA (1928), THE LIFE OF GALILEO (1937–39), MOTHER COURAGE (1941), THE CAUCASIAN CHALK CIRCLE (1948). See *alienation effect*, *Brechtian*, *epic theater*.

Brechtian is a term used to describe plays written or presented according to the theories of *Brecht*. See *alienation effect, epic theater*.

Brenton, Howard (b.1942): English playwright. His very leftwing political drama, heavily influenced by *Brecht*, explores class and culture. Notable works include CHRISTIE IN LOVE (1969), REVENGE (1969), MAGNIFICENCE (1973), THE CHURCHILL PLAY (1974), THE ROMANS IN BRITAIN (1980).

Brink, André (b.1935): South African novelist, Afrikaans writer, and translator. A strong opponent of apartheid, he explores the culture and morals of the Afrikaans world, which led to the banning of LOOKING ON DARKNESS (1974) by the South African government. Other notable works include A DRY WHITE SEASON (1979), A CHAIN OF VOICES (1982), STATES OF EMERGENCY (1988).

Brittain, Vera (1893–1970): English novelist, poet, and autobiographer. She was a highly acclaimed feminist and pacifist author, and was closely associated with *Holtby*. Notable works include TESTAMENT OF YOUTH (1933), a poignant *autobiography* that mourns her generation lost in World War I, and her own lost youth.

Brodber, Erna (b.1940): Jamaican novelist. Her early writing is sociological, after which she began to write *novels* exploring cultural heritage against a modern world, incorporating *stream of consciousness techniques* and drawing on an *oral tradition*. Notable works include ABANDONMENT OF CHILDREN IN JAMAICA (1974), A STUDY OF YARDS IN THE CITY OF KINGSTON (1975), JANE AND LOUISA WILL SOON COME HOME (1980), MYAL (1988), LOUISIANA (1997).

broken rhyme occurs when a word is split in order to create a *rhyme*. It is rare except in comic *verse*, but sometimes *Hopkins* uses it, e.g.

> I caught this morning morning's minion, king-
> dom of daylight's dauphin, dappled-dawn-drawn Falcon, in his riding
> ("The Windhover," 1877)

Brontë family: an English family of writers that included three female novelists and poets who lived with their father and unstable brother Branwell in the parsonage at Haworth, a remote weaving village on the Yorkshire moors. All read widely, and were particularly influenced by *Byron* and *Walter Scott*:

- Charlotte Brontë (1816–55), whose writing has been remarked upon for its emotional *realism*. Notable works include JANE EYRE (1847), which was immediately acclaimed upon publication, VILLETTE (1853)
- Emily Brontë (1818–48), notable works including WUTHERING HEIGHTS (1847), the *tone* of which Charlotte noted as a "horror of great darkness" – a blend of realism, *romance*, and the *gothic* that did not find favor with the public until after her death. Her *poetry* has achieved increasing critical approval
- Anne Brontë (1820–49), some of whose poetry, influenced by *Cowper*, explores religious doubt. Notable works include the *novel* THE TENANT OF WILDFELL HALL (1848), which has attracted the attention of *feminist criticism*.

Brooke, Rupert (1887–1915): English poet. Sometimes classed as a *Georgian poet*, he was for some years a leading light on the Cambridge literary scene and his travels in Germany, the Americas, and the Pacific influenced his *poetry*. His reputation has now faded, but he is still valued for his lighter *verse*, sometimes written in an accessible, colloquial language and often nostalgic. Notable works include POEMS (1911), "The Old Vicarage, Granchester" (1912), "The Dead" (1914), LITHUANIA (1915), NEW NUMBERS (1915, which includes "The Soldier"), 1914 AND OTHER POEMS (1915).

Browning, Elizabeth Barrett (1806–61): English poet. Regarded as the foremost woman poet of her time, and known for her liberal social ideas, she was passionately interested in and venturesome with *verse* construction, e.g. MOTHER AND POET (1861). An invalid for much of her life, she secretly married her fellow poet *Robert Browning*. Other notable works include POEMS (1844), SONNETS FROM THE PORTUGUESE (1850), AURORA LEIGH (1857).

Browning, Robert (1812–89): English poet, influenced particularly by *Keats, Percy Shelley*, and *Byron*. Among his prolific output he excelled in *dramatic monolog*, e.g. "My Last Duchess" (1842), "Andrea del Sarto," "Fra Lippo Lippi," the latter two included along with *poems* such as "Childe Roland to the Dark Tower Came" (1855) in MEN AND WOMEN (1855). Although not as popular in his lifetime as his contemporary *Tennyson*, by the time of his death he had achieved a high critical status that has endured.

Brutus, Dennis (b.1924): South African poet. He draws on his experiences of imprisonment and exile following his resistance to apartheid. Notable works include LETTERS TO MARTHA AND OTHER POEMS FROM A SOUTH AFRICAN PRISON (1968).

Bryant, William Cullen (1794–1878): American poet, editor, and essayist who was his country's leading poetic voice in the first half of the 19th century. His most famous poem is "Thanatopsis" (1817), a somber, *free verse* contemplation of death that is reminiscent of the *neoclassical* poets, especially of the so-called *graveyard school*, but also elevates nature in the spirit of true *Romanticism*. Notable works include THE EMBARGO AND OTHER POEMS (1809), POEMS (1832), THE FOUNTAIN (1842), THE WHITE-FOOTED DEER (1844), HYMNS (1864).

Bunyan, John (1628–88): English writer and preacher. Imprisoned for many years in Bedford jail for preaching without a license, he began to write. Nearly all of his output has a moral or religious basis, and much is presented in a clear and accessible *style*. Notable works include his famous *allegory* PILGRIM'S PROGRESS (1678 and 1684), THE LIFE AND DEATH OF MR. BADMAN (1680), THE HOLY WAR (1682).

Burgess, Anthony (1917–94): English novelist, scriptwriter, biographer, critic, and composer. His *novels* display sharply observed social comment and verbal inventiveness. Notable works include A CLOCKWORK ORANGE (1962), a prophetic vision of the future made into a controversial film in 1971.

burlesque is a term applied to writing that sets out to satirize a subject, work, or literary *style* by making a deliberate mismatch between the *manner* and the matter, usually for *satirical* purposes. *Lampoon, mock heroic, mock epic*, and *parody* are all types of burlesque.

Burns, Robert (1759–96): Scottish poet. Even after he became famous he retained a sense of his humble rural background, and this is reflected in his work. Very personal *poems* sometimes speak of his passionate relationships and financial problems. He is able to write in the formal English of the day and the vernacular Scots, sometimes combining the two. He was also an avid collector, writer, and rewriter of traditional Scottish *songs*, most famously "Auld Lang Syne" and "Red, Red Rose." He achieved a cult status during his lifetime and this has endured, making him widely regarded as the Scottish national poet. Notable works include POEMS CHIEFLY IN SCOTTISH DIALECT (1786, including "The Cotter's Saturday Night" and "Halloween"), "Holy Willie's Prayer" (1789), "Tam o'Shanter" (1790).

Burroughs, John (1837–1921): American journalist, essayist, literary critic, biographer, philosopher, and poet whose appreciation of nature is central to his writing. Notable works include NOTES ON WALT WHITMAN AS POET AND PERSON (1867), WAKE-ROBIN (1871).

Burroughs, William (1914–97): American novelist. One of the *Beat movement* and friends with *Ginsberg* and *Kerouac*, he wrote of his experiences and the culture surrounding his addiction to heroin. Notable works include JUNKIE (1953), NAKED LUNCH (1959), THE SOFT MACHINE (1961), BLADE RUNNER: A MOVIE (1979), QUEER (1984).

Butler, Samuel (1613–80): English poet and *prose* writer best known for his *satirical burlesque* poem HUDIBRAS (1662–78).

Butler, Samuel (1835–1902): English novelist, poet, satirist, philosopher, composer, and art critic. His output is unfocused, a wide variety of subjects being the targets of his *irony* and *satire*. He is best remembered for his semiautobiographical *novel* THE WAY OF ALL FLESH (1903) which reveals an unhappy childhood. Other notable works include EREWHON (1872).

Byatt, A.S. (b.1936): English novelist, *short story* writer, and critic. Her writing is characterized by historical, artistic, and literary perspectives, perceptions, and *allusion*s. Notable works include THE VIRGIN IN THE GARDEN (1978), STILL LIFE (1985), SUGAR AND OTHER STORIES (1987), POSSESSION (1990).

Byron, George Gordon, Lord (1788–1824): English *Romantic* poet and playwright. Among other qualities his *poetry* expresses by turns lyrical beauty and biting *satire*, and its intense popularity, especially among a female readership, became known as "Byronmania." Celebrated for his lifestyle as much as his writing, he doubtless played up to Lady Caroline Lamb's image of him as "Mad, bad, and dangerous to know," and his creation of the *Byronic hero* probably had much to do with his perception of himself. A friend of *Percy Shelley* and possessing the same Romantic ideals of freedom and liberty, he embraced the cause of independence for Greece and died there. Notable works include CHILDE HAROLD'S PILGRIMAGE (1812–18), THE PRISONER OF CHILLON (1816), DON JUAN (1819–24).

Byronic hero is a term given to a *hero* figure who displays the characteristics of Childe Harold, Don Juan, or other heroes of *Byron*'s *narrative poem*s; typically he is a brooding, passionate, solitary, and outcast wanderer in wild, remote lands, rebellious and fascinatingly attractive – in other words a typical *Romantic* figure, alone in the world and finding new pathways that owe nothing to social convention.

Byronic stanza: see *ottava rima*.

cacophony is the same as *dissonance*.

cadence refers to the musical *rhythm* of language in *prose* or *verse*:

- in a general sense
- in particular toward the end of a sentence, line, or short passage, e.g. whether it rises or falls, is questioning or commanding, and so forth. It is a part of a writer's *style*; for instance, the cadences of *Beckett*, *Dickens*, and *Tennyson* are distinctive.

caesura: a natural pause in a line of *verse*, sometimes roughly midway through the line and usually indicated by punctuation. It is frequently used in combination with enjambment to give variety in the pacing of verse and to avoid monotonous regularity. For an example see *enjambment*.

Cambridge School of Critics: an umbrella term given to an opinion-forming group of English academics at Cambridge University between the 1920s and 1950s. See *Empson, Leavisite, Richards*.

Campbell, Roy (1901–57): South African poet, translator, and autobiographer. His reputation was established by THE FLAMING TERRAPIN (1924), a long allegorical *poem*. Sometimes accused of self-congratulatory writing, he took a *satirical* view of South African intellectuals, attacked the *Bloomsbury group*, and was influenced by his experiences as a fascist sympathizer fighting for Franco in the Spanish Civil War. Later writing tends to be more calmly contemplative. Other notable works include ADAMASTOR (1930), THE GEORGIAD (1931), THE FLOWERING REEDS (1933), MITHRAIC EMBLEMS (1936), FLOWERING RIFLE (1939), SONS OF THE MISTRAL (1941), LIGHT ON A DARK HORSE (1951), COLLECTED POEMS (1960).

campus novel: a *novel*, often humorous, exploring university life, e.g. *Kingsley Amis's* LUCKY JIM, *Bradbury's* THE HISTORY MAN, *Lodge's* CHANGING PLACES.

canon: an accepted list of great *literature* that is believed to constitute the essential tradition of English (or any other) culture. See *Leavisite*.

caricature: a *style* of writing (or drawing) that deliberately exaggerates particular features of its subject, usually for comic and/or *satirical* effect, e.g. the portrayal of Sir Andrew Aguecheek in *Shakespeare's* TWELFTH NIGHT. The *novels* of writers such as *Fielding, Smollett, Dickens*, and *Thackeray* are rich in caricatures.

Caroline age generally refers to *literature* written in England during the reign of Charles I (1625–49).

Caroline drama covers plays written during the reign of Charles I (1625–49); however:

- no plays were performed after the closing of the theaters by the Puritans in 1642
- the period 1603–42 is sometimes covered by the term *Jacobean drama*
- the period 1558–1642 is sometimes covered by the overall term *Elizabethan drama*.

carpe diem, meaning "seize the day," is a phrase coined by the Latin poet Horace suggesting that because life is short one must grasp present pleasures. This *motif* is commonplace in *literature*, and was especially popular with the Elizabethan *lyric* poets, e.g. in *Herrick*'s "Gather ye rosebuds while ye may" (in the famous *poem* "To the Virgins, to Make Much of Time") and Feste's song "O Mistress Mine" in *Shakespeare*'s TWELFTH NIGHT. Other notable examples include *Marvell*'s "To His Coy Mistress."

Carter, Angela (1940–92): English novelist, *short story* writer, and essayist. Some of her early works are examples of *magic realism*. Her writing is often humorous and feminist, and challenges ideas of reality, later work mixing *fantasy* with reality in an accessible *style*. Notable works include THE MAGIC TOYSHOP (1967), HEROES AND VILLAINS (1969), THE BLOODY CHAMBER (1979), THE SADEIAN WOMEN (1979), NIGHTS AT THE CIRCUS (1984), WISE CHILDREN (1991), BURNING YOUR BOATS: COLLECTED SHORT STORIES (1995).

Carter, Martin (b.1927): Guyanese poet. His *poem*s are noted for their *rhetoric*, compassion, and startling *imagery*; they are sometimes influenced by his political activity, but also show personal concerns. Notable works include THE HILL OF FIRE GLOWS RED (1951), THE KIND EAGLE (1952), RETURNING (1953), POEMS OF RESISTANCE (1954), POEMS OF SUCCESSION (1977).

Carver, Raymond (1938–88): American *short story* writer and poet. His reputation rests on the former, which are often very short, *minimalist*, tightly written pieces about ordinary people, simple on the surface but containing a concentrated and dark view of lack of communication in the 20th century world. Notable works include WILL YOU PLEASE BE QUIET, PLEASE? (1976), CATHEDRAL (1983), FIRES (1983).

Cary, Joyce (1888–1957): British novelist. His experience in Nigeria affected his early *novel*s looking at the ways in which Africans and their British administrators related to each other. He also explored politics, childhood experiences, and the British empire, but most important to him was the world of art. Notable works include AISSA SAVED (1932), AN AMERICAN VISITOR (1933), MISTER JOHNSON (1939), POWER IN MEN (1939), CHARLEY IS MY DARLING (1940), HERSELF SURPRISED (1941), THE HORSE'S MOUTH (1944), NOT HONOUR MORE (1955).

catalexis: the omission of a syllable from the final *foot* of a line in *verse*, e.g. as happens quite frequently in *trochaic* verse:

> Through the / forest / I have / gone
>> (Puck in *Shakespeare*'s A MIDSUMMER NIGHT'S DREAM)
>
> Tyger / Tyger / burning / bright   (from *Blake*'s "The Tyger")

In these examples the lost syllable creates a *masculine ending*. The use of catalectic lines is also called truncation.

catastrophe: the final *climax* of a play or *story* after which the *plot* is resolved. See also *act, dénouement, resolution*.

catharsis: an emotional release experienced by an audience as they witness the fate of a tragic *hero*. See *Aristotle*.

Cather, Willa (1873–1947): American novelist, poet, and *short story* writer. The experience of the pioneer is central to her wide-ranging and complex work as a woman writer dealing with issues such as contrary impulses toward life (e.g. adventure/safety) and the American frontier. Notable works include O Pioneers! (1913), My Ántonia (1918), Death Comes for the Archbishop (1927), One of Ours (1922).

Causley, Charles (b.1917): English poet and children's *story* writer. Influenced by *Clare*, he makes innocence a frequent *theme* in his *poetry*. His *diction* is direct, and he often uses the straightforward *rhythm* of *ballad* and popular *song*. Notable works include Collected Poems 1951–75 (1975), The Animals' Carol (1978), The Gift of a Lamb (1978), Early in the Morning (1986), Jack the Treacle Eater (1987).

Cavalier is a label given to certain *lyric* poets active during the reign of King Charles I, e.g. Thomas Carew (?1594–1640), *Herrick, Lovelace,* John Suckling (1609–42). Their *verse* is characteristically elegant and *witty love poetry*. The term is also sometimes used of certain court *dramas* of the period.

Caxton, William (?1422–?91): English printer who set up the first printing press in England close to London's Westminster Abbey in about 1471, for the first time making available in print many works including those of the major early English poets such as *Gower, Lydgate,* and *Chaucer.*

Celtic renaissance/revival/twilight: all terms associated with the resurgence of Irish *literature* at the end of the 19th century of which *Yeats* was the leading light.

Chandler, Raymond (1888–1959): American novelist, *short story* writer, and screenwriter, considered one of the greatest practitioners of *detective fiction*. In the *character* of Philip Marlowe, Chandler created a prototype for the "hard-boiled" detective – tough and cynical, but with a strong sense of moral values underneath. Notable works include The Big Sleep (1939), Farewell, My Lovely (1940), The High Window (1942), The Lady in the Lake (1943), and the screenplay Double Indemnity (1946, with Billy Wilder).

Chang, Jung (b.1952): Chinese-born writer and scholar, based in Britain, best known for Wild Swans (1992), which might be described as a *nonfiction saga novel,* part *autobiography*, telling of her family's experiences in 20th century China.

Chapman, George (?1559–1634): English playwright, poet, translator, and collaborator. Friendly with and influenced by *Jonson*, he was highly praised during his lifetime as a writer of *comedies, tragedies,* and *masques* for the stage, but subsequently did not maintain the status of some of his peers. Perhaps now best remembered for his translation of *Homer* which was praised by *Keats* in his *sonnet* "On First Looking into Chapman's Homer" (1816). Other notable works include The Shadow of Night (1594), Ovid's Banquet of Sense (1595), All Fools (?1599), Bussy D'Ambois (?1604), Eastward Ho (1605, with Jonson and *Marston*), The Revenge of Bussy D'Ambois (?1610).

character: a created person in a play or a *story* whose particular qualities are revealed by the *action, description,* and conversation. Not to be confused with the actor in a play, who represents the character.

characterization is the method by which *character*s are established in a *narrative* or *drama*. See *flat characters, round characters, showing and telling*.

Chatterton, Thomas (1752–70): English poet. The "marvellous boy," as *Wordsworth* called him, has become an image of lost talent, his youthful suicide being part of his attraction for poets of the *Romantic period, Keats* dedicating ENDYMION to him. His *poetry*, written in *Spenserian style* using *archaisms*, shows a budding talent. Notable works include "Ethelgar, A Saxon Poem" (1769), ROWLEY POEMS (1777).

Chatwin, Bruce (1940–89): English travel writer and novelist. A versatile and sensitive writer, with notable works including IN PATAGONIA (1977), ON THE BLACK HILL (1982), THE SONGLINES (1987), UTZ (1988).

Chaucer, Geoffrey (?1340–1400): English poet and translator. A superb storyteller, he is generally acknowledged as the greatest English writer of the Middle Ages. He spent much of his life in royal service and this enabled him to travel, his time in Italy bringing him into contact with *Boccaccio* and *Petrarch* by whom his work is much influenced. His decision to write in English rather than Anglo-Norman or Latin did much to establish the former as a literary language. His range extends from the courtly to the earthy, combining philosophy and *realism*, and he is credited with shrewd insights into the enduring traits of human nature. His best-known work is THE CANTERBURY TALES (?1387–1400), a *collection* of *stories* in the *manner* of Boccaccio, in which pilgrims en route from London to the tomb of Thomas à Becket at Canterbury tell stories ranging from *fabliau* to those of *courtly love* in order to pass the time. Notable works include THE BOOK OF THE DUCHESS (?1370), THE HOUSE OF FAME (?1376), THE PARLEMENT OF FOULES (?1382), THE LEGEND OF GOOD WOMEN (?1384), TROILUS AND CRISEYDE (?1385). See also *decasyllabic line, dream vision, exemplum, fable, rhyme royal*.

Chaucerian stanza: see *rhyme royal*.

Chaudhuri, N.C. (1897–1999): Indian historian, biographer, and autobiographer. Much of his work explores Anglo-Indian relationships. Notable works include THE AUTOBIOGRAPHY OF AN UNKNOWN INDIAN (1951), THY HAND, GREAT ANARCH! (1987).

Cheever, John (1912–82): American novelist and *short story* writer. His frequent territory is the well-heeled communities of east-coast modern America, wherein individuals struggle, often in vain, with questions of love, morality, and the meaning of existence. Notable works include the *collection*s THE BRIGADIER AND THE GOLF WIDOW (1964), THE WORLD OF APPLES (1973), and the *novel*s THE WAPSHOT CHRONICLE (1957), THE WAPSHOT SCANDAL (1964), BULLET PARK (1969).

Chesterton, G.K. (1874–1936): English poet, novelist, *short story* writer, critic, journalist, essayist, and autobiographer. His prolific output was invariably colored by his strong moral and politically leftwing views. He made a marked contribution to *detective fiction* with his Father Brown stories. Notable works include CHARLES DICKENS (1906), THE VICTORIAN AGE IN LITERATURE (1913), THE INNOCENCE OF FATHER BROWN (1911), THE FLYING INN (1914), COLLECTED POEMS (1927), CHAUCER (1932), AUTOBIOGRAPHY (1936).

chiasmus: *figure of speech* in which the word order of similar phrases is turned around, e.g. adverb–verb–subject is followed by subject–adverb–verb. Used frequently in 18th century *verse*, it is a *form* of *antithesis*. A famous nonliterary example is President Kennedy's "Ask not what your country can do for you, but what you can do for your country."

Chopin, Kate (1850–1904): American novelist, poet, *short story* writer, and essayist who was influenced by the French writer Guy de Maupassant (1850–93). Notable works include THE AWAKENING (1899) which, like the Norwegian playwright *Ibsen*'s THE DOLL'S HOUSE (1879), was regarded as scandalous in its sympathetic depiction of a woman who breaks the traditional constraints of marriage.

choric figures are *character*s within a play or *novel* who comment upon the *action* while being a part of it, e.g. in *Shakespeare*, the Fool in KING LEAR, Enobarbus in ANTONY AND CLEOPATRA, Thersites in TROILUS AND CRESSIDA (?1602), Tom in *Tennessee Williams*'s THE GLASS MENAGERIE, Alfieri in *Miller*'s A VIEW FROM THE BRIDGE. Examples of choric figures in novels are the rustics in *George Eliot*'s SILAS MARNER or in various of *Hardy*'s novels, and the use of aged African-American women and other figures in some of *Faulkner*'s works.

chorus: a person or group of people which stand outside the *action* of a *drama* and comment upon it. Most *tragedies* in ancient Greece had a chorus of citizens or elders who, as virtual representatives of the audience, react to the events of the *action* but are powerless to affect the course of events. *Shakespeare* occasionally uses choruses of various kinds, as in ROMEO AND JULIET and HENRY V, and among other notable usages are in *Milton*'s SAMSON AGONISTES, *T.S. Eliot*'s MURDER IN THE CATHEDRAL and *Wilder*'s OUR TOWN; but there has not been great use of a chorus in English theater. See *choric figures*.

chronicle: any kind of sequential historical account such as the Anglo-Saxon Chronicle, written in Old English. THE UNION OF THE NOBLE AND ILLUSTRE FAMILIES OF LANCASTRE AND YORK (1542) by Edward Hall (?1513–72) and CHRONICLES OF ENGLAND, SCOTLAND AND IRELAND (1577) by Raphael Holinshed (?d.1580) were important sources for the *chronicle play*s of *Shakespeare* and his contemporary playwrights.

chronicle play: a type of history play that deals with highlighted events from the reign of an English king. Such plays were popular during the closing years of the 16th century, fueled by patriotic enthusiasm after the defeat of the Spanish Armada in 1588, e.g. *Marlowe*'s EDWARD II and *Shakespeare*'s two *cycle*s of eight plays covering seven kings in English history from the 1370s to 1485.

Churchill, Caryl (b.1938): English playwright. Her work is characteristically leftwing and feminist, but not narrowly so: she ranges with *humor* and intelligence over a wide range of social, moral, political, and other subjects. She has worked closely with small theater companies in Britain. Notable works include VINEGAR TOM (1976), CLOUD NINE (1979), FEN (1982), TOP GIRLS (1982), SERIOUS MONEY (1987).

Cibber, Colley (1671–1757): English actor, playwright, adapter, and poet. His LOVE'S LAST SHIFT (1696, satirized by *Vanbrugh* in THE RELAPSE – in which, ironically, Cibber played Lord Foppington) began the vogue for *sentimental comedy*, which lasted through most of the 18th century, and which encouraged Cibber to adapt several of *Shakespeare*'s plays to suit the taste of the time. His literary merit (much mocked by his contemporaries) is considered doubtful, but his contribution to the theater is underrated. In his *autobiography* AN APOLOGY FOR THE LIFE OF MR. COLLEY CIBBER, COMEDIAN (1740), he paints a colorful picture of theater life in his day. He was *poet laureate* from 1730–57. Other notable works include THE CARELESS HUSBAND (1704).

Ciceronian style is an elaborate and florid, yet clear and well-ordered, *prose style* (from the Roman writer, politician, and orator Cicero (106–43BC). It may be regarded as the opposite of the *Senecan style*.

Cisneros, Sandra (b.1945): American poet and novelist. Her work explores poverty, and racial and sexual oppression, drawing on childhood reminiscences and her Mexican/American parentage. Notable works include THE HOUSE ON MANGO STREET (1983) and MY WICKED WICKED WAYS (1987).

citizen comedy was popular in the early 17th century in England, and usually dealt with lower- and middle-class London life. Good examples are *Dekker*'s THE SHOEMAKER'S HOLIDAY, *Jonson*'s BARTHOLOMEW FAIR, and *Middleton*'s A CHASTE MAID IN CHEAPSIDE (?1613). *Shakespeare*'s only citizen comedy is THE MERRY WIVES OF WINDSOR (?1598).

Clare, John (1793–1864): English poet. Usually categorized as a rural poet, he was much attached to his native village of Helpston where he was an agricultural laborer. He wrote with clarity and truth about the coutryside of his corner of North-amptonshire. His *poetry* was at first fashionable, but a decline in the popularity of so-called "ploughman poets" contributed to his growing insanity, and he spent the last years of his life in Northampton General Asylum. Thanks to the attention of *Blunden, Day Lewis*, and others his poetry has once more become known and admired. Notable works include POEMS DESCRIPTIVE OF RURAL LIFE AND SCENERY (1820), THE VILLAGE MINSTREL (1821), THE SHEPHERD'S CALENDAR (1827). The 20th century saw the publication of POEMS (1935), LETTERS (1951), PROSE (1951).

Clark, Bekederemo J.P. (b.1935): Nigerian poet, playwright, and literary critic. His work is rooted in Ijaw culture. Notable works include SONG OF A GOAT (1961), AMERICA THEIR AMERICA (1964), THE EXAMPLE OF SHAKESPEARE (1970), A DECADE OF TONGUES (1981).

Clarke, Gillian (b.1937): Welsh poet. She can focus upon particular moments, arti-facts, or incidents, often inspired by her native Wales, handling them and their sig-nificance with lyricism and within a controlled *structure*. Notable works include LETTER FROM A FAR COUNTRY (1982), SELECTED POEMS (1985), LETTING IN THE RUMOUR (1989), THE KING OF BRITAIN'S DAUGHTER (1993).

classic as a term has developed three broad meanings when applied to *literature*:

- works from ancient Greece or Rome (from "classical" times), whether of high merit or not
- outstanding works from any age

- typical, e.g. *Shakespeare's* HAMLET might be described as a classic *revenge tragedy*, or *Mary Shelley's* FRANKENSTEIN as a classic *gothic novel.*

clerihew: a four-line *verse* of two *couplets*, often comic and sometimes epigrammatic, named after its inventor E. Clerihew Bentley (1875–1956), as in:

George the Third
Ought never to have occurred.
One can only wonder
At so grotesque a blunder.

cliché: a word or phrase that, when first used, may have some freshness and originality but has since become worn out through overuse, e.g. "to turn over a new leaf," "interface," "a whole new ballgame," "over the moon." *Pope* famously satirized the clichés of *poetasters* in his ESSAY ON CRITICISM:

Where'er you find "the cooling western breeze",
In the next line, it "whispers through the trees";
If crystal streams "with pleasing murmurs creep",
The reader's threatened (not in vain) with "sleep".

climax is a term sometimes used interchangeably with *crisis* and *turning point* generally to indicate the arrival of any time of crucial intensity in a play or *story*; but the term is more precisely used to indicate that particular moment when the *rising action* leads to a high point in the fortunes of the *hero* or *heroine*. See *act, anabasis, plot.*

close reading: the focusing upon ways that writers' choices of *form, structure,* and language shape *meanings*. This approach was sometimes disparaged in the 1970s and 1980s, but it is essential to a precise understanding of how writers create their effects. See *explication, intrinsic attitude, Leavisite.* By contrast, see *extrinsic attitude.*

closed couplet: a *couplet* of *verse,* common in the *heroic couplet,* where the sense is complete by the end of the second line, e.g.

Say what strange motive, Goddess! could compel
A well-bred lord to assault a gentle belle?

(from *Pope's* THE RAPE OF THE LOCK)

closet drama may best be described as a dramatic *poem,* as it is intended to be read rather than performed, e.g. *Milton's* SAMSON AGONISTES, *Percy Shelley's* PROMETHEUS UNBOUND.

closure is a sense of conclusion at the end of:

- a *novel* or *drama* when the *resolution* is clear and there are no loose ends
- a line in *poetry* that is *end-stopped* or a *stanza* that finishes with a period.

Clough, Arthur Hugh (1819–61): English poet whose *lyric* ability often conveys characteristic Victorian doubts. Notable works include THE BOTHIE OF TOBER-NA-VUOLICH (1848), AMOURS DE VOYAGE (1858), POEMS (1862), DIPSYCHUS (1865).

cockney school of poetry: a contemptuous and snobbish term that first appeared in the October 1817 edition of the rightwing BLACKMORE'S magazine in England and used to mock a particular group of London-based poets including *Hazlitt, Keats, Lamb,* and *Hunt* who were not considered to be of any social standing.

coda: similar to an *epilog*, a concluding section that rounds off a piece of *literature* in some way, e.g. at the end of *Stoppard's* JUMPERS.

code is a term used in *structuralism* to denote the system of *signs* in a language that the reader must understand, or decode, in order to interpret a *text*. See *hermeneutics*, *interpretation*.

Coetzee, J.M. (b.1940): South African novelist and literary critic. He is a political writer who is also concerned about the *techniques* of *fiction*. Notable works include IN THE HEART OF THE COUNTRY (1977), WAITING FOR THE BARBARIANS (1980), LIFE AND TIMES OF MICHAEL K (1982), FOE (1986), DISGRACE (1999).

Coleridge, Samuel Taylor (1772–1834): English poet, critic, and translator. His relationship with *Wordsworth*, especially their collaboration over the LYRICAL BALLADS, affected the direction of English *poetry* and was a keystone in English *Romanticism*. Inventive, imaginative and exciting, his small but brilliant poetic output is shot through with a sense of insecurity. He was an influential critic and thinker, and his theories on such matters as the poetic *imagination*, *organic form*, and the Elizabethan stage contribute much to literary *criticism* in general and our understanding of Romanticism in particular. Notable works include "Kubla Khan" (1797), "The Rime of the Ancient Mariner" (1798, published in LYRICAL BALLADS), "Frost at Midnight" (1798), "Dejection: An Ode" (1802), BIOGRAPHIA LITERARIA (1817).

collection: a gathering together of all the work of a single writer, usually *poetry* and of a particular period of output, e.g. *Lochhead's* DREAMING FRANKENSTEIN, AND COLLECTED POEMS. Not to be confused with *anthology*. See also *selection*.

Collins, Billy (b.1941): American poet. His accessible *poetry* has achieved both critical and popular acclaim, and he is in demand as a *performance poet*. He has said that his poetry is about dwelling on the interesting side issues that distract us from our planned direction through the day. Notable works include QUESTIONS ABOUT ANGELS (1991), THE ART OF DROWNING (1995), PICNIC, LIGHTENING (1998).

Collins, Wilkie (1824–89): English novelist and playwright. A friend of *Dickens*, whose advice and *criticism* he respected, he is regarded as one of the first *thriller* writers; his complex plots of crime, mystery, and suspense were popular but often criticized for sensationalism. Notable works include THE FROZEN DEEP (1857), THE WOMAN IN WHITE (1860), NO NAME (1862), ARMADALE (1866), THE MOONSTONE (1868). See *novel of sensation*.

Collins, William (1721–59): English poet. He wrote much in his short life, including some fine *odes*. He was technically skillful, but perhaps never quite achieved his potential. Notable works include ODES ON SEVERAL DESCRIPTIVE AND ALLEGORICAL SUBJECTS (1746–47), "Ode on the Popular Superstitions of the Highlands" (1788, published posthumously).

colonial criticism: see *postcolonial criticism*.

Colonial period: often used to define the period of American *literature* covering 1607 (the founding of the settlement at Jamestown) until 1775 (the outbreak of the Revolutionary War).

comedy defines a work that is primarily designed to amuse and entertain, and in which, despite alarms along the way, all ends well for the *characters*. The term is usually applied to a play (originally referring to Greek and Roman *dramas*), sometimes to a *novel*, and very occasionally to *narrative verse*. The *genre* is a wide category covering many different types, and does not necessarily mean that the work intends to provoke laughter.

comedy of humors is a kind of *drama* where the *characters* are constructed upon the old physiological theory of *humors*. The *genre* was particularly popular around the time when *Jonson* wrote EVERY MAN IN HIS HUMOUR (1598) and EVERY MAN OUT OF HIS HUMOUR (1599), and several of his contemporaries such as *Chapman, Fletcher, Massinger,* and *Middleton* exploited the *form*.

comedy of ideas is a term sometimes applied to plays that debate ideas in a *witty* or humorous way, e.g. several of *Shaw's* such as MAN AND SUPERMAN (1905) or BACK TO METHUSELAH (1922).

comedy of manners refers to a type of *drama* where the social behavior of a section of the community is humorously portrayed. *Shakespeare's* LOVE'S LABOUR'S LOST (?1594) and MUCH ADO ABOUT NOTHING (?1598) may be so described, but some critics consider an essential element to be that the audience is composed of the same social class as that depicted on stage; that is, they are induced to laugh at themselves. Most *Restoration comedy* fulfills this requirement, where upper and upper-middle class behavior is portrayed. Later examples include the plays of *Sheridan, Wilde,* and *Coward.* A good example of a modern writer in the *genre* is *Ayckbourn,* whose comedies depict middle-class behavior for a middle-class audience.

comedy of menace is a term originating in the 1950s to denote a type of play in which the *characters* feel, or indeed are, threatened, e.g. *Pinter's* THE BIRTHDAY PARTY.

comic relief is a term given to an episode in an otherwise serious play, even a *tragedy,* in order to provide one or more of the following:

- relief from the intensity of the *drama,* e.g. the Porter scene in act II, scene 3 of *Shakespeare's* MACBETH
- a contrast to the *tone* of the surrounding drama, e.g. the Gravediggers' scene in act V, scene 1 of Shakespeare's HAMLET
- a pause before the final *climax* of the drama, e.g. the appearance of the Clown in act V, scene 2 of Shakespeare's ANTONY AND CLEOPATRA.

Only the MACBETH instance above is not an example of all three cases. Comic relief fails if it is merely that and is not integrated into the scheme of the drama as a whole.

commedia dell'arte: a *form* of comic *drama* developed in Italy during the 16th century and involving stock *characters* such as a young daughter, a lover, an old father (Pantaloon), a cunning servant (Harlequin), a hunchback clown (Punch), the *action* being improvised around a standard *plot*. The *genre* influenced Elizabethan writing, e.g. *Shakespeare's* THE TAMING OF THE SHREW (?1592), and also French playwrights such as Molière (1622–73), and *opera*.

Commonwealth literature is *postcolonial literature* from member countries of the British Commonwealth of Nations.

Commonwealth period: generally refers to *literature* written in England between 1649 and 1660 (the Puritan Interregnum).

comparative literature: a study of similarities and parallels in the *literature* of different cultures and countries.

complaint: a melancholy subgenre of *lyric* poem, typically mourning the loss of a lover or the sad state of the world, e.g. *Chaucer*'s "A Complaint unto Pity" (14th century), *Wyatt*'s "They Flee from Me," *Surrey*'s "Complaint by Night of the Lover Not Beloved," Abraham Cowley's (1618–87) *ode* "The Complaint" (1656). See *dirge, elegy, lament.*

conceit: a clever or *witty* thought, often conveyed by a surprising image. In Elizabethan *poetry* "conceit" simply referred to a *simile, metaphor,* or any extended *figure of speech*; in later *metaphysical* poetry it increasingly indicated ingenious, striking use of *figurative language.*

concrete language is that which refers to things rather than ideas (which are *abstract*), e.g. "There is a willow grows aslant a brook" (*Shakespeare*, HAMLET).

concrete poetry is a *form* of *poetry* in which the typography and/or the shape of the *poem* on the page creates a pattern or picture that has immediate impact and is very much a part of the *meaning*. The fashion for such poetry grew in the 20th century, but poets such as *Herbert*, with his pattern poetry, and *Hopkins* had experimented with it in earlier centuries. Good modern examples include John Hollander's "Swan and Shadow" (1969 – words in the shape of a swan and its reflection in the water) and *McGough*'s "40-Love" (1971). (See page 34.)

confessional literature is a term covering self-revelatory *prose* such as *De Quincey*'s CONFESSIONS OF AN ENGLISH OPIUM EATER and THE PRIVATE MEMOIRS AND CONFESSIONS OF A JUSTIFIED SINNER (1824) by James Hogg (1770–1835). See *confessional poetry.*

confessional poetry is a term used to describe *poetry* that reveals, sometimes in explicit detail, the personal life of the poet. Although *Coleridge, Wordsworth* (THE PRELUDE), and others had written of their personal responses to life, this term is usually applied to the very candid American *narrative* and *lyric verse* that emerged with *Robert Lowell*'s LIFE STUDIES in the late 1950s, partly in reaction against the idea of *T.S. Eliot* and the *new critics* that poetry should be impersonal. Those who have been classified as confessional poets include Robert Lowell, the *Beat movement* poets, *Plath, Berryman, Rich, Sexton.* See *confessional literature.*

Congreve, William (1670–1729): English playwright. Considered one of the best writers of *Restoration comedy*, his *comedy of manners* dealing subtly and humorously with the social tensions of romance and marriage in the upper-class society of his day. Notable works include LOVE FOR LOVE (1695), THE WAY OF THE WORLD (1700).

connotation: an implication, suggestion, or *association* that a word or string of words conveys to an individual, or to people in general, beyond the literal, surface *meaning* (or *denotation*) of the word(s). Connotations make *metaphors* possible. See also *referential language.*

```
                        Dusk
                     Above the
                  water hang the
                         loud
                         flies
                         Here
                        O so
                        gray
                        then
            What              A pale signal will appear
            When         Soon before its shadow fades
            Where        Here in this pool of opened eye
         In us       No Upon us As at the very edges
            of where we take shape in the dark air
             this object bares its image awakening
                ripples of recognition that will
                 brush darkness up into light
even after this bird this hour both drift by atop the perfect sad instant now
                 already passing out of sight
               toward yet-untroubled reflection
             this image bears its object darkening
          into memorial shades Scattered bits of
       light       No of water Or something across
       water          Breaking up No Being regathered
        soon            Yet by then a swan will have
          gone              Yes out of mind into what
                         vast
                         pale
                         hush
                         of a
                        place
                         past
                  sudden dark as
                    if a swan
                       sang
```

Concrete poetry (see page 33)

Conrad, Joseph (1857–1924): Polish-born British novelist, considered to be a leading *modernist.* His experience as a sailor inspired his writing. The stylistic beauty of his own writing may be a result of his not being a native speaker. *Leavis* considered him one of the greatest novelists in the English language (see *Leavisite*). He often explores the psychological and the mythic, although some recent readings of his work tend to focus on *postcolonial* and gender aspects. He constantly criticizes colonial powers for their treatment of the undeveloped world; yet HEART OF DARKNESS (1902) has recently been criticized as racist (although it could be read as a trenchant *criticism* of racism). Other notable works include LORD JIM (1900), NOSTROMO (1904), THE SECRET AGENT (1907), UNDER WESTERN EYES (1911).

consonance: repetition of the same consonant sounds before and after a different vowel, e.g. clip-clop, crust crest, stop step, leader loader louder. In *poetry* it is a variety of *half rhyme*. See also *alliteration, assonance*.

content, in a literary sense, is any *theme*, idea, *argument, action, story*, or *moral* message that is contained within a literary *form*.

context: this term has traditionally been used to indicate the placing of a given passage or section of a literary work in relation to the parts that immediately precede and follow it. However, for the wider sense in which the term is currently applied, see *contextuality*.

contextuality: the idea that writers, readers, and *texts* function within personal, biographical, political, social, literary, cultural, and/or historical *contexts*, and are influenced by the beliefs and assumptions of the times in which they are written and read.

convention: the term is used in two main senses; it describes

- an agreed method of conveying an idea between the writer and reader (or audience). The term is often used when the *manner* of presentation is not realistic. For instance, when watching a play, an audience suspends disbelief, knowing that what it is watching is only a representation of a certain scene; or accepts the convention that in *soliloquy* a *character* is speaking thoughts aloud (see *suspension of disbelief*)

- any accepted recurrent feature in writing, such as the use of *meter* in *verse*, or the convention that a *sonnet* has 14 lines, or the appearance of certain minor *stock characters* in *fiction* in order to move the *plot* along.

Structuralist critics frequently point out that all *literature* is written in conventions or *codes* that are not realistic.

conversation piece/poem: writing, usually *blank verse poetry*, that in an informal *style* and *tone* conveys a *mood* often by *association*. *Coleridge* and *Wordsworth* wrote many such *poems*, e.g. respectively "This Limetree Bower My Prison" and "Tintern Abbey," and among others who wrote in this *genre* were *Robert Browning, Frost, Auden*.

Cooper, James Fenimore (1789–1851): American novelist best known for his portrayal of Native Americans and pioneer life, and for his development of the *character* known as Leatherstocking. Notable works include THE PIONEERS (1823), THE LAST OF THE MOHICANS (1826).

Cope, Wendy (b.1945): English poet. She writes reflective *poetry* on a wide range of topics, and is particularly skilled at *witty*, sensitive, and technically clever *parodies* of other modern poets. Notable works include MAKING COCOA FOR KINGSLEY AMIS (1986), IF I DON'T KNOW (2001).

Copernican revolution: a term given to describe the explosion of ideas following the theory proposed by Nicolas Copernicus (1473–1543), in which the earth and other planets were seen to revolve around the sun. This superseded the *Ptolemaic system* in astronomy in which the earth was believed to be at the center of the universe, making way for modern ideas of cosmology. In THE FIRST ANNIVERSARY (1611) *Donne* wrote that the "new Philosophy calls all in doubt," and indeed it had a profound effect on *Renaissance literature*. For decades after the Ptolemaic system was scientifically accepted as dead, writers often used the old cosmology imaginatively, e.g. *Milton* in PARADISE LOST (1667). Donne blends attachment to the old system with grasp of the new when he begins "Holy Sonnet 7" (1635) "At the round earth's imagined corners…"

correctness is conforming to rules and *conventions*. Writers in the 17th and 18th centuries tended to think that this was a good idea; but in general the English, unlike the French and mindful of *Shakespeare*'s lack of concern with rules such as the *dramatic unities*, have valued appropriateness as more important.

Corso, Gregory (1930–2001): American poet, novelist, and playwright. He is the best-known and most widely read of the *Beat movement* poets, and in his prodigious output he aimed at the *rhythm*s of speech. Anarchic in *style* and often politically motivated, his *poems* are generally more humorous, lighter of touch, and sometimes more exuberant than others in the group. Notable works include "Gasoline" (1958), "Bomb" (1958, an example of *concrete poetry*), THE HAPPY BIRTHDAY OF DEATH (1960), MINDFIELD: NEW AND SELECTED POEMS (1989).

counterpoint, a term adopted from music, is applied to *verse* to indicate the introduction of metrical variation; e.g. if the *meter* is basically iambic, and then trochaic, dactylic, or anapestic variations are introduced, the effect may be said to be counterpoint.

coup de théâtre: a strikingly theatrical twist in the *plot* of a play that changes the direction of the *action*.

couplet: a pair of lines, usually rhyming, in *verse*, e.g.

> O body swayed to music, O brightening glance
> How can we know the dancer from the dance?

> (from *Yeats*'s "Among School Children," 1928)

courtly love refers to a kind of idealized love portrayed in *poems*, *romance*s, and *song*s of the Middle Ages. The lovers are always of a high social class, and their love is ennobling despite being outside marriage (which was likely to be an arranged marriage of economic and/or political convenience between powerful families, and little to do with love). By *convention* the lady is worshipped by the lover, who suffers constantly in body and mind, at some point making an extended lover's *complaint*, and is tested by a very arduous task or quest on behalf of the beloved. The pattern of courtly love was that of Lancelot for Guinevere in *Arthurian legend*. It is unlikely that the concept is a realistic picture of medieval love. *Feminist criticism* tends to view it as yet another way of subordinating women to men. There are aspects of courtly love in many works, and also criticism and even mocking of the convention, in *Chaucer*'s TROILUS AND CRISEYDE and in several of THE CANTERBURY TALES. *Sidney, Spenser,* and *Shakespeare* also depict courtly love, especially in their *sonnet*s.

Couzyn, Jeni (b.1942): Canadian poet. Her work, much of it introspective, tends to focus with clarity and directness upon various aspects of womanhood, and on the difficulties of living. Notable works include FLYING (1970), CHRISTMAS IN AFRICA (1975), A TIME TO BE BORN (1981), LIFE BY DROWNING: SELECTED POEMS (1983), THAT'S IT (1993).

Coward, Nöel (1899–1973): English playwright, *short story* writer, composer, and lyricist. Characteristically he portrays a society where all are out for pleasure, the sophisticated and the unconventional showing *wit* and elegance, winning the audience's admiration at the expense of the boring, sober, and conservatively puritanical. Notable works include THE VORTEX (1924), HAY FEVER (1925), PRIVATE LIVES (1930), DESIGN FOR LIVING (1933), BLITHE SPIRIT (1941), PRESENT LAUGHTER (1942).

Cowleyan ode: see *irregular ode.*

Cowper, William (1731–1800): English poet and translator. His *poetry*, often dealing with the helpless isolation of the individual, is by turns direct, simple, quietly *witty*, and powerful, pointing toward *Romanticism* through his frequent focus upon rural subjects. Notable works include "God Moves in a Mysterious Way" (1779, a hymn), THE TASK (1785), "The Castaway" (1799).

Crabbe, George (1754–1832): English poet. Much of his early *poetry* is *Augustan* in the *manner* of *Pope*, later *narrative verse* being more akin to contemporary *Romantics*; yet he continued to write in *heroic couplets*. Inspired by the landscape of his native Suffolk, he creates a picture of an often poor and degraded rural life. Among his friends or admirers he numbered *Austen, Byron, Johnson, Walter Scott, Southey, Wordsworth*. Notable works include THE VILLAGE (1783), THE BOROUGH (1810, including "Peter Grimes").

Crane, Hart (1899–1932): American poet. His most important work is the long *poem* THE BRIDGE (1930), a celebration of modern America that uses Brooklyn Bridge as its central *metaphor* but ranges across many images, urban and natural, to present the poet's "mythological synthesis" of his country. Other notable works include WHITE BUILDINGS (1926) and the posthumously published SEVEN LYRICS (1966), TEN UNPUBLISHED POEMS (1972).

Crane, Stephen (1871–1900): American novelist, journalist, *short story* writer, and poet. His experiences of traveling as a journalist were used in his writing, although he had not encountered war before he wrote his best-known work, THE RED BADGE OF COURAGE (1895), hailed as a masterpiece of *realism. Conrad* and *Henry James* became friends and admirers. Other notable works include MAGGIE (1893), THE BLACK RIDER (1895), THE OPEN BOAT AND OTHER STORIES (1898), ACTIVE SERVICE (1899), THE MONSTER (1899), WAR IS KIND (1899).

crime novel: a very general term covering both *detective fiction* and *police procedural* and other kinds of crime *stories*. Often the psychological state of the criminal and her or his attempts to elude the law is of prime interest, e.g. in *Highsmith*'s Ripley *novels*.

crisis is a term generally used to denote any important moment or *turning point* in a play or *story*. Several crises may lead up to a *climax*, and may follow thereafter. For instance, in *Shakespeare*'s HAMLET there may be said to be a crisis when in act I Hamlet hears from the Ghost of his uncle's guilt, a climax in act III when he "proves" that guilt by means of the play-within-the-play, and another crisis soon afterward when he kills Polonius in mistake for his uncle. However, some critics use the two words interchangeably.

critical theory: see *literary/critical theory.*

criticism is a term that refers to the whole business of the analysis, evaluation, and interpretation of works of *literature*. The long history of criticism starts with classical theorists such as *Aristotle, Plato,* Horace (65–8BC), and Cicero (106–43BC). Writers in English who have made important contributions to theories of criticism include *Sidney, Jonson, Dryden, Johnson, Coleridge, Percy Shelley, Poe, Arnold, Bradley, Richards, T.S. Eliot, Leavis, Raymond Williams.* See *extrinsic attitude, intrinsic attitude, Leavisite, literary/critical theory* (and all the cross-references listed thereunder), *new critics, objective criticism, practical criticism.* Two Frenchmen, Roland Barthes (1915–80) and Jacques Derrida (b.1930), have made crucial contributions to modern critical theory.

critique: a detailed analysis of a work, sometimes adversely critical but implying that this standpoint is carefully reasoned.

Crozier, Lorna (b.1948): Canadian poet. Much of her work is inspired by her native prairies, but her lyricism, passion, and *humor* take her observation of humanity beyond the merely local and onto a universal plane. Notable works include THE WEATHER (1983), THE GARDEN GOING ON WITHOUT US (1985), ANGELS OF FLESH, ANGELS OF SILENCE (1988), INVENTING THE HAWK (1992).

Cruden's Concordance is an invaluable cross-reference source to all the main words used in the *Bible.*

cruelty, theater of: see *theater of cruelty.*

cultural materialism: the idea that the time and place in which the *text* is written and being read is vitally important. Cultural materialists argue that gender, race, age, class, educational background, sexual orientation, and many other factors influence the writer and the reader. See *hermeneutics, reader-response theory, Shakespeare.*

cummings, e. e. (1894–1962): American poet. Radical and antiestablishment in his choice of subject matter, he developed his own *style* of *poetry* with his unconventional punctuation and typography as seen in the use of lower case letters for his name. He was influenced by jazz and contemporary slang, and his work as a graphic artist stimulated experimentation with the *form* and layout of his poetry. Notable works include the autobiographical narrative, THE ENORMOUS ROOM (1922), and the poetry *collection*s & (1925), IS 5 (1926).

cyberpunk is a subspecies of *science fiction*. The setting is often located within a virtual reality created by computers. The *character*s are bizarre, whether real or artificial intelligences. The *genre* adapts very well to cinema. Cyberpunk has been seen as an aspect of *postmodernism.*

cycle: another word for a group of linked works, e.g. the cycle of *mystery plays* from the Creation to the Last Judgment, or *Shakespeare*'s history play cycles such as the HENRY VI trilogy, or his *sonnet sequence*. A *collection* like *Chaucer*'s CANTERBURY TALES may also be classed as a cycle.

D

Dabydeen, David (b.1956): Guyanese poet and novelist. He presents the East Indian colonial legacy in a harsh light, is concerned with the experience of migration, and sometimes writes in Creole dialect. He claims to have been particularly influenced by *Shakespeare*'s THE TEMPEST and *Conrad*'s HEART OF DARKNESS. Notable works include SLAVE SONG (1984), THE INTENDED (1990), DISAPPEARANCE (1993), TURNER: NEW AND SELECTED POEMS (1994). See *D'Aguiar*.

dactyl: a *foot* in *verse* consisting of one stressed syllable followed by two unstressed, thus:

- Cánnon to \ ríght of them,
- Cánnon to \ léft of them
  (from *Tennyson*'s "The Charge of the Light Brigade")

dactylic: see *meter*.

D'Aguiar, Fred (b.1960): Guyanese poet, novelist, and playwright. His *poem*s are often humorous, compassionate, and written in the Creole dialect. Notable works include MAMA DOT (1985), AIRY HALL (1989), A JAMAICAN AIRMAN FORSEES HIS DEATH (1991), DEAR FUTURE (1996). See *Dabydeen*.

Dante, Alighieri (1265–1321): Italian poet whose long *poem* THE DIVINE COMEDY (written *c.*1307–21) had a considerable influence on European *literature*. It consists of three sections – the INFERNO, the PURGATORIO, and the PARADISO – all written in a scheme of *terza rima*. Dante's impact on world literature has been compared to that of *Homer* and *Shakespeare*.

Davie, Donald (b.1922): English poet and literary critic. Influenced as a student by *Leavis*, he was a part of and wrote much for *the Movement*, but was later critical of its English parochialism. Notable works include BRIDES OF REASON (1955), A WINTER TALENT (1957), ESSEX POEMS (1969), IN THE STOPPING TRAIN (1977), COLLECTED POEMS (1990).

Davies, John (1569–1626): English poet. Notable works include ORCHESTRA: OR, A POEM OF DANCING (1596), which presents a celebration of Elizabethan life as a courtly, well-ordered, and harmonious dance. See *Tillyard*.

Davies, Robertson (1913–95): Canadian novelist, playwright, and journalist. Heavily influenced by the philosophy of Carl Jung (1875–1961), his works often deal with *myth*, magic, and wonder, and frequently place provincial Canada within the *context* of the psychic *imagination* of a wider world. Notable works include THE SALTERTON TRILOGY (1951–58), THE DEPTFORD TRILOGY (1970–75), THE CORNISH TRILOGY (1981–88), THE CUNNING MAN (1994).

Day Lewis, C. (1904–72): British poet, novelist, critic, and writer of *detective fiction* under the *pseudonym* Nicholas Blake. Associated with *Auden*, *Spender*, and *MacNeice*, he is praised mainly for his early *verse*, in which the *paradox* of Day Lewis as a Marxist with *Romantic* tendencies is sometimes evident. After World War II he increasingly became one of the literary establishment. He was *poet laureate* from 1967–72. Notable works include TRANSITIONAL POEM (1929), THE MAGNETIC MOUNTAIN (1933), A QUESTION OF PROOF (1935), OVERTURES TO DEATH (1938).

de la Mare, Walter (1873–1956): English poet, novelist, literary critic, children's, and *short story* writer associated with the *Georgian* poets. Many of his *poem*s explore childhood and, although sometimes regarded as lightweight, some are enduring. Notable works include THE LISTENERS AND OTHER POEMS (1912), PEACOCK PIE: A BOOK OF RHYMES (1913), MEMORY AND OTHER POEMS (1938), THE BURNING GLASS AND OTHER POEMS (1945), THE WINGED CHARIOT (1951).

De Quincey, Thomas (1785–1859): English literary critic and journalist who was friends with *Coleridge* and *Wordsworth*. His writing on aspects of the way that the mind works had considerable influence on *Poe*, among others. Notable works include the autobiographical CONFESSIONS OF AN ENGLISH OPIUM EATER (1822).

death of the author: a concept advanced by Roland Barthes (1915–80) in his DISCOURSE (1968), as a key aspect of *structuralism*. The idea is that readers respond to *text*s regardless of *authorial intention*. Barthes argues that "the death of the author" leads to "the birth of the reader" in the sense that the reader should not be trying to solve the puzzle of what the *author* means, but should feel free to react with the text in a way that creates a variety of possible and personal interpretations. See *poststructuralism, semiotics*.

decadence: see *aestheticism*.

decasyllabic line: a *verse* line containing ten syllables, the most common line in English *meter* and most often found in the *form* of *iambic pentameter*. Sometimes the line is irregular and carries a syllable more or less than ten. *Chaucer*'s discovery of this line from continental sources was vital and led to the development of, among other things, the *sonnet*, *Spenserian stanza*, and *blank verse*, the medium in which *Shakespeare* and his contemporaries mainly wrote.

deconstruction is a central word in *poststructuralist criticism*, and it has taken on many *meaning*s. At its simplest it may be used as a word that implies analysis with the knowledge that all *text*s depend on interpretation and how both writer and reader variously interpret language, and hence with an awareness that the same text is capable of an enormous multiplicity of possible meanings. Where *poststructuralism* differs from *structuralism* is that the latter holds, in general terms, that rigorous analysis will ultimately fix upon a definite meaning of a text; the former holds that no fixed meaning can ever be found. The French philosopher Jacques Derrida (b.1930) is the foremost figure in the development of deconstruction.

Defoe, Daniel (1660–1731): English novelist, journalist, and poet whose output was among the most prolific of all writers in English. His early work consists largely of *satirical poem*s and political *essay*s in which, in contrast to most of his *Augustan* contemporaries, his *prose style* is plain and direct. He later turned to social, moral, and historical essays, and then late in life discovered his talent for *narrative*. He is now often regarded as the first English novelist, best known for works such as ROBINSON CRUSOE (1719) and MOLL FLANDERS (1722); at the very least he is an important experimenter and innovator in the *genre*, and his lively subject matter set the pattern of *novel* writing for years to come. Other notable works include JOURNAL OF THE PLAGUE YEAR (1722) and ROXANA (1724).

Dekker, Thomas (?1570–1632): English playwright who collaborated with many of his contemporaries, and pamphleteer. His work is vivid, realistic, and, on the whole, cheerful. Notable works include THE SHOEMAKER'S HOLIDAY (1600), THE WITCH OF EDMONTON (1621, in collaboration with *John Ford* and *Rowley*).

Delaney, Shelagh (b.1939): English playwright and scriptwriter. Notable works include A TASTE OF HONEY (1957), which established her at only 17 years old as one of the new breed of so-called "kitchen sink" dramatists. See *kitchen sink drama*.

DeLillo, Don (b.1936): American novelist whose writing is acclaimed as a notable example of a *postmodern* reading of contemporary American society. Notable works include AMERICANA (1971), GREAT JONES STREET (1973), RUNNING DOG (1978), LIBRA (1988), MAO II (1991), UNDERWORLD (1997).

denotation: the simplest and most literal *meaning* of a word, without any further *connotation* or *association*. See *referential language*.

dénouement: the final unraveling of the *plot* to the audience or reader's delight or sadness. See also *act, catastrophe, resolution*.

Desai, Anita (b.1937): Indian novelist and *short story* writer. She often explores the interface between the cultures of the East and the West. Notable works include CRY, THE PEACOCK (1963), FIRE ON THE MOUNTAIN (1977), CLEAR LIGHT OF DAY (1980), IN CUSTODY (1984), BAUMGARTNER'S BOMBAY (1988), FASTING, FEASTING (1999).

description is the word used to denote passages of writing, most often (but by no means always) in *prose*, that tell of places (in order to create *setting*), people, objects, social manners, and so forth. Unlike *narrative*, description may not strictly advance the *story*, although it may have an explicit or implicit impact upon it. The selection of descriptive detail may well tell the reader something about the *author*'s *viewpoint*.

desert island fiction: *stories* in which the *setting* is an isolated wild island. It is a *genre* that includes *tales* of adventure, exploration, paradise, and savagery, e.g. *Defoe*'s ROBINSON CRUSOE, *Golding*'s LORD OF THE FLIES, *Huxley*'s ISLAND.

detachment: see *distance*.

detective fiction is *fiction* in which the mystery is solved by a detective. *Poe* did much to encourage the *genre*, creating the solitary, detached but sharply observant detective Dupin. He was followed by the more down-to-earth figures of *Dickens*'s Bucket in BLEAK HOUSE and *Wilkie Collins*'s Sergeant Cuff in THE MOONSTONE. Poe's kind of detective was revived by *Arthur Conan Doyle* in the figure of Sherlock Holmes, and thereafter most English detectives were in this mold, from Agatha Christie's (1890–1976) Poirot to *P.D. James*'s Dalgleish and Colin Dexter's (b.1930) Inspector Morse (although the latter two, as usual from the mid-20th century onwards, are of the *police procedural* type). Among others, *Chandler* and Dashiell Hammett (1894–1961) produced a distinctively American detective fiction genre, their detectives becoming known as of the "hard-boiled" variety – tough, ruthless, and "seen-it-all."

deus ex machina: the mechanism by which the *plot* takes an unexpected turn in order to solve a tricky situation, and literally meaning "god from the machine." In Greek *drama* a god was mechanically lowered by means of a crane onto the stage in order to intervene in human affairs and assist in the *resolution* of the plot.

device is a word used to describe any literary *technique*.

dialectics can refer to:

- a question-and-answer method of discussion
- a thematic line of reasoning that runs through and unifies a work or works, e.g. in the *love poetry* of *Donne*
- the German philosopher Georg Hegel's (1730–1831) idea, which draws on the foregoing definitions, that all ongoing human thought, ideas, and history develop a *thesis*, against which there develops an inevitable rebellion or *antithesis*, a clash that in time develops a synthesis, which in turn becomes the new thesis; against which... and so on through history.

dialog is

- speech between two or more *character*s in any kind of *literature*
- a literary *genre* in which characters discuss a *theme*. *Plato* was one of the earliest writers to use this *form*. Notable examples in English include *Dryden*'s *essay* of DRAMATIC POESY (1668), *Hopkins*'s ON THE ORIGIN OF BEAUTY (1865), *Wilde*'s THE ARTIST AS CRITIC (1891).

diary (or journal): personal observations of events in the *form* of a day-to-day record, usually not intended for others to read or for publication, but sometimes written with an eye to posterity. Notable examples are those of Samuel Pepys (1633–1703), John Aubrey (1626–97), John Evelyn (1620–1706), *Boswell*, Fanny Burney (1752–1840), and *Dorothy Wordsworth*. The diary form has also been used by novelists as way of telling a *story*, for instance *Richardson*'s PAMELA OR VIRTUE REWARDED (1740–41), or THE DIARY OF A NOBODY (1892) by George Grossmith (1847–1912) and Weedon Grossmith (1852–1919). The *epistolary novel* is another form of the same *genre*. See *autobiography, memoir*.

Dickens, Charles (1812–70): English novelist and journalist. Despite or perhaps because of some sensation and sentimentality in his works, Dickens was an immensely popular *author* during his lifetime, and has since steadily grown in academic approval. In general his early work is full of vitality, vivid *character*s and *caricature*s, and atmospheric *setting*s – all things that gave rise to the adjective "Dickensian"; his later *novel*s are darker in *tone*, more disciplined and with a greater sense of *unity*, and of increasing thematic and psychological complexity. His characterization of women is sometimes regarded as unconvincing. Notable works include THE PICKWICK PAPERS (1836–37), OLIVER TWIST (1837–38), NICHOLAS NICKLEBY (1838–39), A CHRISTMAS CAROL (1843), DAVID COPPERFIELD (1849–50), BLEAK HOUSE (1852–53), LITTLE DORRIT (1855–57), GREAT EXPECTATIONS (1861), OUR MUTUAL FRIEND (1864–65).

Dickinson, Emily (1830–86): American poet whose two thousand *poem*s contribute greatly to 19th century American *literature*. She endured inner torment for much of her life. She described her *poetry* as "New Englandy," and her subject matter was influenced by a Puritan outlook. In her poetry simple *imagery* and melancholic *theme*s of death and loss of love have a powerful effect, and her experiments with punctuation, typography, grammar, *meter* and use of *metaphor* influenced much 20th century poetry. Notable works include "I Like a Look of Agony" (*c.*1861) and "I Heard a Fly Buzz – When I Died" (*c.*1862).

diction: a term sometimes used to describe the language, or choice of words, in which a *text* is written. See *poetic diction*.

didactic: a term used of writing that aims to instruct, or even to preach.

Didion, Joan (b.1934): American essayist and novelist. Her *essays* are good examples of *new journalism* and her *novels* of *postmodernism*, although it is limiting wholly to define her work by such labels. Much of her writing is a powerful critique of aspects of American society. Notable works include RUN, RIVER (1963), SLOUCHING TOWARDS BETHLEHEM (1968), THE WHITE ALBUM (1979), SALVADOR (1983), JOAN DIDION: ESSAYS AND CONVERSATIONS (1984), MIAMI (1987).

différance is a term important in *poststructuralism*, coined by the French philosopher Jacques Derrida (b.1930) to indicate the instability of *meaning* in language. The word does not exist in French, but contains elements of several French words that do exist (différence, différer, différent), generating complications and difficulty in establishing meaning.

digression: a sidetracking from the main *theme* or *story*; e.g. *Chaucer* frequently breaks up his *narrative* with the *rhetorical device* of digression.

Dillard, Annie (b.1945): American novelist, essayist, poet, and literary critic who writes in a polished and individual *style*. Notable works include PILGRIM AT TINKER'S CREEK (1974), the semiautobiographical AN AMERICAN CHILDHOOD (1987).

dimeter: see *meter*.

Dinesen, Isak (1885–1962): the *nom de plume* of Danish *short story* writer and essayist Karen Blixen who wrote mainly in English and was particularly popular in America. Her skillfully told *tales* often deal with mental disturbance and *grotesque characters*. Notable works include SEVEN GOTHIC TALES (1934), the autobiographical OUT OF AFRICA (1937, about her life in Kenya and which was made into a successful film), ESSAYS (1965).

dirge: a *song* of mourning or *lament*, shorter than an *elegy*, as in Ariel's song "Full Fathom Five Thy Father Lies" in *Shakespeare's* THE TEMPEST. See *monody, threnody*. See also *complaint*.

dirty realism: an American *style* of *fiction* typically featuring tough *characters* speaking terse *dialog* and involved in violent *action*, often in a rural setting. Writers associated with the *genre* include *Carver, Hemingway, Wolff*.

discourse may mean:

- a learned discussion (see *dissertation, thesis, tract, treatise*)
- a specialized language or jargon that is used in any subject of interest, from literary *criticism* to football. In this sense the word often crops up in discussions concerning such areas as *linguistics, structuralism,* and *poststructuralism*.

discovery, in *literature* studies, is another word for *anagnorisis*.

dissertation: a written discussion, usually scholarly, on some learned topic. See *discourse, thesis, tract, treatise*.

dissonance is the deliberate or inadvertent use in *poetry* or *prose* of discordant or clashing sounds. Examples are frequent in the writings of, among others, *Berryman, Hardy, Ted Hughes, Robert Lowell, Tennyson*.

distance, sometimes referred to as *aesthetic distance*, is a term used to indicate the detachment with which either the writer or the reader views a piece of *literature*. For instance, a writer might view her/his *characters* from an objective, disinterested distance, as in *existentialist* literature or *satire* (as opposed to *involvement*). Likewise, a reader may remain detached or emotionally involved in a *story*. The idea of aesthetic distance may be summed up thus:

- in a real fog we are emotionally involved because of the anxiety of coping with a real situation that may be dangerous
- in a fictional fog, such as in the opening to *Dickens*'s BLEAK HOUSE, we can enjoy in a detached way Dickens's artistic creation and the *symbolism* of the fog because we are not directly involved.

See *alienation effect*.

document: a written record giving information or evidence, e.g. gazette, *diary*, state paper, will, archive.

documentary novel: fiction based on documentary evidence with the intention of recreating an event from an historical aspect, e.g. *Dreiser*'s AN AMERICAN TRAGEDY. See also *thesis novel*.

documentary theater: *drama* based on documentary evidence as found in newspapers, *diaries*, reports, and so forth. *Edgar*'s MARY BARNES (1977) and THE JAIL DIARY OF ALBEE SACHS (1978) are examples of the *genre*. See *drama of ideas*.

doggerel is a term for poorly constructed, bad light *verse*, sometimes deliberately so for comic effect and usually on a trivial subject. The term may come from "dog-Latin," which means bad Latin.

domestic comedy: a *form* of *drama* about family life in the higher social classes, popular since the 18th century, e.g. *Goldsmith*'s SHE STOOPS TO CONQUER. Modern *dramatists* using this *genre* include *Ayckbourn, Coward, Tennessee Williams*.

domestic tragedy focuses upon middle or lower-middle class family life, as opposed to *tragedy* in the grand manner involving important people (such as kings) and great enterprises. Examples from *Elizabethan* and *Jacobean drama* include the anonymous ARDEN OF FEVERSHAM (1592), A WOMAN KILLED WITH KINDNESS (1603) by Thomas Heywood (1573–1641), the anonymous A YORKSHIRE TRAGEDY (1608), *Middleton*, and *Rowley*'s THE CHANGELING. The *genre* had some popularity in the 18th and 19th centuries, and it saw a notable revival with some of the plays of *Ibsen* and *Strindberg*, and particularly with 20th century American *dramatists* such as *Miller, O'Neill*, and *Tennessee Williams*, who did much to broaden the traditional concept of tragedy.

Donne, John (1572–1631): English poet, generally regarded as the foremost of the *metaphysical* poets. In his early years he wrote mainly *love poetry*, which was by turns ironic, passionate, erotic (he was the first writer to use the word "sex" in its modern sense), psychological, intellectually and syntactically complex; but always vigorous, with the direct, colloquial language grabbing the reader's attention. The religious *poetry* of his mature years, especially after his ordination in 1615, is more reflective, less sure, showing a struggle for faith. His religious *prose* is some of the most effective written in the English language. His reputation has declined in recent years, but he is still counted as one of the most original of English poets. Notable works include DEVOTIONS (1624), POEMS (1633, which contains many but not all of his best-known works such as "The Good-Morrow," "Go and Catch a Falling Star," "The Sun Rising," "The Canonization," "The Ecstasy," "The Relic," "At the Round Earth's Imagined Corners," "Death be not Proud"), "Elegy XIX, To His Mistress Going to Bed" (1669).

Dos Passos, John (1896–1970): American novelist, playwright, essayist, and historian. Influenced by the modernist intellectual movements of the day, he applied a wide range of artistic and journalistic *techniques* to present a chronicle of early 20th century America in the landmark *trilogy* U.S.A. (1930–36). Other notable works include THREE SOLDIERS (1921), MANHATTAN TRANSFER (1925).

double meter occurs when each *foot* is made up of two syllables, as in *iambs* and *trochees*. It is much more common in English *verse* than the *triple meter* of *dactyls* and *anapests*.

double plot is a term used of plays that have a main and a *subplot*. Some plays even have triple or multiple *plots*.

double rhyme is another term for *feminine rhyme*.

Douglass, Frederick (1817–95): American writer, freed slave, and famous anti-slavery orator who founded an antislavery journal called THE NORTH STAR (1847–64), later renamed FREDERICK DOUGLASS' PAPER. In 1845 he published the landmark *autobiography*, NARRATIVE OF THE LIFE OF FREDERICK DOUGLASS. In 1858 he established the *periodical* DOUGLASS' MONTHLY (published until 1863). He was important in American political life, organizing two African-American regiments during the Civil War, and holding various public offices. Other notable works include the revised and enlarged editions of his autobiography, MY BONDAGE AND MY FREEDOM (1855) and THE LIFE AND TIMES OF FREDERICK DOUGLASS (1881), plus *collections* of his *essays* published in the 20th century under the titles DOUGLASS ON WOMEN'S RIGHTS (1976) and A BLACK DIPLOMAT IN HAITI (1977).

Dove, Rita (b.1952): American poet, novelist, *short story* and *verse drama* writer. Her *poetry* is distinguished for its lyrical and *narrative* qualities. Notable works include THOMAS AND BEULAH: POEMS (1987), GRACE NOTES (1989), SELECTED POEMS (1993).

Doyle, Arthur Conan (1859–1930): Scottish novelist, *short story* writer, playwright, and essayist. Best known as the creator of the amateur detective Sherlock Holmes, he was irritated that the popularity of this *character* obscured his other *historical novels*, *science fiction*, and *romances*. Notable works include THE ADVENTURES OF SHERLOCK HOLMES (1892), THE EXPLOITS OF BRIGADIER GERARD (1896), THE HOUND OF THE BASKERVILLES (1902), THE LOST WORLD (1912). See *detective fiction*.

Doyle, Roddy (b.1958): Irish novelist and playwright. Often locating his *stories* in working-class northern Dublin, he has a *style* that is invigoratingly freewheeling and colloquial, his tone compassionate, his *characters* memorable. Notable works include THE BARRYTOWN TRILOGY (1992) and PADDY CLARKE HA HA HA (1993) in which he memorably captures the world as seen through the eyes of a lively child.

Drabble, Margaret (b.1939): English novelist. Her early *novels* focus upon the situation of modern educated young women coming to terms with conflicting needs, demands, and aspirations, but more recent work uses a broader canvas. Notable works include THE MILLSTONE (1965), THE WATERFALL (1969), THE NEEDLE'S EYE (1972), THE ICE-AGE (1977), THE RADIANT WAY (1987), THE GATES OF IVORY (1991), THE WITCH OF EXMOOR (1996), THE PEPPERED MOTH (2001). She has also edited THE OXFORD COMPANION TO ENGLISH LITERATURE (1985; concise edition, 1987).

drama may be described as any kind of performance designed for an audience in some kind of theater, characteristically showing an *action* by *character*s covering an imagined length of time within a *setting* or settings. The script of a play is somewhat like an architect's drawing, which comes to life when actors adopt characters, and speak the words and perform the actions indicated by the playwright. A reader of a play needs to be "theater-literate" in order to visualize it successfully in her or his head. In talking or writing about drama, students should focus less on the work as a "book" and more on the concept of "the play": it is important to have a sense of the piece as something that has reality in performance, involving presentation and action as well as words. Sometimes the word "drama" is used to indicate a relatively serious play, as opposed to a light piece. See also *unities, dramatic.*

drama of ideas is a term used to define plays that deal with problems, often of a social rather than individual nature. Plays have dealt with social issues over the centuries, but it is in the late 19th century with the work of *dramatist*s like *Ibsen* and *Shaw* that a sense of debate within a *drama* emerged. During the 20th century *Brecht* encouraged explicit debate on stage and had a considerable influence upon drama in the second half of the century. Among notable "ideas" playwrights since the 1960s are *Howard Barker, Bond, Brenton, Churchill, Edgar, Hare,* and *McGrath* whose concerns have ranged over subjects including the class system, racism, feminism, the press, hypocrisy, and political corruption. See *agitprop.*

dramatic irony: in *drama*, where a *character* is unaware of the *irony* of her/his words or situation and other characters on stage or, more especially, the audience are (or soon will become) aware, e.g. in act II, scene 5 of TWELFTH NIGHT when Malvolio reads aloud a letter believing it to be a declaration of love from Olivia, the other characters listening to him and the audience knowing that he is being tricked. In *comedy*, this gives rise to mirth; in *tragedy*, to pain. See *tragic irony.*

dramatic monolog: see *monolog.*

dramatic unities: see *unities, dramatic.*

dramatis personae: list of *character*s who take part in a play.

dramatist is another word for "playwright," sometimes used to describe those who also write *drama* for media other than the stage, e.g. film, radio, television.

dramatization is any kind of conversion into *drama* of work in another medium, e.g. the adaptation of *Bible* stories into *mystery plays*, or the conversion of *novel*s into television drama or screenplay.

dramaturgy is the art of dramatic composition.

drawing room comedy is a semidisparaging term for a pleasant, often undemanding, *comedy of manners*, usually concerning the English middle classes, the best examples of which are plays such as *Shaw*'s CANDIDA and *Coward*'s HAY FEVER.

dream vision refers to a kind of *literature*, most popular in the Middle Ages, in which a *character* falls asleep, often in pleasant, rural surroundings, and has a dream in which s/he is guided through a landscape. This *genre* often provides a good vehicle for *allegory*. Medieval writers were much influenced by the French 13th century ROMANCE OF THE ROSE, and the Italian *Dante*'s DIVINE COMEDY is a dream vision. Examples in English include *Langland*'s PIERS PLOWMAN, *Chaucer*'s THE BOOK OF THE DUCHESS and THE HOUSE OF FAME; and later examples include *Bunyan*'s THE PILGRIM'S PROGRESS, *Keats*'s "The Fall of Hyperion: A Dream" (1819). ALICE'S ADVENTURES IN WONDERLAND (1865) by Lewis Carroll (1832–98) is in the same genre, as is *Joyce*'s FINNEGANS WAKE.

Dreiser, Theodore (1871–1945): American novelist, journalist, playwright, *short story* writer, poet, essayist, and autobiographer. *Sinclair Lewis* considered Dreiser's first *novel* SISTER CARRIE (1900) to be "the first book free of English literature's influence." This book and his next, JENNIE GERHARDT (1901), were unpopular on account of their uncompromising *realism*. He became increasingly socialist in outlook. Other notable works include his *documentary novel* AN AMERICAN TRAGEDY (1925).

Dryden, John (1631–1700): English poet, playwright, critic, and translator. His interests were wide, and his writing often considers philosophical or political questions. A polished, exact, and versatile craftsman in *verse, prose,* and *drama,* Dryden today maintains a reputation that is as high as ever, but he is more admired than read for pleasure. His *poetry* is often noted for its mastery of the *heroic couplet.* He was the first official *poet laureate.* Notable works include the *essay* of DRAMATIC POESY (1668), the plays MARRIAGE À LA MODE (1672), ALL FOR LOVE (1678, a reworking of *Shakespeare*'s ANTONY AND CLEOPATRA), and the *poems* ABSALOM AND ACHITOPHEL (1681) and MAC FLECKNOE (1682).

Du Bois, W.E.B. (1868–1963): American historian, essayist, and editor, famous for his work on the position of African-Americans. Notable works include THE SUPPRESSION OF AFRICAN SLAVE-TRADE (1896), SOULS OF BLACK FOLK (1903), BLACK RECONSTRUCTION IN AMERICA (1935). From the 1930s his politics grew increasingly radical and in 1960, at the age of 92, he joined the Communist Party and went to live in Ghana.

Duffy, Carol Ann (b.1955): Scottish-born poet and playwright. Her *poems* are at the same time sensitive and unsentimental. Notable works include STANDING FEMALE NUDE (1985), SELLING MANHATTAN (1987), SELECTED POEMS (1994).

dumb show is a term used to describe a mimed dramatic *action* that is intended to prepare the audience for the main action of the play that follows. It is mainly used in *Elizabethan* and *Jacobean drama,* derived from the *tragedies* of the Roman Seneca, the most famous example being the dumb show that precedes the play-within-the-play in *Shakespeare*'s HAMLET. Other examples are to be found in *Norton* and *Sackville*'s GORBODUC, *Kyd*'s THE SPANISH TRAGEDY, and in *Webster*'s THE WHITE DEVIL and THE DUCHESS OF MALFI.

Dunbar, William (?1460–?1513): Scottish poet. Sometimes classified with *Henryson* in a group known as Scottish Chaucerians, he wrote in a range of *styles*, humorous and serious, courtly and low, religious and secular. Some of his *poems* are *allegories* and *satires*. Notable works include "The Thrisill and the Rois" (1503), "Lament for the Makaris" (1508), "Done is a Battle" (?1510).

Dunn, Douglas (b.1942): Scottish poet, *short story* writer, translator, and editor. Influenced by *Larkin*, his *poems* often contain clearly observed depictions of ordinary people and their lives, and his focus ranges from the local to wider political and aesthetic considerations. Notable works include TERRY STREET (1969), ELEGIES (1985, a commemoration of his wife who died in 1981, and which has been hailed as the finest work of its kind since *Tennyson*'s IN MEMORIAM).

duolog: a conversation between two *characters* in any kind of *literature*.

Durrell, Gerald (1925–95): English travel and natural history writer, journalist, and novelist. His writing is light and readable. Notable works include THE BAFUT BEAGLES (1953), MY FAMILY AND OTHER ANIMALS (1956), ISLAND ZOO (1961).

Durrell, Lawrence (1912–90): English poet, travel writer, and novelist. The people and locations around the Mediterranean, where he spent most of his life, provide the subject matter for much of his writing. His major *novels* are THE BLACK BOOK (1938), THE ALEXANDRIA QUARTET (1957–60), THE REVOLT OF APHRODITE (1968–70), and THE AVIGNON QUINTET (1974–85). Durrell called the "investigation of modern love" one of his central *themes*. Other works include A PRIVATE COUNTRY (1943), PROSPERO'S CELL (1945), BITTER LEMONS (1957).

dystopia: very unpleasant fictional world that is, literally, the opposite of *utopia*. It is often the writer's projection into the future of ominous tendencies in contemporary society, e.g. *Huxley*'s BRAVE NEW WORLD, *Orwell*'s NINETEEN EIGHTY-FOUR, *Burgess*'s A CLOCKWORK ORANGE, *Atwood*'s THE HANDMAID'S TALE. *Science fiction* often depicts dystopian cultures.

Eagleton, Terry (b.1943): English literary critic. He is a controversial opposer of conventional orthodoxies, and is recognized as a foremost influence in *Marxist criticism*. Notable works include LITERARY THEORY: AN INTRODUCTION (1983).

early national period: sometimes used to cover American *literature* written between approximately 1775 (the beginning of the Revolutionary War) and 1828 (the emergence of Jacksonian democracy).

Eden, Emily (1797–1869): English travel writer and novelist. She writes about India from her experiences of living there for 14 years with her brother while he was governor general. Influenced by *Austen*, her writing is *witty*, observant, and an excellent record of the attitudes and manners of fashionable society of the day. Notable works include PORTRAITS OF THE PEOPLE AND PRINCES OF INDIA (1844), UP THE COUNTRY (1866), LETTERS FROM INDIA (1872), and the *novels* THE SEMI-DETACHED HOUSE (1859), THE SEMI-ATTACHED COUPLE (1860).

Edgar, David (b.1948): English playwright with a reputation for deft presentation of socialist ideas. Notable works include DESTINY (1976), THE JAIL DIARY OF ALBIE SACHS (1978), PENTECOST (1994), THE PRISONER'S DILEMMA (2001).

edition: a printing of a *text* from which future impressions or reprintings or reissues may be made. If there are substantial changes in a further printing, this printing is referred to as the "second edition," and so forth. The printing history of a text is normally detailed on one of the initial pages of the book.

Edwardian period: used to refer to *literature* written in England between the death of Queen Victoria (1901) and the start of World War I (1914), during most of which time Edward VII was on the throne (1901–10). In American literature roughly the same timespan is referred to as the naturalistic period.

Ekwensi, Cyprian (b.1921): Nigerian novelist and *short story* writer. He writes in an engaging, energetic, and realistic way about city life in West Africa. Notable works include JAGUA NANA (1961).

elegiac: a term used to describe any *poem*, not necessarily a strict *elegy*, that has a sadly reflective *tone* and/or deals with the transience of things, e.g. *Gray*'s "Elegy Written in a Country Churchyard."

elegy: a *poem* of mourning for an individual, e.g. "Adonais" (1821), *Percy Shelley*'s lament for *Keats*. See *complaint, dirge, monody, threnody.*

Eliot, George (real name Mary Ann Evans; 1819–80): English novelist, critic, and poet. Well educated, she was influenced by the *Romantic* poets, German *literature*, and an interest in religion, toward which she had a liberal attitude. Moving in intellectual circles in London, she became assistant editor of the *Westminster Review*. She met George Henry Lewes and lived happily with him (despite the fact that he was already married) from 1854 until his death in 1878. In some senses a feminist, she is regarded by many as the foremost woman novelist of the 19th century, *Leavis* praising her "luminous intelligence" and ranking her in THE GREAT TRADITION as central within the *canon* of great English novelists. Notable works include ADAM BEDE (1859), THE MILL ON THE FLOSS (1860), SILAS MARNER (1861), MIDDLEMARCH (1871–72), DANIEL DERONDA (1874–76).

Eliot, T.S. (1888–1965): American-born British poet, playwright, and literary critic. Encouraged and influenced by *Pound*, Eliot began to write *poetry* that, in its use of cosmopolitan subject matter, allusiveness, stark images, and fragmentary *free verse*, led to his being regarded as a central figure in *modernism*, especially after the publication of THE WASTE LAND (1922). His critical writings show great admiration for the Elizabethan *dramatists* and *metaphysical* poets, and he was in the forefront of a mid-20th century revival of *verse drama*. In various ways he had the greatest impact of any 20th century poet; but his increasingly rightwing political and cultural views and his emphasis on *tradition* in his critical writings limited his influence over younger writers. Other notable works include PRUFROCK AND OTHER OBSERVATIONS (1917), THE SACRED WOOD (1920), ASH-WEDNESDAY (1930), MURDER IN THE CATHEDRAL (1935), FOUR QUARTETS (1935–42). See also *objective correlative.*

elision: the running together or eliding of two syllables to make the right number of syllables in a line, e.g. "o'er" instead of "over," or "e'er" in place of "ever." See *synaeresis, syncope.*

Elizabethan age: used to refer to *literature* written in England during the reign of Elizabeth I (1558–1603).

Elizabethan drama: strictly speaking referring only to *drama* written during the *Elizabethan age*, the term has also come to cover the whole of the great age of English drama from early in the Elizabethan era until the closing of the theaters in 1642 (again, drama written during the reign of James I should technically be referred to as *Jacobean* and that during Charles I's reign as *Caroline*).

Ellison, Ralph (1914–94): American novelist, essayist, and *short story* writer. Literary heir to *Richard Wright*, he writes of African-American culture and conditions. Notable works include INVISIBLE MAN (1952, a semiautobiographical *novel*).

emblem: an *allegorical* picture or *symbol*. Scales may be emblematic of the scales of justice, and the spear on *Shakespeare*'s coat of arms is emblematic of his name. In THE PRELUDE *Wordsworth* writes of the prospect of a moonlit mountain range as "the emblem of a mind/That feeds upon infinity."

emblem book: a book of symbolic pictures explained by accompanying *verses*. Images from these books were frequent in 16th and 17th century *poetry* and *drama*, *Shakespeare* making much use of Geoffrey Whitney's A CHOICE OF EMBLEMES (1586), for instance in act I, scene 7 of MACBETH, where Lady Macbeth tells her husband to "Look like the innocent flower,/But be the serpent under it" (see illustration opposite, taken from Whitney). Quarle's EMBLEMES (1635) was also most popular.

Emecheta, Buchi (b.1944): Nigerian novelist and writer of children's *literature* and television scripts. Her writing shows her feminist concern for women's rights, and mostly she sets her *novels* in West Africa. Notable works include the semi-autobiographical SECOND-CLASS CITIZEN (1974), THE BRIDE PRICE (1976), THE JOYS OF MOTHERHOOD (1979).

Emblem book (see page 50)

Emerson, Ralph Waldo (1803–82): American essayist and poet. A leading member of the transcendentalists, he was very interested in philosophy and religion, and attracted to a Wordsworthian reverence for nature which has become very important in American thought. He became committed to the abolition of slavery. Notable works include NATURE (1836), REPRESENTATIVE MEN (1850). See *transcendentalism*.

empathy is a term used in *literature* to describe an emotional (and sometimes physical) identification with a *character* which goes beyond *sympathy*. *Keats* claims that he becomes "a part of all I see" and expresses his empathy thus: "if a sparrow comes before my window I take part in its existence and pick about the gravel." In act V, scene 1 of *Shakespeare*'s MACBETH the Doctor may be said to empathize not only with the sleepwalking Lady Macbeth but with all humanity when he says "God, God forgive us all!"

Empson, William (1906–84): English critic and poet. Taught and influenced by *Richards*, he was one of the founders of the English Literature degree course at Cambridge University. In his SEVEN TYPES OF AMBIGUITY (first published in 1930) he advocated such ultraclose analysis of the *text* that *T.S. Eliot* called his *method* "the lemon squeezer school of criticism." Other notable works include THE STRUCTURE OF COMPLEX WORDS (1951), COLLECTED POEMS (1949, revised 1955), MILTON'S GOD (1961). His *poetry* influenced younger poets such as those associated with *the Movement*, and the critic John Wain (1925–94) praised it for its "passion, logic and formal beauty."

encomium has come to mean any piece or writing of praise, and was very popular in the 17th and 18th centuries, as in *Dryden's* "A Song for Saint Cecilia's Day" or *Gray's* "Hymn to Adversity."

end rhyme is rhyming at the end of lines, and hence the most common kind of rhyming. See *rhyme*.

end-stopping/end-stopped: where the end of a *verse* line is marked by a pause, usually indicated by punctuation. For an example see *enjambment*. End-stopped lines tend to emphasize the *rhythm* in verse that has a regular *structure*. See *versification*.

English language: brought to the British Isles by Germanic tribes in AD449, the language we call Anglo-Saxon developed and was enriched by a series of infusions such as the arrival of Christianity (and hence many additional Latin words), by the Viking invasions of the 8th and 9th centuries, and the Norman invasion of 1066 (bringing French). During the later Middle Ages the language settled down into what we call Middle English (the language of *Chaucer*). Recognizably modern English emerged during the *Renaissance*, after which the vocabulary was further expanded by the development of the British Empire, drawing on words from other languages worldwide and giving English a far larger vocabulary than any other language. This has been consolidated in modern times by the powerful influence of the United States as an English-speaking country and by the development of computer and other technical languages based upon English.

English sonnet: another name for the *Shakespearean sonnet*.

English Stage Company: an influential theater company operating at the Royal Court Theatre, London, during the mid-20th century, and responsible for innovative plays by *Osborne, kitchen sink drama*, and other *avant-garde* work.

enjambment is the running-on of the sense of one line of *verse* into the next without *end-stopping*. It is often used together with *caesura* in order to lend variety and a natural effect to the *rhythm* of verse. In the following example there is enjambment between lines 3 and 4, a caesura in line 4, and lines 1 and 2 are end-stopped:

> The thirtieth of November.
> Snow is starting to fall.
> A peculiar silence is spreading
> over the fields, the maple grove.

> (from *Rich's* TOWARD THE SOLSTICE, 1978)

Enlightenment: a western European literary, intellectual, philosophical, and cultural climate that prevailed between roughly 1660 and 1770, and advocated clarity of thought and word, and good sense in all affairs. The period is sometimes known as the age of reason as it was thought that human reason would solve all problems, stimulating scientific discoveries and all other kinds of progress. The thinking and writing of *Johnson* is sometimes seen as characterizing the English spirit of that age.

Enright, D.J. (b.1920): English poet and editor. Using *understatement* and *irony*, he tends to combine anger over social inequality with compassion for the human condition. He often uses an Eastern location. Notable works include THE LAUGHING HYENA (1953).

envoi (or **envoy**), in English, is a message (literally "send-off") at the end of a piece of *literature*. Originally a four-line *stanza* to conclude a certain *form* of French *poem*, it has been used in English literature in *poetry*, as in *Chaucer*'s THE CLERK'S TALE (one of the CANTERBURY TALES), and in *prose*, as in *A.N. Wilson*'s THE HEALING ART. Among others *Swinburne* and *Wilde* have employed the *device*.

epic: a long, *narrative poem* recounting heroic achievements and great events in a grand, elevated *style* of writing. Some epics spring from an *oral tradition*, e.g. *Homer*'s ILIAD and ODYSSEY or the anonymous Old English BEOWULF; others, such as the Latin AENEID by Virgil (70–19BC) or *Milton*'s PARADISE LOST, are literary. Although the word has become widened to embrace anything on a large scale (e.g. epic scale, epic imagery, epic film, epic voyage), students should be careful before using it in other than its strict literary sense. See also *mock epic*.

epic (or **extended) simile:** a long *simile* that characteristically interrupts the *narrative* of an *epic poem*. Much used, for example, by *Milton* in PARADISE LOST. There is another good example in *Arnold*'s "Sohrab and Rustum" (1853).

epic theater has much in common with *documentary theater* in that it uses *devices* such as *song*, *plot* summaries, film and slide projection, and/or a *chorus* to present a *story* that often ranges over a wide period of time, geographic area, and/or cast of *characters*, with frequent doubling up of parts, all of which encourages an *alienation effect* on the part of the audience. This type of theater was developed by *Brecht* between the 1920s and 1950s. See *Brechtian, distance*.

epigram: a short *witty* statement in *prose* or *poetry*. The *form* became popular in the 17th and 18th centuries with writers such as *Jonson, Herrick, Donne, Dryden, Jonathan Swift*, and *Pope*; and there was a revival of interest by later 19th and 20th century writers, e.g. the American writers *Emerson, Dickinson, Pound, Nash*. *Wilde* used many epigrams in his plays, an epigram in prose sometimes being called an *apothegm*. See *aphorism, clerihew, maxim*.

epigraph: in a literary sense, a phrase used to hint at the significance of what follows by means of a quotation or motto at the beginning of a book, chapter, section or *poem*, e.g. "Mistah Kurtz – he dead," *T.S. Eliot*'s quotation from *Conrad*'s HEART OF DARKNESS at the beginning of THE HOLLOW MEN; "Ours was the marsh country," *Graham Swift* quoting from *Dickens*'s GREAT EXPECTATIONS at the beginning of WATERLAND; or *Fowles* quoting from various sources at the beginning of every chapter of THE FRENCH LIEUTENANT'S WOMAN.

epilog is either:

- a passage that concludes and often comments upon the preceding work, e.g. the Doctor's speech that emphasizes the *moral* of the anonymous *morality play*, EVERYMAN. With a play it is often a plea for applause, e.g. Puck at the end of *Shakespeare*'s A MIDSUMMER NIGHT'S DREAM. Sometimes an epilog is a summary of what has gone before, or is an afterthought; or
- the name of the *character* who speaks the epilog.

See *coda, prolog*.

epiphany in a literary sense has come to mean a sudden experience of revelation or understanding. *Joyce* used it in this sense in A PORTRAIT OF THE ARTIST AS A YOUNG MAN.

Wordsworth experiences many so-called epiphanies in THE PRELUDE, calling such moments "spots of time." *Characters* frequently experience epiphanies in *Murdoch's novels*, e.g. Jake Donaghue in UNDER THE NET.

episode is a term that may indicate:

- a single incident or relatively self-contained passage within a longer work
- a single section of a serialized work.

episodic describes the *structure* of a work consisting of a sequence of loosely connected events, usually happening to the same person. The term is often applied to *picaresque novels*.

epistolary novel: a kind of *novel*, made popular in the 18th century, in which the story is told through the letters or *diary* of the *protagonist*, e.g. *Richardson's* PAMELA, *Walker's* THE COLOR PURPLE.

epithalamium: a *poem* celebrating marriage, e.g. *Spenser's* EPITHALAMIUM, written for his own marriage.

epithet: an adjective or adjectival phrase used to describe a particular characteristic. The term is variously used in connection with:

- a person, e.g. Long John Silver, Richard the Lionheart
- a thing, e.g. when Falstaff talks of "grinning Honour" in *Shakespeare's* HENRY IV PART 1
- 18th century *poetic diction*, where an epithet was attached to almost every noun, sometimes to ludicrous effect, e.g. "fish" were described as the "finny tribe"
- Homeric epithets, often compound adjectives in the style of the Greek *Homer*, wherein a recurrent formula is used in description, e.g. "fleet-foot Achilles," "wine-dark sea." This kind of epithet was often used in Anglo-Saxon *poetry*.

eponymous: when the main *character* gives his or her name to the title of a work, e.g. King Lear, Silas Marner, or Gatsby in *F. Scott Fitzgerald's* THE GREAT GATSBY. Hamlet might be referred to as the "eponymous hero" of *Shakespeare's* HAMLET.

Equiano, Oloudah (1745–c.1801): an African of the Ibo people who was captured and enslaved, and worked for masters in Barbados, Virginia, and England. He saved money, bought his freedom, and then worked with others in Britain for the abolition of slavery. His THE INTERESTING NARRATIVE OF THE LIFE OF OLOUDAH EQUIANO, OR GUSTAVUS VASSA, THE AFRICAN, WRITTEN BY HIMSELF (1789) has become a *classic* of autobiographical writing.

Erdich, Louise (b.1954): American novelist and poet of German and Native American descent. Using her knowledge of Native American life, tribal issues, and ancestry to develop her *themes*, she often locates her *novels* in North Dakota. Her *method* is sometimes compared to *magic realism*. Notable works include LOVE MEDICINE (1984), THE BEET QUEEN (1986), TRACKS (1988), CROWN OF COLUMBUS (1991), THE BINGO PALACE (1994).

essay: a term used mainly to describe a discursive piece of writing, or a short *prose* piece of an informal nature, as made popular in the 18th century by writers such as *Addison*, *Steele*, and *Lamb*, and still featuring in some modern literary *periodicals*.

Etherege, George (1636–92): English playwright of *Restoration comedy* in the *comedy of manners style*. Notable works include THE MAN OF MODE (1676).

euphuism: an elegant and elaborate *prose style* (not to be confused with "euphemism"). See *Lyly*.

exegesis is a detailed critical analysis and explanation of difficulties in a literary *text* (the term was originally confined to examination of the *Bible*).

exemplum: a short *tale* illustrating a *moral* point. Exempla were frequent in sermons and medieval *literature*. Examples are to be found in much of *Chaucer's* work.

existentialism is a philosophy that proposes that every individual must assume responsibility for the nature of her or his existence in a dangerous and meaningless universe. These ideas had their origins in the 19th century and rose to prominence in the mid-20th century through the writings of, among others, the Frenchmen Albert Camus (1913–60) and Jean-Paul Sartre (1905–80). See *absurd, theater and literature of the*.

exordium: in *rhetoric*, the introductory part of a speech or *essay*.

explication is the kind of *close reading* advocated by the *new critics*. See *intrinsic attitude, Leavisite*.

exposition: the *setting* of the scene in a play or *story*, sometimes dealing with essential events prior to the opening of the *narrative*, e.g. the information revealed in the opening scene of *Shakespeare's* HAMLET. See *act*.

expressionism is a movement in *literature* and art, mainly German in origin, which rejects *realism* and objective portrayal, preferring to depict inner states of mind by distorted images. In art Edvard Munch's painting THE SCREAM (1894) is probably the most famous expressionist image, and Vincent Van Gogh's turbulent landscapes are also characteristic. Among other areas of literature, expressionism had some impact upon American *dramatists* such as *O'Neill* in THE EMPEROR JONES, *Wilder* in THE SKIN OF OUR TEETH and *Miller* in DEATH OF A SALESMAN; and *Tennessee Williams* uses expressionist *techniques*, for example in THE GLASS MENAGERIE. Expressionism also had an impact upon *Beat movement* writers (such as *Ginsberg*) and the *theater of the absurd*.

extenuatio is an alternative term for *meiosis*.

extrinsic attitude embraces the idea that an objective scrutiny of a *text* is not enough and that the historical *context* in which a text is produced decides *meaning*. Many of the newer *literary theories* assume an extrinsic attitude, e.g. *psychoanalytic criticism, feminist criticism*. This approach is also known as *historicism*.

eye rhyme, sometimes called "sight *rhyme*," is when words look as if they rhyme, but they do not (as in "come/home"), e.g.

> …Until this morning and this snow.
> If anything might rouse him now…

> (from *Owen's* "Futility")

Half rhyme is created by eye rhyme, but the reverse is not necessarily true, e.g. "once/France" is a half rhyme, but not an eye rhyme.

Ezekiel, Nissim (b.1924): Indian poet, playwright, and editor, who is often regarded as the "Grand Old Man" of Anglo-Indian *literature*. Notable works include THE UNFINISHED MAN (1960), THE EXACT NAME (1965), THREE PLAYS (1969), HYMNS IN DARKNESS (1976).

fable: a *short story* in *prose* or *verse* that concludes with a *moral*. Often it takes the *form* of a "beast fable," where animals assume human characteristics. The Greek writer Aesop (?620–560BC) is the earliest well-known writer of this kind of fable; a modern example is *Orwell*'s ANIMAL FARM. Other fables include *Chaucer*'s THE NUN'S PRIEST'S TALE (from THE CANTERBURY TALES), *Kipling*'s JUST SO STORIES, *Thurber*'s FABLES FOR OUR TIME. See *allegory*.

fabliau: a short, *satirical*, earthy, bawdy *story* about ordinary folk, often portraying promiscuous women and cuckolded husbands. In *tone* and subject matter the *genre* is the *antithesis* of *courtly love tales*. Fabliaux were popular in 14th century England, *Chaucer*'s MILLER'S TALE and REEVE'S TALE (from THE CANTERBURY TALES) being *classic* examples of the type.

fabulation is a modern term to describe a *method* of *narrative* that deliberately defies a reader's traditional expectations of storytelling, by experimenting with subject matter, *form*, and *style*, and combining all kinds of realistic and nonrealistic elements in a self-consciously surprising – even shocking – way. See *antinovel*.

faction is *literature* or other media that incorporate fact within *fiction*, or combine fact and fiction, e.g. *Mailer*'s ARMIES OF THE NIGHT. See *new journalism*.

fallible narrator: see *narrator/narrative voice*.

falling action is when the *action* of a play falls away from its *climax*.

falling rhythm: see *rising rhythm*.

fancy is another word for *imagination*, although *Coleridge* drew a fine distinction between the two terms. The word is sometimes used to denote the creative faculty that produces light or humorous writing, whereas the imagination produces the more serious and passionate. In this *context*, it is interesting to read *Keats*'s "Fancy" (1820).

fantastic is a term applied to *literature* where the reader is unsure whether events can be explained by natural causes/psychological explanations, or whether the supernatural is involved, e.g. *Henry James*'s THE TURN OF THE SCREW, or *Emily Brontë*'s WUTHERING HEIGHTS.

fantasy, in a literary sense, refers to *short stories* or *novels* that create an alternative world imaginatively apart from the ordinary experience of the reader. It could describe *gothic* horror such as *Mary Shelley*'s FRANKENSTEIN; or *science fiction* such as *Wells*'s THE WAR OF THE WORLDS; or *utopias* and *dystopias* such as are found in *Jonathan Swift*'s GULLIVER'S TRAVELS, *Huxley*'s BRAVE NEW WORLD, and *Orwell*'s ANIMAL FARM. Fantasies are often also *allegories*.

Fanthorpe, U.A. (b.1921): English poet. With *objectivity* and compassion her incisive *poetry* observes and explores the everyday. Prolific and popular, she is at times both disarmingly humorous and disturbingly direct. Notable works include SIDE EFFECTS (1978), SELECTED POEMS (1986), CONSEQUENCES (2000).

farce is a type of *drama* where comic situations are pushed to the point of hilarious absurdity. Unlike *satire*, farce is usually simple entertainment, and it may include any or all of the following: complicated *plots* (often involving mistaken identity), exaggerated *characters*, bizarre situations, and knockabout *action*. Many English *dramatists* have employed farce, for instance *Shakespeare* in THE TAMING OF THE SHREW (?1592), THE COMEDY OF ERRORS (?1594), and THE MERRY WIVES OF WINDSOR (1602), *Jonson* in BARTHOLOMEW FAIR, *Wilde* in THE IMPORTANCE OF BEING EARNEST, and *Orton* and *Stoppard* in most of their plays. Farce is often an element in *theater of the absurd*. See also *black comedy*.

Farquhar, George (?1677–1707): Irish playwright of *Restoration comedy* in the *comedy of manners style*. He is often more concerned with romantic love than is usual in the cynical world of Restoration comedies, and he broadened their scope by sometimes using locations in the provinces away from fashionable London. His plays are marked by a sense of reality, vitality, and good *humor*. Notable works include THE RECRUITING OFFICER (1706), THE BEAUX' STRATAGEM (1707).

Farrell, J.G. (1935–79): English novelist. Through meticulous research, a *witty* and *ironic style*, a symbolic approach, and a wide range of *characters*, he explores his main *theme* of British imperial decline, especially in his "Empire trilogy." Notable works include TROUBLES (1970), THE SIEGE OF KRISHNAPUR (1973), THE SINGAPORE GRIP (1978).

fatal flaw: see *Bradley, tragic flaw*.

Faulkner, William (1897–1962): American novelist, poet, *short story* writer, and journalist. He created a fictionalized *setting* called Yoknapatawpha County (based on Mississippi, his home state), and in his many *novels* he developed a complex *style* that sometimes involves *stream of consciousness* and multiple *narrators*. He was at first regarded as a merely regional writer, but in various of his writings he describes the decline of the Southern states with somber lyricism. He is now generally recognized as one of America's greatest 20th century novelists. Notable works include THE SOUND AND THE FURY (1929), AS I LAY DYING (1930), LIGHT IN AUGUST (1932), ABSOLOM, ABSOLOM! (1936), COLLECTED STORIES (1950, a *collection* of *detective fiction*), A FABLE (1954), THE RECEIVERS (1962). See also *regional novel*.

feeling is a notion applauded by writers of the *Romantic period* who elevated the benefits of feeling (that is, responding through the emotions) above those of the intellect. For instance, in "To My Sister" (1798) *Wordsworth* emphasizes the value of leaving behind books on a mild March day, going out into nature, and experiencing an "hour of feeling."

feet: see *meter*.

feminine ending: see *weak ending*.

feminine rhyme occurs when accented rhyming syllables are followed by unaccented rhyming syllables (survìval, revìval; clìpper, dìpper, fìnding, bìnding), as in this anonymous epitaph:

> Here I lie and my four daughters.
> Killed by drinking Cheltenham waters.

See *rhyme*.

feminist criticism sets out to redress what is regarded as the patriarchal, *phallo-centric* nature of society and *literature*, especially the *novel*. It covers both attitudes toward female writers and the treatment of women as role models (or, more often, their marginalization) in literature. One of its basic beliefs is the *poststructuralist* notion that the very language in which literature is written is based on a male-dominated society, and therefore that the subordination of women is reinforced by the repeated use of an inherited language. The roots of feminism go back to the 18th century and to *texts* such as A VINDICATION OF THE RIGHTS OF WOMAN (1792) by Mary Wollstonecraft (1759–97), and may be traced via books such as *Woolf*'s A ROOM OF ONE'S OWN and *Rich*'s ON LIES, SECRETS, AND SILENCE. See also *postmodernism*.

Ferlinghetti, Lawrence (b.1919): American poet. A leading figure in the 1950s *Beat movement*, he wrote *poetry* that was characteristically light and *satirical*, sometimes experimental. Notable works include A CONEY ISLAND OF THE MIND (1958), STARTING FROM SAN FRANCISCO (1961, revised 1967).

Fermor, Patrick Leigh (b.1915): English travel writer of elegance, lyricism, and vividness. Notable works include THE TRAVELLER'S TREE (1950), MANI (1958), ROUMELI (1966), A TIME OF GIFTS (1977).

fiction is a general word covering any imaginative work, but is usually applied to *novels* and *short stories* (in order to distinguish them from such works as *biographies*, *travel literature*, and so forth) rather than to *drama* and *poetry*. See also *faction*.

Fielding, Henry (1707–54): English novelist, playwright, poet, and essayist. A lawyer by training, his early literary work was nearly all *drama*, often political *satire*. After the passing of a stage censorship law in 1737 he turned to journalism as a satirical outlet. He is best remembered now for his *novels* which, while still satirical in their attacks upon corruption and hypocrisy, show sharp observation and a generous compassion for the foibles of human beings, and have strong *narrative* lines. His flair for the broad comic sweep, using a multiplicity of *characters* and a sense for the *picaresque*, makes him an important writer in the development of the novel in England. Notable works include JOSEPH ANDREWS (1742), THE HISTORY OF TOM JONES, A FOUNDLING (1749).

figurative language (figures of speech): language with a meaning beyond the literal, usually involving *simile* and *metaphor*, and sometimes other *devices* such as *hyperbole*.

Findley, Timothy (b.1930): Canadian novelist, *short story* and television script writer. He often explores the borderlines between *fiction* and history and truth. See *fabulation*. Notable works include THE WARS (1977), FAMOUS LAST WORDS (1981).

first-person narrative/point of view: see *narrator/narrative voice*.

Fitzgerald, F. Scott (1896–1940): American novelist, *short story* writer, playwright, and screenwriter. He wrote about and was a leading light of "The Jazz Age," a term that he himself coined, and his writing gives a vivid picture of the social behavior of his times. His fast-living lifestyle and neuroses, and those of his wife, are reflected in the *characters* and *action* of many of his *novels*, as is the deterioration caused by such a manner of living. Notable works include THIS SIDE OF PARADISE (1920), THE

BEAUTIFUL AND DAMNED (1922), THE GREAT GATSBY (1925), TENDER IS THE NIGHT (1934), THE LAST TYCOON (1941).

Fitzgerald, Penelope (1916–2000): English novelist and biographer. Her writing ranges over mystery, *romance, comedy,* history, and social *realism.* Notable works include OFFSHORE (1979), THE GATE OF ANGELS (1990), THE MEANS OF ESCAPE (2000).

fixed form refers to any *form* in *poetry* that is bound by established *rules* determining such things as *meter, rhyme scheme,* line length, and so forth.

flashback, probably a term borrowed from films, is the appearance during any kind of *literature* of a *scene* or *episode* that returns to an earlier time, e.g. in *Graham Swift's* WATERLAND. No doubt thanks to its use in the movies, this *technique* has become increasingly common since the early 20th century. Sometimes called *analepsis.* See also *anachorism, in media res.*

flashforward: the corollary of *flashback.* Also known as *prolepsis.* See also *anachorism.*

flat characters, as defined by *E.M. Forster* in ASPECTS OF THE NOVEL, are *characters* who are two-dimensional and do not develop during the course of the *story.* He cites Mrs. Micawber from *Dickens's* DAVID COPPERFIELD as an example. See *round characters.*

Fletcher, John (1579–1625): English playwright. A skilled professional man of the theater, he collaborated with many other playwrights, including almost certainly *Shakespeare* on THE TWO NOBLE KINSMEN (?1613) and HENRY VIII (1613). Other notable works include THE FAITHFUL SHEPHERDESS (?1609), PHILASTER (?1609), THE MAID'S TRAGEDY (?1611), the latter two in collaboration with *Beaumont.*

folio: a large page formed by a printer's sheet that has been folded once only, thus creating four pages. The First Folio edition of *Shakespeare's* plays (1623) was printed in this size.

foot: see *meter.*

Ford, Ford Madox (1873–1939): English novelist, poet, and editor. He had a powerful and positive influence upon his contemporaries, and as editor of THE ENGLISH REVIEW (a literary magazine founded in 1908) he did much to encourage previously unknown writers such as *Pound* and *Lawrence.* Notable works include THE GOOD SOLDIER (1915), PARADE'S END (1924–28).

Ford, John (?1586–?1640): English playwright. His plays show interest in moral *paradoxes* and in the position of women in society. Notable works include THE BROKEN HEART (?1627), TIS PITY SHE'S A WHORE (?1629).

foregrounding is a technical term denoting language that draws attention to itself as consciously literary, hence pushing its "literariness" into the foreground and demanding the attention of the reader. *Sterne's* TRISTRAM SHANDY is often cited as an example.

foreshadowing occurs when a writer prepares the reader or audience in any way for later events in a *narrative* or *drama.*

form is the shape of a piece of *literature* as opposed to its *content.* Although for academic purposes each needs to be analyzed in its own right, form and content are inseparable and depend upon one another, and the form is usually determined by the content. (The same is often true in other arts; hence the architectural notion that "form follows *function*" – that is, the shape of a building should be determined by its purpose or content.) As a secondary meaning the word form is sometimes used to denote the kind or *genre* of work; but it is best avoided in this sense. See *mechanic form, organic form, structure.*

formalism: see *intrinsic attitude.*

format refers to the physical size and/or layout of a book.

Forster, E.M. (1879–1970): English novelist, critic, essayist, and biographer. He was influenced by the philosophers G.E. Moore (1873–1958) and Bertrand Russell (1872–1970) and had close contact with members of the *Bloomsbury group.* He actively opposed censorship, and among other things his writing is noted for its gentle *satire,* humane liberal tolerance, and sense that it is possible to rise above politics through love. Notable works include WHERE ANGELS FEAR TO TREAD (1905), A ROOM WITH A VIEW (1908), HOWARDS END (1910), THE CELESTIAL OMNIBUS (1911), A PASSAGE TO INDIA (1924), ASPECTS OF THE NOVEL (1927), ABINGER HARVEST (1936).

Fowles, John (b.1926): English novelist and essayist. His *novels* often show an interest in experimenting with the conventional *narrative structures* of *fiction.* Notable works include THE MAGUS (1966, revised 1977), THE FRENCH LIEUTENANT'S WOMAN (1969).

Frame, Janet (b.1924): New Zealand novelist, *short story* writer, and poet. Influenced by the time she spent in institutions for the mentally ill, her writing can be disturbing; she often explores questions of the human identity and the borderline between reality and madness. She is also concerned with whether language can truly communicate her experience. Notable works include her autobiographical books TO THE ISLAND (1982), AN ANGEL AT MY TABLE (1984, made into a film in 1990), THE ENVOY FROM MIRROR CITY (1985).

Franklin, Benjamin (1706–90): American journalist, essayist, and autobiographer. A key figure in the movement for American independence, he possessed a widely admired *prose style,* once described by the Irish historian W.E.H. Lecky as "terse, luminous, simple, pregnant with meaning, eminently persuasive." Notable works include POOR RICHARD'S ALMANACK (1732–58), AUTOBIOGRAPHY (1793).

Franklin, Miles (1879–1945): Australian novelist. Renowned for her unconventional life and radical attitudes, she explores among other things feminism, Australian nationalism, and the impact upon her as a writer of being brought up in the remote bush. Notable works include MY BRILLIANT CAREER (1901, made into a film in 1979).

Frayn, Michael (b.1933): English playwright, journalist, and novelist, best known for his humorous stage *comedies* with a serious *satirical* edge. Notable works include the *novels* THE RUSSIAN INTERPRETER (1966), A VERY PRIVATE LIFE (1968), and the plays ALPHABETICAL ORDER (1975), MAKE AND BREAK (1980), NOISES OFF (1981).

free indirect style/free indirect discourse: see *narrator/narrative voice.*

free verse, sometimes referred to by the French term "vers libre," is *verse* that does not conform to any fixed *meter,* pattern, *rhyme,* or line length (although all these may partly be in evidence), relying upon the natural *rhythms* and *stresses* of the language. However, the use of *caesura* and *enjambment* are as significant as in more conventional verse. Most notably *Whitman* wrote LEAVES OF GRASS in free verse, and *Hopkins* used it in an innovative way. The *form* (or rather, lack of form) became increasingly popular with *modernist* poets during the 20th century, and *T.S. Eliot*'s THE WASTE LAND is often cited as a free verse *classic*. Other notable exponents include *Pound, Lawrence, Ginsberg, Langston Hughes*, and *William Carlos Williams*, whose "This is Just to Say," quoted in full under *minimalism*, is also a good example of a free verse *poem*.

Friel, Brian (b.1929): Irish playwright and *short story* writer. Much of his sensitive, lyrical writing explores personal, family, and Irish situations. He often locates his plays in and around Ballybeg, an imaginary village in Donegal. Notable works include TRANSLATIONS (1980), DANCING AT LUGHNASA (1990).

Frost, Robert (1874–1963) is a very popular American poet, localizing a great deal of his writing in rural New England. He received much of his initial encouragement from England, notably through the poet *Edward Thomas*. His *poems* often concern the individual trying to come to terms with the world, and tend to employ a conversational *diction* and *tone* characteristic of New England speech patterns. Notable works include MOUNTAIN INTERVAL (1916), NEW HAMPSHIRE (1923), COLLECTED POEMS (1930), IN THE CLEARING (1962). His best-known poem is probably "The Road Not Taken" (1916).

Fugard, Athol (b.1932): South African playwright, novelist, and screenwriter. His father was of English descent, his mother an Afrikaner. He founded his "poor theatre" in black townships, and his plays are often powerful yet compassionate explorations of what it was like to be a black South African living under apartheid. Notable works include THE COAT (1966), SIZWE BANSI IS DEAD (1972), THE ISLAND (1973), A LESSON FROM ALOES (1978), "MASTER HAROLD" AND THE BOYS (1982).

Fuller, Roy (1912–91): English poet and novelist. Influenced by *Auden* and *Spender*, he is noted for his objective, refined, *ironic* view and his skillful poetic *technique* which combines traditional and innovative *form*s. Notable works include THE MIDDLE OF A WAR (1942), COLLECTED POEMS: 1936–1961 (1962), THE REIGN OF SPARROWS (1980), AVAILABLE FOR DREAMS (1989).

function is a term sometimes used to denote any event or *action* which moves along the *plot*.

G

Galsworthy, John (1867–1933): English novelist, playwright, and poet. In many of his works there is commentary on social injustice of one type or another, and his work had an impact upon contemporary attitudes, as when his play JUSTICE (1910) was influential in the abolition of solitary confinement in prisons. Other notable works include THE SILVER BOX (1906), THE FORSYTE SAGA (1906–21), STRIFE (1909), THE SKIN GAME (1920), COLLECTED POEMS (1934).

Gardam, Jane (b.1928): English novelist, *short story* writer, and children's *author*. Her *novel*s often have young protagonists, and are characterized by deft scene-setting, period detail, literary allusiveness, and emotional scenes. Notable works include GOD ON THE ROCKS (1978), CRUSOE'S DAUGHTER (1985), THE QUEEN OF THE TAMBOURINE (1991), FAITH FOX (1996).

Gardner, Helen (1908–86): extremely influential English critic, specializing in *metaphysical literature*. Notable works include THE BUSINESS OF CRITICISM (1960) in which she underlined that the *function* of a critic is to "shine a torch," not "wield a sceptre" (in other words, to illuminate rather than attack).

Gaskell, Elizabeth (1810–65): English novelist and biographer. She was a friend of *Charlotte Brontë* and encouraged by *Dickens*, and her work shows a marked development in *structure*, becoming more disciplined as her writing career progressed. She carefully researched all background aspects of her *character*s, whether industrial workers or country folk, especially their speech. Among other things she has been noted for her *narrative* skill and her compassionate treatment of the less fortunate in society. Notable works include MARY BARTON (1848), CRANFORD (1851–53), RUTH (1853), NORTH AND SOUTH (1855), THE LIFE OF CHARLOTTE BRONTË (1857), WIVES AND DAUGHTERS (1866). See also *regional novel*.

Gatheru, Mugo (b.1925): Kenyan novelist. Among other things he deals with the social frictions between a traditional and a modern society. Notable works include CHILD OF TWO WORLDS (1964).

genre: a category into which types of *literature* may be placed, e.g. *metaphysical poetry, revenge tragedy, science fiction, short story.*

Georgian period, in *literature*, is generally considered to cover writing in England during the reign of George V (1910–36). In historical terms the term Georgian applies to the consecutive reigns of the first four Georges in England (1714–1830).

Georgian poetry covers poets who wrote fairly traditional work, often rural in *setting* and delicate in touch, during the early part of the *Georgian period*, e.g. *Blunden, Brooke, de la Mare, Graves, Housman, Lawrence, Masefield, Owen, Sassoon,* and *Edward Thomas,* many of whom were featured in *anthologies* published between 1912 and 1922 called GEORGIAN POETRY. The Georgians were considered to be minor and conventional by *modernist*s such as *T.S. Eliot.*

Ghosh, Amitav (b.1956): Indian novelist and travel writer. His sometimes complex writings show his experience of various cultures. Notable works include THE CIRCLE OF REASON (1986), THE SHADOW LINES (1988).

ghost story: a *genre* popular since Anglo-Saxon times, consisting of stories of spirits who return to haunt the living, and are usually, but not exclusively, in the *form* of *short stories* in *prose*. Notable writers of such stories include *Irving* ("The Legend of Sleepy Hollow," 1820), *Poe, Dickens, Stevenson, Kipling, Henry James, Wilde* (THE CANTERVILLE GHOST, 1891), *Wharton* (TALES OF MAN AND GHOSTS, 1910), *de la Mare*. *Mary Shelley* began writing FRANKENSTEIN in response to a ghost story competition organized by *Byron*. A ghost story has traditionally been thought most fit for telling on or about Christmas Eve, *Dickens's* A CHRISTMAS CAROL (1843) being the most famous of these. *Novel*-length ghost stories are rare, an exception being *Susan Hill's* THE WOMAN IN BLACK. See also *gothic novel*.

ghost writer: a professional writer who does most or all of the writing for a celebrity who then usually takes the credit for her or his "*autobiography*."

Gibbons, Stella (1902–89): English novelist and *short story* writer. Most of her output consisted of sentimental social *comedies*, but COLD COMFORT FARM (1932) is a very successful *parody* of the kind of popular rural *fiction* written by *Webb*. See also *rural novel*.

Ginsberg, Allen (1926–97): American poet who was influenced by, among others, *William Carlos Williams*, especially in his precise, short *lyrics* and use of *free verse*. A relentless critic of middle-class American values, he protested in the 1960s against the Vietnam War and was a leading light in the "flower power" movement, a phrase of his own coining. Notable works include HOWL AND OTHER POEMS (1956), KADDISH AND OTHER POEMS (1961).

Globe Theatre: the famous Bankside theater, near to the *Rose Theatre* and the River Thames, for which *Shakespeare* wrote many of his plays. Built in 1599, it was rebuilt after a fire in 1613, and dismantled in 1644 after all the theaters were closed. It has now been reconstructed near to the old site in the Southwark area of London, and it is once again possible to see the plays of Shakespeare and his contemporaries performed in the theatrical circumstances for which they were written.

glossary: a list of explanations of difficult words in a *text*.

Glück, Louise (b.1943): American poet. Influenced by *Plath*, she often treats auto-biographical experience with intensity yet objectiveness. Notable works include THE TRIUMPH OF ACHILLES (1985).

Godwin, William (1756–1836): English novelist, philosopher, and biographer. A radical, almost anarchic, thinker in the *age of reason*, admired by *Coleridge* and *Wordsworth*, he became an atheist and believed that humans were rational beings capable of continually improving themselves and thus in no need of institutions or laws. By the 1820s his radicalism had dimmed and he became antireform. Notable works include AN ENQUIRY CONCERNING POLITICAL JUSTICE (1793), CALEB WILLIAMS (1794).

Golding, William (1911–93): English novelist, essayist, playwright, and poet whose reputation rests on his work as a novelist. His work is often centered upon the darker impulses at the core of human existence. Notable works include LORD OF THE FLIES (1954), THE SPIRE (1964), RITES OF PASSAGE (1980).

Goldsmith, Oliver (?1730–74): Irish playwright, poet, novelist, and essayist. Although he has been dismissed by some as lightweight, his most inventive work has nonetheless endured. He is difficult to classify as he could write on a variety of subjects and in a diversity of *manners*, and thus perhaps it is unsurprising that best-known works are in different *genres* – a *novel*, a *poem*, and a play, respectively THE VICAR OF WAKEFIELD (1766), THE DESERTED VILLAGE (1770), SHE STOOPS TO CONQUER (1773). Other notable works include THE GOOD NATURED MAN (1768).

Goodison, Lorna (b.1947): Jamaican poet and *short story* writer. She combines the Jamaican *oral tradition* with conventional poetic *forms*, and uses powerful *imagery* (influenced by her painting) to depict *viewpoints* of Jamaican women. Notable works include TAMARIND SEASON (1980), I AM BECOMING MY MOTHER (1986), HEARTEASE (1988), TO US ALL FLOWERS ARE ROSES (1990).

Gordimer, Nadine (b.1923): South African novelist and *short story* writer. Much of her work reflects her interest in politics and her stand against apartheid and censorship and, more recently, the time leading up to the democratic elections in her country. Notable works include THE SOFT VOICE OF THE SERPENT (1952), FRIDAY'S FOOTPRINT (1960), A GUEST OF HONOUR (1970), THE CONSERVATIONIST (1974), BURGER'S DAUGHTER (1979), JULY'S PEOPLE (1981), MY SON'S STORY (1990), NONE TO ACCOMPANY ME (1994).

Gosse, Edmund (1849–1928): English biographer, essayist, translator, and poet. He helped to establish the reputation of *Ibsen* in Britain, and was a prolific poet and biographer, but he is best known for his masterpiece, the *autobiography* FATHER AND SON (1907).

gothic novel/fiction/romance refers to *literature* that deals with the passionate, mysterious, horrific, and/or the supernatural, often in a medieval *setting*. It was especially popular between the 1760s and 1820s. The word "Gothic" is derived from the Germanic tribe, the Goths, but came to denote the style of flying buttresses and pointed windows, arches, and vaulting of medieval architecture. *Walpole's* THE CASTLE OF OTRANTO is generally considered the earliest in the *genre*, and is subtitled A GOTHIC STORY on account of its medieval setting. Other notable examples include THE MYSTERIES OF UDOLPHO (1794) by Ann Radcliffe (1764–1823), *M.G. Lewis's* THE MONK, *Beckford's* VATHEK and *Mary Shelley's* FRANKENSTEIN. *Austen* pokes fun at the genre in NORTHANGER ABBEY, as does *Peacock* in NIGHTMARE ABBEY. Later *novels* with gothic elements include *Emily Brontë's* WUTHERING HEIGHTS, *Charlotte Brontë's* JANE EYRE, *Dickens's* GREAT EXPECTATIONS, and the stories of *Poe, Faulkner, Dinesen,* Mervyn Peake (1911–68), and *Angela Carter.* See also *ghost story*.

Gower, John (?1330–1408): English poet who was much admired in the 15th century and sometimes regarded, along with *Chaucer, Langland,* and *Lydgate,* as a founding father of English *poetry*. Like many of his contemporaries, he was concerned with the corruption of the times. Notable works include CONFESSIO AMANTIS (*c.*1386–93), which contains many *courtly love stories*, one used by *Shakespeare* as a basis for PERICLES (?1608) where Gower appears in the *character* of the Chorus.

Granville-Barker, Harley (1877–1946): English playwright and literary critic. He dealt with political and social issues that at the time were rarely dealt with on stage, and some of his contemporaries regarded his work as too intellectual and untheatrical. On the other hand *Shaw*, in whose plays Granville-Barker acted, admired him. Notable works include THE VOYSEY INHERITANCE (1905), WASTE (1907), THE MADRAS HOUSE (1910).

Graves, Robert (1895–1985): English poet, novelist, literary critic, and translator. Early *poems* are predominately concerned with his experiences in World War I. A dissident in many respects, he is noted for his *love poems* and use of plain language within traditional *verse forms*. He often drew upon classical culture and *myth* for inspiration. Notable works include the *autobiography* GOODBYE TO ALL THAT (1929), I, CLAUDIUS (1934), THE GREEK MYTHS (1955).

graveyard school refers to certain 18th century poets who wrote reflectively about mortality and death, as in THE GRAVE (1743) by Robert Blair (1699–1746). For a time this *style* was moderately fashionable. See also *black comedy*.

Gray, Thomas (1716–71): English poet. Friends, among others, with *Smart* and *Walpole*, he represents part of a movement away from the *neoclassical* and toward the *picturesque*, accelerated by his visit to the Lake District as recorded in his JOURNAL (1775). His *verse* is characteristically polished, precise, and readable. Notable works include the *mock heroic* "Ode on the Death of a Favorite Cat, Drowned in a Tub of Gold Fishes" (1748), "Elegy Written in a Country Churchyard" (1751), which owes something to the *graveyard school* of *poetry*, "The Bard" (1757), "The Progress of Poetry" (1757), POEMS (1868).

great chain of being: this refers to the notion, popular from ancient times and still current during the *Renaissance*, that all life makes up a hierarchical chain from God at the top down to the lowest life form on earth at the bottom. This kind of ordering is expressed in such as Ulysses' speech on "degree" in act I, scene 3 of *Shakespeare's* TROILUS AND CRESSIDA (?1602) and epistle 1, section 8 of *Pope's* ESSAY ON MAN (1732–34).

Great Tradition, The refers to the concept of an essential *canon* in *fiction*, including the work of five novelists (*Austen, George Eliot, Henry James, Conrad, Lawrence*) upon which *Leavis* based his approach to the study of *literature*. It is also the title of a seminal work by Leavis, explaining this concept, published in 1948. See *Leavisite*.

Greene, Graham (1904–91): English novelist, playwright, *short story* and travel writer, and essayist. His writings often show *characters* in run-down or out-of-the-way places in various parts of the world who are presented with a moral dilemma involving a sense of failure and/or guilt. Notable works include BRIGHTON ROCK (1938), THE POWER AND THE GLORY (1940), THE HEART OF THE MATTER (1948), THE THIRD MAN (1950), THE QUIET AMERICAN (1955), OUR MAN IN HAVANA (1958), TRAVELS WITH MY AUNT (1969), THE HONORARY CONSUL (1973), THE LAST WORD (1990).

Greene, Robert (?1558–92): English playwright, *prose* writer, and pamphleteer who was associated with the *university wits* and led a dissipated life, dying in poverty. Notable works include FRIAR BACON AND FRIAR BUNGAY (?1589), GREENE'S GROATSWORTH OF WIT (1592), containing his attack upon that "upstart crow"

Shakespeare, who later based THE WINTER'S TALE on Greene's prose *romance* PANDOSTO (1588).

Griffiths, Trevor (b.1935): English playwright and television *dramatist*. His early work often adopts a Marxist standpoint and contains elements of political debate between the *characters*. Notable works include THE PARTY (1973), COMEDIANS (1975).

grotesque is a term denoting bizarre, macabre, exaggerated, *fantastic*, aberrant, unpleasant, sick and/or pornographic elements in any art *form*. Writers in English who have employed elements of the grotesque include *Webster, Tourneur, Jonathan Swift, Smollett, Byron, Poe, Dickens, Robert Browning, Beckett, Waugh.*

Gunn, Thom (b.1929): English poet. Influenced by 16th and 17th century *poetry* and identified with *the Movement*, his early work is noted for its disciplined use of conventional *forms* and objective view of its subject matter. Over the years he has developed his technical and thematic range, and later *verse* has become more flexible. He was drawn into the Californian alternative culture of the late 1960s. Notable works include FIGHTING TERMS (1954), JACK STRAW'S CASTLE (1975), THE PASSAGE OF JOY (1982).

Gurney, Ivor (1890–1937): English poet who also composed and sometimes set his work to music. Influenced by *Hopkins, Whitman,* and *Edward Thomas,* he writes of rural Gloucestershire and of trench life during World War I, when he was wounded and gassed, and which he deals with objectively but with a remarkable lyricism. Committed to a mental institution from 1922 until his death, he wrote *poetry* that can be uneven, but does not often show signs of his instability. Notable works include SEVERN AND SOMME (1917), WAR'S EMBERS (1919), COLLECTED POEMS (1982, ed. P.J. Kavanagh).

H

haiku: a Japanese verse *form* comprising a single three-line *stanza* of seventeen syllables, the lines containing five, seven, and five syllables respectively. Designed in its brevity to capture the essence of the poet's mood toward an idea, object, season, or scene, a haiku can lose its concision in translation since it is difficult to replicate fully the poet's intention. The form interested the *imagists*, e.g. in *Pound*'s "In a Station of the Metro" (1913). Among others *Frost* and *Yeats* were also influenced by the haiku.

half rhyme, sometimes called "near," "imperfect," or partial *rhyme*, or off-rhyme, occurs when two words rhyme, but not perfectly. Its effect can be gentler and more subtle in pattern than a full rhyme. For example:

> Move him into the sun –
> Gently its touch awoke him once,
> At home, whispering of fields unsown,
> Always it woke him, even in France…

> (from *Owen*'s "Futility")

Here "sun/unsown" and "once/France" are half rhymes. See *consonance*.

hamartia is an error of judgment that leads to the downfall of a tragic *hero*. In his POETICS *Aristotle* says that hamartia is not a moral failing: for instance, Oedipus kills his father on impulse and marries his mother through ignorance. It is close to, but not quite the same as, a *tragic flaw* (see *Bradley*).

Harbage, Alfred (1901–76): American scholar and literary critic who specialized in Shakespearean research. Notable works include SHAKESPEARE'S AUDIENCE (1941).

hard ending: see *masculine ending*.

Hardy, Thomas (1840–1920): English novelist, poet, *short story* writer, and *dramatist*. Broadly speaking he devoted the first part of his creative life to writing the *novels* for which he is best known, the second part to *poetry*, which he regarded, as do many critics, as his most important contribution to *literature*. He placed his novels into three categories:

- novels of *character* and environment, e.g. THE MAYOR OF CASTERBRIDGE (1886)
- *romances* and *fantasies*, e.g. THE TRUMPET-MAJOR (1880)
- novels of ingenuity, e.g. A LAODICEAN (1881).

His predominant *theme* tends to be the struggle of men and women in the face of an ironic fate. He locates many of his novels in a region he calls Wessex, which, roughly speaking, extends from the counties of Oxfordshire and Hampshire westward down to Cornwall (see also *regional novel*). His poetry may in some senses be seen as early *modernist* in its challenging of contemporary Victorian *convention*. He claimed that he wrote "for poetic *texture* rather than poetic veneer," and his strong *imagery* stemmed from his passion and consideration for the natural world. Other notable works include FAR FROM THE MADDING CROWD (1874), THE RETURN OF THE NATIVE (1878), THE WOODLANDERS (1887), TESS OF THE D'URBERVILLES (1891), LIFE'S LITTLE IRONIES

(1894), JUDE THE OBSCURE (1895), WESSEX POEMS (1898), THE DYNASTS (1904–08), SATIRES OF CIRCUMSTANCE (1914).

Hare, David (b.1947): English playwright and screenwriter. Many of his plays concern the greed and corruption that he sees as characteristic of British society in the second half of the 20th century. Notable works include BRASSNECK (1973, with *Brenton*), KNUCKLE (1974), FANSHEN (1975), TEETH 'N' SMILES (1975), LICKING HITLER (1978), PLENTY (1978), A MAP OF THE WORLD (1982), PRAVDA (1985, with Brenton), RACING DEMON (1990), SKYLIGHT (1995).

Harlem Rennaissance is a term applied to the emergence of the first definable generation of African-American writers in the 1920s and 1930s in the Harlem district of New York City. They began to promote black consciousness and established a body of published writings that were mindful, among other things, of their African heritage. Leading writers include Countee Cullen (1903–46), *Du Bois, Langston Hughes, Hurston,* and Claude McKay (1890–1948).

Harrison, Tony (b.1937): English poet, translator, and playwright. His *poetry* sometimes reflects his wide travels and is usually politically committed, often using tightly controlled elements of colloquial speech and skillful rhyming. Notable works include THE LOINERS (1970), THE SCHOOL OF ELOQUENCE AND OTHER POEMS (1978), V. (1985), A COLD COMING: GULF WAR POEMS (1991), THE GAZE OF THE GORGON (1992).

Harte, Bret (1836–1902): American *short story* writer, poet, novelist, and playwright, mainly noted for his neatly structured short *tales*. A friend of *Twain*, his notable works include THE LUCK OF ROARING CAMP AND OTHER SKETCHES (1870), MRS. SKAGGS'S HUSBANDS (1873).

Hartley, L.P. (1895–1972): English novelist, *short story* writer, literary critic, and essayist. Influenced by *Henry James* and Sigmund Freud (1856–1939), frequent *themes* in his writings, which show a strong moral concern, are of childhood memories and the search for personal identity. Notable works include EUSTACE AND HILDA (1947), THE GO-BETWEEN (1953).

Harwood, Gwen (1920–95): Australian poet who often conveys the anguish of life, yet has a fundamentally positive outlook. Her *lyric poetry* is markedly controlled. Notable works include POEMS (1963), THE LION'S BRIDE (1981), BONE SCAN (1988).

Hawthorne, Nathaniel (1804–64): American novelist, *short story* writer, and children's *author*. Associated with *transcendentalism*, his writing is often *allegorical*, and explores guilt, sin, redemptive dreams, and other aspects of the American conscious and subconscious, showing some fascination with the effects of Puritanism on the morality of New Englanders. Notable works include TWICE-TOLD TALES (1837, revised 1842), THE SCARLET LETTER (1850), THE HOUSE OF THE SEVEN GABLES (1851), TANGLEWOOD TALES (1853).

Hazlitt, William (1778–1830): English literary critic and essayist. His *prose* is highly regarded in its analysis of contemporary *authors*, politics, and Elizabethan playwrights. He is a fine critic of the early *Romantics*. Notable works include AN ESSAY ON THE PRINCIPLES OF HUMAN ACTION (1805), LECTURES ON THE ENGLISH POETS (1818), THE SPIRIT OF THE AGE (1825), THE PLAIN SPEAKER (1826).

Head, Bessie (1937–86): South African novelist. She writes about experiences of exile together with the problems created by racism, town and rural values, male domination, and tribal partisanship. Notable works include WHEN THE RAIN CLOUDS GATHER (1968).

headless line: an *iambic verse* line whose first syllable is missing, thus creating an initial *foot* containing a single stressed syllable.

> I'm / a means, / a stage, / a cow / in half
>
> (from *Plath*'s "Metaphors," 1965)

Heaney, Seamus (b.1939): Irish poet and critic. In his *poetry* he draws on his childhood experiences of life on an Irish farm and on many other aspects of Irish life. As the situation in Northern Ireland deteriorated during the 1970s his writing became more political. He is usually economic with words, and he has a facility for striking *metaphor*s. Notable works include DEATH OF A NATURALIST (1966), NORTH (1975), THE GOVERNMENT OF THE TONGUE AND OTHER CRITICAL WRITINGS (1988), BEOWULF (1999, translation), COLLECTED POEMS 1966–96 (1999), ELECTRIC LIGHT (2001).

Heller, Joseph (1923–99): American novelist, *short story* writer, and playwright. His best-known *novel*, CATCH-22 (1961), is a zany *satire* on the folly and turmoil of war that drew on his air force experiences in World War II. Other notable works include GOOD AS GOLD (1979).

Hellman, Lillian (1905–84): American playwright whose taut and intensely dramatic plays often focus on the use of power in personal, social, and political relationships. Hellman testified before the notorious House Un-American Committee in 1952, and wrote about her encounter with McCarthyism in SCOUNDREL TIME (1976). Other notable works include the plays THE CHILDREN'S HOUR (1934), THE LITTLE FOXES (1939), WATCH ON THE RHINE (1941).

Hemingway, Ernest (1899–1961): American novelist, journalist, and *short story* writer. Influenced by such writers as *Pound* and *Ford Madox Ford*, his *prose style* became famous for its laconic, "tough guy" terseness, which matched his often very masculine subject matter such as big-game hunting and bullfighting. His work reflected mid-20th century disillusionment and enjoyed both popular and critical acclaim. Notable works include IN OUR TIME: STORIES (1925), A FAREWELL TO ARMS (1929), FOR WHOM THE BELL TOLLS (1940), THE OLD MAN AND THE SEA (1952).

hendecasyllable: a *verse* line of eleven syllables, e.g.

> To be, or not to be: that is the question
>
> (from act III of *Shakespeare*'s HAMLET)

See also *meter*.

hendiadys is a *figure of speech* whereby two nouns are brought together to express one idea, e.g. "life and soul," "doom and gloom."

Henri, Adrian (b.1932): English poet, one of the *Liverpool poets* of the 1960s and 1970s. Influenced by pop, rock, and jazz music, and by the methods of poets and writers such as *William Burroughs*, his *poetry*, often impressionistic or surreal, is very varied in *style* and *theme*. Notable works include AUTOBIOGRAPHY (1971), COLLECTED POEMS (1986), NOT FADING AWAY: POEMS 1989–1994 (1994).

Henry, O. (real name William Sydney Porter, 1862–1910): American *short story* writer. He is a master of surprise, often introducing ironic twists at the end of his *tales*. Notable works include CABBAGES AND KINGS (1904), THE TRIMMED LAMP (1907), THE VOICE OF THE CITY (1908).

Henryson, Robert (?1436–?1504): Scottish poet. Almost nothing is known of his life. Sometimes classified with *Dunbar* in a group known as Scottish Chaucerians, he wrote *pastorals* and *allegories*, his *tone* often strictly moral yet compassionate. Notable works include THE TESTAMENT OF CRESSEID (written as a sequel to *Chaucer's* TROILUS AND CRISEYDE), ROBENE AND MAKYNE, MORALL FABILLIS OF ESOPE.

Henslowe, Philip (?1557–1616): English theater manager. In 1587 he built the *Rose Theatre* on *Bankside*, and was also involved in the Hope and Fortune theaters. He successfully ran *The Admiral's Men* and other acting companies. Many playwrights wrote for him, but not *Shakespeare* (despite what the film SHAKESPEARE IN LOVE would have us believe!). His *diaries* are an invaluable source of information about the Elizabethan theatrical life.

heptameter: see *meter*.

heptastich: a seven-line *stanza* used by many English poets, e.g. *Chaucer, Spenser, Percy Shelley, Robert Browning, Longfellow, Auden*.

heptasyllable: a *verse* line of seven syllables, e.g.

> Through the forest have I gone
> > (from act II, scene 2 of *Shakespeare's* A MIDSUMMER NIGHT'S DREAM)

See also *meter*.

Herbert, George (1593–1633): Welsh *metaphysical* poet whose works were often brief but distinguished by their careful construction, ingenious *conceits*, and deep religious faith. Notable works include THE TEMPLE: SACRED POEMS AND PRIVATE EJACULATIONS (1633). See also *concrete poetry*.

hermeneutics, originally applied to interpreting the *Bible*, now refers in general to the study of the *interpretation* of *texts*. See *code*.

hero/heroine: the leading *character* or *protagonist* in a *story*. Although, strictly speaking, it does not matter in literary criticism if s/he is good or bad (therefore Macbeth may be described as the hero), in this kind of case it has become the practice to refer to the *antihero*.

heroic couplets: pairs of rhyming *iambic pentameters*. *Chaucer* first made extensive use of them (they are sometimes known as "riding *rhyme*," possibly because Chaucer's pilgrims tell their stories in this *meter* as they ride toward the shrine of St. Thomas à Becket in THE CANTERBURY TALES). Many poets have employed them through the centuries. *Dryden* used them with skill (e.g. in MACFLECKNOE), helping to make them popular in the *neoclassical period*. *Pope* excelled in their use, and *Crabbe* frequently employed them, as in

> Old Peter Grimes made fishing his employ
> His wife he cabined with him and his boy...

> > (the opening of THE BOROUGH)

heroic drama/tragedy: a term applied to a kind of *drama* popular during the *Restoration period* and influenced by French classical drama. In the *preface* to his heroic tragedy THE CONQUEST OF GRANADA (1672) *Dryden* states that "an heroic play ought to be an imitation, in little, of an heroic poem; and consequently... love and valour ought to be the subject of it." This play, together with his ALL FOR LOVE and *Otway's* VENICE PRESERVED, are the best of this type, but many were overblown *bombast*, satirized by *Fielding* in TOM THUMB (1730) and *Sheridan* in THE CRITIC (1779). See *Restoration tragedy*.

heroic poetry: another term for *epic poetry*.

heroic quatrain: a set of four *iambic pentameters* rhyming abab, e.g. in *Gray's* "Elegy Written in a Country Churchyard."

Herrick, Robert (1591–1674): English poet. Associated with *Jonson* and in some respects a *Cavalier* poet, Herrick was called by *Swinburne* "the greatest songwriter ever born of English race." His versatility enabled him to write in a variety of *forms*, among them *epigram*, *song*, hymn, *elegy*, epitaph, *love poetry* (sometimes sensuously erotic) and, above all, *lyric poems* at which he was a master craftsman. Notable works include HESPERIDES (1648), "Noble Numbers" (1660). See also *carpe diem*.

hexameter: see *meter*.

hexastich: a six-line *stanza*.

high comedy is a term sometimes applied to *witty*, sophisticated *comedy* such as *Shakespeare's* MUCH ADO ABOUT NOTHING, *Congreve's* THE WAY OF THE WORLD, *Wilde's* A WOMAN OF NO IMPORTANCE. The term can also be applied to *novels*, e.g. *Austen's* PRIDE AND PREJUDICE, or *poems*, e.g. *Pope's* THE RAPE OF THE LOCK. See *low comedy*.

Highsmith, Patricia (1921–95): American novelist and *short story* writer. One of the most highly acclaimed *crime novel* writers of our time, best known for her Tom Ripley *novels*. Although writing in third-person *narrative*, Highsmith leads the reader into seeing the world through the eyes of her amoral, psychopathic *antiheroes*. Notable works include STRANGERS ON A TRAIN (1950), THE TALENTED MR. RIPLEY (1955), DEEP WATER (1957), THE STORYTELLER (1965), PEOPLE WHO KNOCK ON THE DOOR (1983).

Hill, Geoffrey (b.1932): English poet and critic. Initially influenced by, among others, *Blake* and *Housman*, he writes richly textured *verse* in which religious and historical *themes* and *settings* predominate. Notable works include FOR THE UNFALLEN (1959), KING LOG (1968), MERCIAN HYMNS (1971), TENEBRAE (1979), THE MYSTERY OF THE CHARITY OF CHARLES PEGUY (1983), ENEMY'S COUNTRY (1991), COLLECTED POEMS (1994).

Hill, Susan (b.1942): English novelist, *short story* and children's writer, playwright, and autobiographer. She can generate considerable *atmosphere* in her writing, which often shows acute psychological insight into loneliness. Notable works include GENTLEMEN AND LADIES (1968), I'M THE KING OF THE CASTLE (1970), THE BIRD OF NIGHT (1972), THE WOMAN IN BLACK (1983).

historical novel: a kind of *faction* in which historical events or backgrounds are used as the basis for a fictional story. Much *gothic fiction* was set in the Middle Ages, and then *Walter Scott* wrote the first of many of his historical novels with WAVERLEY (1814), since when the *genre* has remained popular. Notable among such works are

Thackeray's VANITY FAIR, *Dickens*'s A TALE OF TWO CITIES (1859), *George Eliot*'s ROMOLA (1863), *Graves*'s I, CLAUDIUS, GONE WITH THE WIND (1936) by Margaret Mitchell (1900–49), THE KING MUST DIE (1958) by Mary Renault (1905–83), *Farrell*'s THE SIEGE OF KRISHNAPUR, *Golding*'s RITES OF PASSAGE.

historicism/new historicism: the critical view that all *literature* must be studied with regard to the historical *context* within which it was produced, an approach that reacts against that of the *new critics*, and conflicts with some aspects of *structuralism* and *deconstruction*. See *extrinsic attitude.*

history play: broadly speaking, any play set in a historical period, although the term is often used to refer to the *chronicle plays* written by *Shakespeare* and his contemporaries.

Hoffman, Eva (b.1945): Polish-born Canadian writer, journalist, and editor. As a Jewish displaced person she is concerned with issues of adjustment to a different culture and language. Notable works include LOST IN TRANSLATION: A LIFE IN A NEW LANGUAGE (1989), EXIT INTO HISTORY (1993), SHTETL (1997).

Holtby, Winifred (1898–1935): English novelist, journalist, literary critic, and *short story* writer. Interested in pacifism, women's rights, and racial tolerance, she is at her best depicting the doings of local communities within the *setting* of her native East Yorkshire. Her friend *Brittain* wrote much about her in TESTAMENT OF YOUTH. Notable works include ANDERBY WOLD (1923), THE LAND OF GREEN GINGER (1927), SOUTH RIDING (1936). See also *regional novel.*

Homer: the name given to the supposed ancient Greek author(s) of two *epics*, THE ILIAD and THE ODYSSEY. Nothing is known about him (or her – research by the 19th century *Samuel Butler* led him to believe that the author was female). These *poems*, possibly written between 800 and 700BC, were central to the culture of ancient Greece, and their impact and influence has survived through all ages to the present day.

Hopkins, Gerard Manley (1844–89): English poet. His early *poetry* is noted for its sensuous detail, and all his output is marked by sensitivity to aural and rhythmical effects. He coined the terms *inscape, instress,* and *sprung rhythm,* which are important in understanding his *verse.* He converted to Roman Catholicism and then became a Jesuit, never managing to reconcile service to God with writing poetry. Notable works include "The Wreck of the Deutschland" (written 1875–76), "The Windhover," "Spring," "Pied Beauty," "Binsey Poplars." None of his *poems* was published in his lifetime.

Horation ode: an *ode* written in the *style* of the Roman poet Horace (65–8BC).

Hospital, Janette Turner (b.1942): Australian novelist and *short story* and *detective fiction* writer. In some respects a postmodernist, she locates her *stories* in various places around the world, and her subjects often include dislocated wanderers. Notable works include TIGER IN THE TIGER PIT (1983), DISLOCATIONS (1986).

Housman, A.E. (1859–1936): English poet and literary critic. His love for an idealized English countryside, mellowed by a dark nostalgia, made his work very popular around the time of World War I. Notable works include A SHROPSHIRE LAD (1896), LAST POEMS (1922).

Hove, Chenjerai (b.1956): Zimbabwean poet and novelist. His writing explores the Zimbabwean situation during the war of liberation, and issues of pre- and post-independence society. Notable works include BONES (1988).

hovering stress/accent occurs in *poetry* when it is unclear whether or not a syllable should be stressed.

Howard, Henry: see *Surrey, Earl of.*

Howells, William Dean (1837–1920): American novelist, critic, editor, *dramatist*, travel and *prose* writer. A friend of *Henry James*, he wrote many *romances*, but later work moves toward *realism* and a concern for social issues. Notable works include A MODERN INSTANCE (1882), THE RISE OF SILAS LAPHAM (1885), INDIAN SUMMER (1886), A HAZARD OF NEW FORTUNES (1889).

hubris: a weakness in a Greek tragic *hero* which means he fails to take notice of the warnings of the gods and disobeys their laws. This leads to his downfall and *nemesis*, e.g. Oedipus in *Sophocles'* OEDIPUS THE KING, Creon in his ANTIGONE, Pentheus in Euripedes' THE BACCHAE (5th century BC). See also *tragedy, tragic flaw.*

Hughes, Langston (1902–67): American novelist, *short story* writer, poet, journalist, and playwright. An important figure in the *Harlem Renaissance*, he often uses jazz rhythms to explore African-American consciousness and became known as the Negro Poet Laureate. He can be a shrewd observer of black/white relationships. Notable works include NOT WITHOUT LAUGHTER (1930), THE WAYS OF WHITE FOLKS (1934), SHAKESPEARE IN HARLEM (1942, poems), BLACK NATIVITY (1961).

Hughes, Richard (1900–76): English novelist, playwright, and poet. His *themes* include the extreme severity of nature, and the ways in which apparent innocence is disturbed, and sometimes destroyed, by violent events. Notable works include A HIGH WIND IN JAMAICA (1929, published in America as THE INNOCENT VOYAGE), THE FOX IN THE ATTIC (1961).

Hughes, Ted (1930–98): English poet, children's writer, critic, translator, and editor. His *poetry* often concerns nature and the harsh, disturbing, violent, and highly imaginative aspects of the animal world, but emphasizes the necessity of struggling to endure in the face of adversity. Some of his work may be classed as *topographical poetry*, drawing on his native Yorkshire and adopted Devon. His *style* was influenced by *Hopkins* and *Lawrence*. He was *poet laureate* from 1984–98. Notable works include THE HAWK IN THE RAIN (1957), LUPERCAL (1960), WODWO (1967), CROW (1970), CAVE BIRDS (1975, revised 1978), NEW SELECTED POEMS 1957–1994 (1995).

Hulme, Keri (b.1947): New Zealand novelist, *short story* writer and poet who is of mixed English, Maori and Scots ancestry and who draws on a wide range of approaches and *techniques* in her writing. Notable works include THE BONE PEOPLE (1983), THE WINDEATER/TE KAIHAU (1986).

humanism/humanist: terms that, in a literary sense, are most often used to apply to the moral and philosophical ideas (that is, "humanities" as opposed to "sciences") of *Renaissance* writers and thinkers such as Erasmus (1456–1536), *More, Sidney, Spenser* and, later, *Milton*. Classical and Christian ideas were blended, placing at the center of thinking the achievements, dignity, and positive aspects of human beings in this world, rather than their innate corruption and the spiritual afterlife. The attitude may be typified by the Prince's speech, beginning "What a piece of work is man. How noble in reason, how excellent in faculty…" in act II, scene 2 of *Shakespeare*'s HAMLET. Later on these terms came to refer to the ideas of those such as *Johnson* and *Arnold* who advocated a liberal philosophy of mankind, adopting in general the views of Renaissance humanists. During the 20th century the terms began to denote a non-religious, even antireligious, moral philosophy of the kind that *Marxists* consider feebly liberal and bourgeois.

humor, in a literary sense, has since the 18th century tended to indicate the quality of anything that gives rise to laughter, as distinct from *wit*, which has a more intellectual appeal.

humors: the essential elements of a theory, current from ancient times until the 17th century in England, that held that people's physiology was composed of four liquids, or "humours," which determined their character. These were black bile, blood, choler, and phlegm; excess of any one of these led respectively to a temperament that was melancholic, sanguine, choleric, or phlegmatic. When Duke Ferdinand in *Shakespeare*'s AS YOU LIKE IT is described as "humorous" it means not that he is funny, but that his humors are out of balance, and thus that he is dangerously "ill-humoured." Robert Burton (1577–1640) describes the qualities of the different humors in his ANATOMY OF MELANCHOLY (1621). See also *comedy of humors*.

Hunt, Leigh (1784–1859): English poet, journalist, critic, essayist, and autobiographer. Among his friends he counted *Byron*, *Lamb*, and *Keats*. In THE EXAMINER, his radical weekly *journal*, he printed works by *Percy Shelley*, Keats, other *Romantics*, and also *Tennyson*, all of whom owed Hunt much for his support. Notable works include "Abou Ben Adhem," published in the *anthology* BOOK OF GEMS (1838), POETICAL WORKS (1819, revised 1832, 1844), TABLE TALK (1851).

Hurston, Zora Neale (*c.*1901–60): American novelist, playwright, *short story* writer, and essayist. Associated with *Langston Hughes* she wrote, among other things, about the black experience and that of black women in particular, with an emphasis on the importance of black folklore. Notable works include MULES AND MEN (1935), THEIR EYES WERE WATCHING GOD (1937), MOSES, MAN OF THE MOUNTAIN (1939), and the *autobiography* DUST TRACKS ON A ROAD (1942).

Huxley, Aldous (1894–1963): English novelist, *short story* writer, journalist, and poet. Several of his *novels* challenge the accepted notions of his time through sharp, sometimes bleak, *satire* on the state of contemporary humanity, and BRAVE NEW WORLD (1932), his best-known work, portrays a *dystopia* that can be read as a stark warning. Religious mysticism and the use and abuse of drugs are other interests that feature in his fictional and nonfictional writings. Other notable works include CROME YELLOW (1921), POINT COUNTER (1928), EYELESS IN GAZA (1936), THE DEVILS OF LOUDUN (1952), ISLAND (1962).

hypallage: another term for *transferred epithet*.

hyperbaton: a technical term for the reversal of usual word order for poetic effect, e.g. in *Surrey*'s *sonnet* "Complaint by Night of the Lover Not Beloved," he writes "Calm is the sea" rather than "The sea is calm," breaking the *meter* and throwing a trochaic *stress* on "Calm" in order to emphasize the calmness of the sea in contrast to the disturbance of his mind. See also *anastrophe, inversion*.

hyperbole: a literary word for "exaggeration." It is common in everyday speech ("I've told you a million times") and *literature*, e.g.

> Will all great Neptune's ocean wash this blood
> Clean from my hand? No, this my hand will rather
> The multitudinous sea incarnadine
> Making the green one red.
>
> (from act II, scene 2 of *Shakespeare*'s MACBETH)

The opposite of hyperbole is *litotes*.

iamb: a single iambic foot. See *meter*.

iambic: see *meter*.

iambic pentameter: the most common rhythmical pattern in English, and the *meter* in which *Shakespeare* and his contemporaries wrote the vast majority of their plays. Playwrights found the iambic rhythm sufficiently akin to the *rhythms* of English speech to sound natural yet at the same time providing musicality; and the five-foot line carried a dignity and weight suitable for dramatic purposes. The development and refinement of its use can be traced from plays such as GORBODUC by *Norton* and *Sackville*, through *Marlowe* (who is credited with perfecting the *form*, *Jonson* calling the iambic pentameter "Marlowe's mighty line") to Shakespeare.

Ibsen, Henrik (1828–1906): Norwegian playwright who is generally regarded as the founder of modern *prose drama*. His work has been much translated into English, and among other things, his *realism*, exploration of the unconscious mind, concern for human rights and the tragedies of ordinary people, and innovative staging have made him a very important influence upon the English-speaking theater. Notable works include PEER GYNT (1867), A DOLL'S HOUSE (1879), GHOSTS (1881), AN ENEMY OF THE PEOPLE (1882), THE WILD DUCK (1885), HEDDA GABLER (1890), THE MASTER BUILDER (1894), JOHN GABRIEL BORKMAN (1896).

identical rhyme: the use of the same word as a *rhyme* in order to create emphasis, e.g.

> All close they met again, before the dusk
> Had taken from the stars its pleasant veil
> All close they met, all eves, before the dusk
> Had taken from the stars its pleasant veil…

(from *Keats*'s "Isabella")

idyll: a pictorial *poem* usually with a peaceful, happy *pastoral setting* (hence the adjective "idyllic"). *Tennyson*'s THE IDYLLS OF THE KING are *stories* of *Arthurian romance*.

imagery is, strictly speaking, a picture in the mind that arises through the use of words. However, the literary term is extended to cover language that evokes elements of any of the five senses – hearing, touch, taste, and smell, as well as sight. Imagery may be evoked by a direct description, or by *figurative language*. In considering the role of imagery students should not just think of the images in themselves, but view them in the *context* of the writer's purpose within the *text* as a whole.

imagination: the mental faculty that creates objects, *characters*, *scenes*, and all things not actually visible and present. *Coleridge*, who used the word *Romantic* to mean "imaginative," considered the imagination the key element in the creative process, and one that underlies and harmonizes literary and all other artistic creation.

imagists: a group of early 20th century poets whose leading light was *Pound*. They aimed to use *free verse* in order to depict with exactness subjects drawn from all areas of life.

Imbuga, Francis (b.?1945): Kenyan playwright and novelist. His plays are interesting for their portrayal of leadership figures, and he has said that he is glad to see theater "take up issues of social misbehavior, political oppression, religious bigotry, [and] betrayal at all levels." Notable works include THE BURNING OF RAGS (1980), BETRAYAL IN THE CITY (1987), AMINATE: A PLAY (1988).

imitation carries four broad senses. It can mean:

- a re-creation of the *style, tone,* or subject matter of another writer, such as *Pope*'s IMITATIONS OF HORACE (1733–38) or *Robert Lowell*'s IMITATIONS (1961)
- the following of good examples, based on the notion that all art should imitate the standards of excellence achieved by previous "masters"
- the effort toward exactitude, based on the notion that all art should imitate nature and human actions as exactly as possible (in his POETICS *Aristotle* calls this "mimesis," that is, imitation)
- *plagiarism* of the literary work of others.

imperfect rhyme: see *half rhyme.*

impersonal narrator: see *narrator/narrative voice.*

impersonality in *literature,* is the absence of a discernible authorial personality, such as is found in *confessional poetry,* in order to focus on the work itself. Its use is based on the general belief that a writer's personality should in no way intrude upon her/his work. The point is well expounded in *T.S. Eliot*'s *essay* TRADITION AND THE INDIVIDUAL TALENT (1919).

implication is when words imply a *meaning* beyond their literal meaning.

implicit metaphor: a *metaphor* in which the *tenor* is implied, e.g. in *Shakespeare*'s "Sonnet 18" where "the eye of heaven" is understood to be the sun, but not explicitly stated.

implied author: the sense of the *author*'s *voice* and presence that every reader has when reading a work.

implied reader: the "ideal" reader for whom a writer constructs her or his *text* in anticipation of a specific reader response that is objective and free of the reader's own assumptions and prejudices. On the other hand there is the "actual reader," who inevitably brings to a text her or his own subjective experience, knowledge, and prejudices.

impressionism is a term from art that describes paintings in which the artist has used the effects of light to create a personal, subjective view of the subject. The application of the term to *literature* is vague, but writing such as the *poetry* of *Wilde* and the *prose* of *Woolf* has been described as impressionist.

in media res means, in Latin, starting a *text* in the middle of the *story* and later going back to cover the early stages. This device was often used in *epic poetry.* See also *anachorism, analepsis, flashback, flashforward, prolepsis.*

incident: a single occurrence in the *action* of a play or the *plot* of a *story,* possibly the entire matter of a *short story.*

incremental repetition occurs when a line or *stanza* in a *ballad* is repeated as a *refrain* but slightly altered in order to advance the *action* or comment upon it. It was popular in English and Scottish ballads.

index may refer to:

- a page-referenced alphabetical list of main items in a *text*, normally located at the end
- a list of texts or passages that were formerly forbidden reading for members of the Roman Catholic Church
- a category of *sign* in *semiotics*.

induction: another term for a *prolog*. See *Shakespeare's* THE TAMING OF THE SHREW (?1592).

influence, in literary terms, is the conscious or unconscious impact that previous or current cultures, and specifically writers, have upon the writer in question.

initiating action denotes the event or events that create tension and act as a trigger to the *plot*.

inscape and **instress:** respectively, the unique spiritual shape of something that makes it beautiful to the beholder, and the internal tensions that create that image. Both of these difficult terms were invented by *Hopkins*.

inspiration: the idea of a helping spirit, either external or from within a person, that gives a writer the impetus to write. See *spontaneity*.

instress: see *inscape*.

intention: see *authorial intention*.

intentional fallacy: a term introduced by the *new critics* to describe the mistaken belief, in their view, that what a writer explicitly or implicitly intended to convey when s/he wrote a *text* is important. They considered that the text itself, viewed objectively, is the only proper interest of the reader. See *authorial intention, death of the author*.

interior monolog is taken by some critics to mean the same as *stream of consciousness*; but others see the term as an aspect of stream of consciousness whereby the *author* attempts to recreate, with all its randomness, the process of thought precisely as it occurs in a person's mind.

interlude: a short entertainment, often humorous and sometimes moral (see *morality plays*) staged between the courses of a meal or the *acts* of a play, and popular in Tudor times, e.g. John Heywood's THE PLAY OF THE WETHER (1533). See *Medwall*.

internal rhyme is rhyming within lines, e.g.

> I sift the snow on the mountains below,
>   And their great pines groan aghast;
> And all the night 'tis my pillow white,
>   While I sleep in the arms of the blast.

> (from *Percy Shelley's* "The Cloud")

See *rhyme*.

interpolation occurs when a section not by the writer has been inserted into the *text*. There are many claimed examples in *Elizabethan drama*, e.g. the comic *scenes* in

Marlowe's DOCTOR FAUSTUS, the Hecate scene in *Shakespeare*'s MACBETH, a *song* in *Webster*'s THE DUCHESS OF MALFI.

interpretation is a term to describe the process of explaining, and the different methods of explaining, literary *texts*. Traditional attitudes hold that it is possible to interpret texts in such as way that the puzzle of *meaning* is solved and the meaning arrived at. The *new critics* reacted against this, *MacLeish* declaring that a *poem* simply "is," and that it does not "mean." Recent *literary theory* such as *structuralism, poststructuralism* and *deconstruction* hold that all interpretations are impossible – yet, paradoxically, these very theories are themselves interpretations. See *code, hermeneutics, sign*.

intertextuality: the idea that *texts* do not exist in a literary vacuum, but that writers and readers are aware of the relationship between texts and that making comparisons between them can be illuminating. For instance, *Marvell* wrote "The Definition of Love" (1681) in the light of *Donne*'s earlier "A Valediction of Forbidding Mourning" (1633); and *Day Lewis* wrote "Song" (1935) as a *parody* of *Marlowe*'s "A Passionate Shepherd to His Love," written almost 400 years earlier, and possibly with "The Nymph's Reply to the Shepherd" (1600) by Walter Ralegh (*c.*1552–1618) in mind (who himself was probably replying to Marlowe's *poem*). See *allusion*.

intrinsic attitude toward a *text*, sometimes called *formalism*, concentrates upon an objective scrutiny of *form, structure*, and language; that is, upon the words on the page, regarding the text as standing alone and ignoring external and historical influences. Such an approach may be regarded as a relatively traditional way of viewing *literature*, and is fundamental to *Richards*'s method of *practical criticism*. See *close reading, Leavisite*. By contrast, see *extrinsic attitude*.

intrusive narrator: see *narrator/narrative voice*.

invention, a term derived from *rhetoric*, refers to the *originality* of a work that may not rely on *imitation* or established *convention*. Inevitably, innovative writers through the ages such as *Donne, Whitman, Joyce*, and *Woolf* have created conventions that others have imitated.

inversion is a reversal of normal word order for impact. *Donne* quite often uses inversion in his *poetry* to draw attention to the words, as in

> She's all states, and all princes, I,
> Nothing else is.
>
> (from "The Sun Rising," 1633)

See also *anastrophe, hyperbaton*.

invocation: an appeal to a god or muse for *inspiration*, usually by a poet, at the beginning of a work, e.g. *Milton*'s appeal to the Holy Spirit at the beginning of PARADISE LOST. See also *apostrophe*.

involvement is a term used to indicate the emotional involvement in the subject matter of a piece of *literature* by either the writer or the reader. This may occur because the *character*s and circumstances of the *story* are close to those of the reader's or writer's own life. See *alienation, distance*.

Irish revival: see *Celtic renaissance/revival/twilight*.

irony is a term used to describe words or situations that are charged with a layer of *meaning* different from the literal or straightforward one, the subtler interpretation of which the speaker or participant may or may not be aware. The least subtle *form* of irony is blatant sarcasm. Among many great writers who have made much use of irony in their writings are *Austen, Chaucer, Dryden, Fielding, Hardy, Henry James, Jonson, Milton, Pope, Shakespeare, Jonathan Swift, Waugh*. A good example comes from the famous sentence,

> It is a truth universally acknowledged that a single man in possession of a good fortune must be in want of a wife.
>
> (from *Austen*'s PRIDE AND PREJUDICE)

The irony here is based on the assumption, from a feminine *viewpoint*, that such a man must wish to marry, the reader understanding that this "truth" is by no means true. The "truth" is that unmarried women want rich husbands, and the irony of *Austen*'s way of putting it would not have been lost on the readership of her time. See *dramatic irony*.

irregular ode: an *ode* in which the number and length of lines and the *rhyme* scheme are different in each *stanza*, e.g. *Coleridge*'s "Dejection: An Ode," *Wordsworth*'s "Ode: Intimations of Immortality." It is sometimes called a Cowleyan ode, Abraham Cowley (1618–67) being credited with devising the *form*.

Irving, Washington (1783–1859): American *short story* writer, editor, and essayist. He was admired widely in his own time, including by *Poe* and *Hawthorne*, for his captivating *style* and rich descriptive *imagery*. He achieved international fame with his *tales* "Rip Van Winkle" (1820) and "The Legend of Sleepy Hollow" (1820), which borrowed Germanic folk tales and adapted them to American *settings*. Other notable works include BRACEBRIDGE HALL (1822), TALES OF A TRAVELLER (1824), THE ALHAMBRA (1832).

Isherwood, Christopher (1904–86): English-born novelist, playwright, *short story* writer, and screenwriter who became a US citizen in 1946. Friends with *Spender* and *Auden*, with whom he collaborated (see Auden entry for these), he is candid in his writings about his homosexuality. Notable works include MR. NORRIS CHANGES TRAINS (1935) and GOODBYE TO BERLIN (1939), two semiautobiographical works based upon his experiences of the disintegrating fabric of society in Berlin in the early 1930s. The latter was adapted by John Van Druten into a play called I AM A CAMERA (1951), and into the musical CABARET (1968).

Ishiguro, Kazuo (b.1954): Japanese-born British novelist, *short story* writer, and screenwriter. His early work is influenced by Japanese culture, although he left Japan at the age of six and did not revisit until briefly in 1989. His novels frequently concern the self-deceptions of the central figure, and the process of self-discovery. Notable works include A PALE VIEW OF HILLS (1982), AN ARTIST OF THE FLOATING WORLD (1986), THE REMAINS OF THE DAY (1989), WHEN WE WERE ORPHANS (2000).

Italian sonnet: see *sonnet*.

Jacobean age: generally considered to cover *literature* written in England during the reign of James I (1603–25).

Jacobean drama covers plays written during the reign of James I; however, the period 1558–1642 is sometimes covered by the overall term *Elizabethan drama*.

Jacobson, Dan (b.1929): South African-born British novelist and *short story* writer. Much of his writing explores aspects of being a South African or living in South Africa. Notable works include Beggar My Neighbour (1964), Her Story (1987).

James, C.L.R. (1901–89): Trinidadian novelist, political essayist, and literary critic. His work is regarded as documentary and socialist realist, and as part of the anti-colonial feeling that became evident during the 1930s and 1940s. Notable works include Triumph (1929) and Minty Alley (1936), which had a considerable influence upon Caribbean *fiction*.

James, Henry (1843–1916): American-born British novelist, *short story* and travel writer, critic, essayist, and playwright. He was influenced by his friendship with *Howells*, and later by his growing knowledge of continental European *literature*. In 1876 he settled in England, and in his early *novels* such as The Portrait of a Lady (1881) he often observes and studies experiences of Americans among Europeans, subtly comparing the New World values of the former with the older civilization of the latter. For Washington Square (1880) and The Bostonians (1886) he reverted to an American *setting*, and for works such as The Aspern Papers (1888) he adopted what he called his "international *theme*." Other notable works include What Maisie Knew (1897), The Turn of the Screw (1898), The Wings of the Dove (1902), The Ambassadors (1903), The Golden Bowl (1904).

James, P.D. (b.1920): English crime writer. Her *style* is often harsh and realistic, and her experience of forensic science aids the use of close factual detail in her *stories*. Notable works include Cover Her Face (1962, which introduces the poetry-writing police detective Adam Dalgleish, who features in many of her stories – see *police procedural*), Death of an Expert Witness (1977), Innocent Blood (1980, not a *crime novel*), Children of Men (1991), Death in Holy Orders (2001).

jazz poetry is *poetry* that is recited to the accompaniment of jazz. *Langston Hughes* in the 1930s was one of the first poets to collaborate with musicians, and the poets of the American *Beat movement* experimented with the *form*. In Britain, Christopher Logue (b.1926) was a leading figure.

Jellicoe, Ann (b.1927): English playwright. Early writing included youthful, energetic pieces for the *English Stage Company*, since when she has become very active in community *drama* in the west of England. Notable works include The Sport of My Mad Mother (1958), The Knack (1961), Shelley: Or The Idealist (1965).

Jennings, Elizabeth (b.1926): English poet and critic associated with *the Movement*. Noted for the clarity and discipline of her *verse*, and her *metaphysical* interests, her subjects range from childhood, love, and friendship to religion and art. She has written candidly about her personal experience of mental illness. Notable works include SONG FOR A BIRTH OR A DEATH AND OTHER POEMS (1961), COLLECTED POEMS (1986).

Jhabvala, Ruth Prawer (b.1927): British-American novelist, *short story* writer, adapter, and screenwriter. Born in Germany of Polish parents and educated in England, she has lived for long periods in India and America, and is fascinated by the interface between East and West. Notable works include THE HOUSEHOLDER (1960), SHAKESPEARE WALLAH (1963, screenplay), HEAT AND DUST (1975), THREE CONTINENTS (1987).

Johnson, age of: a term once used to define *literature* written during the 18th century and roughly contemporary with the life of *Johnson*. Nowadays the terms *Augustan* and *age of sensibility* tend more often to be used to cover two halves of the same period.

Johnson, Samuel (1709–84): English critic, lexicographer, scholar, essayist, translator, poet, biographer, editor, and playwright. His prolific output was in his early years stimulated by lack of money. During his time he was influenced by or friends with most of the important literary and artistic figures of his age. He was a brilliant conversationalist in an age when this was valued. Much of his writing radiates good sense, and his literary *criticism*, while superseded by subsequent thinking, is still well worth reading. *Boswell's biography*, which did as much to flesh out Johnson as a colorful, eccentric, larger-than-life personality as to praise his writings, has helped to raise him to almost legendary status as England's greatest all-round man of letters. Notable works include THE VANITY OF HUMAN WISHES (1749), A DICTIONARY OF THE ENGLISH LANGUAGE (1755), RASSELAS (1759), A JOURNEY TO THE WESTERN ISLES OF SCOTLAND (1775, an account of a tour accompanied by Boswell, who wrote his version under a different title), THE LIVES OF THE ENGLISH POETS (1781).

Johnsonian is a term given to writing in the *manner* and *style* of Johnson.

Jones, David (1895–1974): English poet and graphic artist. IN PARENTHESIS (1937), considered a work of genius by *T.S. Eliot*, combines his World War I experiences with Welsh legend and *Malory's* LE MORTE D'ARTHUR and, as sometimes with his other *poetry*, moves in *form* between *prose* and *free verse*. Other notable works include THE ANATHEMATA (1952), THE SLEEPING LORD (1974).

Jonson, Ben (1572–1637): English playwright and poet. Friends with, among others, *Bacon, Beaumont, Chapman, Donne, Fletcher*, and *Shakespeare*, he became foremost in a literary club that met at the Mermaid Tavern in London. His forceful personality led to frequent clashes with his fellow actors and playwrights, and with the authorities. In 1597 he began work for *Henslowe*. His *comedy of humors* EVERY MAN IN HIS HUMOUR (1598), in which Shakespeare acted, was popular and helped to make him famous. He devised several *masques* in collaboration with the architect Inigo Jones (1573–1652). He excelled in creating *satirical* portraits of the grasping and self-interested. In 1616 he published a folio of his works which helped to establish *drama* as a respected literary *form*, and became unrivaled as the leading literary figure of his day, greatly influencing various younger poets who became known as "the tribe of Ben." During the 18th and 19th centuries his reputation diminished as Shakespeare's increased, but his standing has since in some measure been restored, mainly on the basis of the great *comedies* VOLPONE (?1605), THE ALCHEMIST (1610), and BARTHOLOMEW FAIR (1614). Unofficially he was England's first *poet laureate*.

journal:

- any kind of magazine, newspaper, or *periodical*
- a *diary*.

journalese: *style* of compressed writing employed by journalists that generates *clichés* and was famously parodied by *Waugh* in SCOOP (1938).

Joyce, James (1882–1941): Irish novelist, *short story* writer, and poet. He is perhaps best known for his influence on *modernism,* especially in the development of his *stream of consciousness technique,* with the term "Joycean" coming to mean a *style* of *prose.* He often uses Dublin as a *setting.* Notable works include DUBLINERS (1914), A PORTRAIT OF THE ARTIST AS A YOUNG MAN (1916), ULYSSES (1922), FINNEGANS WAKE (1939).

Kafkaesque: a term sometimes applied to the characteristic *tone* and the nightmarish insecurity of *character*s as in the works of the Czech writer Franz Kafka (1883–1924).

Kavanagh, Patrick (1904–67): Irish poet. Influenced in part by *T.S. Eliot*, he in turn has influenced such poets as *R.S. Thomas* and *Heaney* in his determination that *regional* writing need not be narrow and parochial (see *local color*). His realistic view of rural life is partly a reaction to *Yeats*'s lyrical treatment. Notable works include THE GREAT HUNGER (1942), COME DANCE WITH KITTY STOBLING (1960).

Keats, John (1795–1821): English poet. Trained as an apothecary-surgeon, he abandoned medicine to write *poetry* and became a leading figure of *Romanticism*, highly regarded by contemporaries like *Percy Shelley*, although attacked as a "Cockney poet" by rightwing reviewers. His status as a foremost English poet has remained high. His versatility covers *sonnet*s, *ode*s, *narrative poem*s, children's poetry, and other *form*s. His work is noted, among other things, for its sensitivity, use of the senses, medievalism, creation of interior landscapes, and escapism. The latter is debatable, but it is true that he was not so directly political or social in his comments as were some of his contemporary Romantics such as *Blake*, Percy Shelley, or *Byron*. He thought deeply about literary concepts, including his widely discussed notion of "negative capability." His letters to Fanny Brawne and others are highly readable, *T.S. Eliot* considering them significant documents. His early death from tuberculosis has tended to add to his Romantic mystique. Notable works include "Endymion" (1818), "To Autumn" (1819), "The Eve of St. Agnes" (1819), "Hyperion" (1819), "La Belle Dame sans Merci" (1819), "Lamia" (1819), "Isabella" (1820), "Ode on a Grecian Urn" (1820), "Ode to a Nightingale" (1820), "Ode to Psyche" (1820).

Keene, Molly (1904–96): Irish playwright and novelist, who also wrote under the *pseudonym* M.J. Farrell. She is a successful writer of *drawing room comedy*, and her *novel*s document with sharp observation and caustic *humor* a departed upper-class world of hunting, fishing, servants, and large country houses, which was her own background. Her writing career was interrupted by the death of her husband in the 1950s, but she was persuaded to resume and more recent notable works include GOOD BEHAVIOUR (1981), TIME AFTER TIME (1983), LOVING AND GIVING (1988).

Keiller, Garrison (b.1932): American *short story* writer and novelist. His *tales* are often gently humorous, notable works including LAKE WOBEGON DAYS (1985).

Kempinski, Tom (b.1938): English playwright, in whose writings an interest in psychoanalytical theory is apparent. Notable works include DUET FOR ONE (1980), WHEN THE PAST IS STILL TO COME (1992).

Keneally, Thomas (b.1935): Australian novelist, playwright, and travel writer. Many of his books have Australian *theme*s or subject matter, and sometimes show an interest in moral failure. Notable works include SCHINDLER'S ARK (1982, retitled SCHINDLER'S LIST after the success of the film version of that name), THE PLAYMAKER (1987, adapted for the stage by *Wertenbaker* as OUR COUNTRY'S GOOD).

kenning: in Old Norse and Old English *literature*, a word compound that creates a standard *metaphor*, e.g. helmet-bearer ("helm-berend" in Old English) for warrior, sea-wood ("sae-wudu") for ship, whale-road ("hron-rad") for sea.

Kermode, Frank (b.1919): English scholar, literary critic, and editor whose main focus is the *Renaissance*. His liberal-minded curiosity led him to reject any dogmatic approach to literary studies. He has done much to advance thinking in, among other things, the fields of *hermeneutics, reader-response theory, structuralism.* Notable works include ROMANTIC IMAGE (1957), THE SENSE OF ENDING (1967).

Kerouac, Jack (1922–69): American novelist and poet. A leading light of the *Beat* generation, he developed a characteristically freewheeling *style* of *prose.* Notable works include ON THE ROAD (1957), LONESOME TRAVELLER (1960).

Kesey, Ken (1935–2001): American novelist, *short story* writer, and essayist. His 1960s reputation as a West Coast cult figure and social rebel with a wild lifestyle endures to this day. Notable works include ONE FLEW OVER THE CUCKOO'S NEST (1962), in which he utilized his experiences as a ward attendant in a Californian hospital.

Kincaid, Jamaica (b.1949): Antiguan-born American novelist, *short story* writer, and essayist. Her writing sometimes uses a Caribbean *setting*, and often concerns the adjustments to the modern world of those with an Antiguan cultural background. Notable works include AT THE BOTTOM OF THE RIVER (1983), ANNIE JOHN (1985), LUCY (1990).

King's Men, The: founded in 1594 as the Lord Chamberlain's Men, they were the Elizabethan theater company of which *Shakespeare* was a member and shareholder.

Kingsley, Mary (1862–1900): English travel writer. Her tough-minded writing on such matters as missionaries' inappropriate attempts to change the ways of African people had some political impact. Notable works include TRAVELS IN WEST AFRICA (1897), WEST AFRICAN STUDIES (1899), THE CONGO SCANDEL (1900).

Kingston, Maxine Hong (b.1940): Chinese-American novelist, autobiographer, and essayist. Among other things she is noted for her *poetic diction* and generally experimental *style.* She uses Chinese folklore, blending it into American *setting*s. Notable works include THE WOMAN WARRIOR, MEMOIRS OF A CHILDHOOD AMONG GHOSTS (1976), CHINA MEN (1980).

Kipling, Rudyard (1865–1936): English poet, *short story* and children's writer, novelist, autobiogapher, and journalist. As a reporter in India he acquired knowledge of Anglo-Indian life, which inspired many of his carefully crafted *poem*s and *stories*, gaining for him a reputation as the "Poet of Empire." Back in England he made friends with *Henry James* and others in the literary world. His early stories of British-ruled India were noted for skeptical *realism*, but later he was accused of jingoism, and with the onset of more *modernist* ideas he began to go out of fashion. KIM (1901), a *picaresque novel* set in India, is generally considered to be his masterpiece. Other notable works include PLAIN TALES FROM THE HILLS (1888), LIFE'S HANDICAP (1891), BARRACK-ROOM BALLADS AND OTHER VERSES (1892), MANY INVENTIONS (1893), STALKY AND CO. (1899), JUST SO STORIES (1902), PUCK OF POOK'S HILL (1906).

kitchen sink drama: a term applied to plays of the 1950s and 1960s in England that centered upon the domestic problems of ordinary people, the kitchen sink being taken as a metaphorical focus. They were in part a reaction against the so-called drawing room *drama*s of playwrights such as *Rattigan*. *Osborne's* LOOK BACK IN ANGER (1956) is credited with beginning the fashion for such plays, with radio and the rise of television drama giving them impetus. See *angry young men*.

Kopit, Arthur (b.1939): American playwright. Influenced by *Brecht* and *Pirandello*, his social concerns are often expressed through *satire*. Notable works include OH DAD, POOR DAD, MAMA'S HUNG YOU IN THE CLOSET AND I'M FEELIN' SO SAD (1961, a parody of the *theater of the absurd* and the *avant-garde* theater of the 1960s), INDIANS (1968), WINGS (1978).

Kureshi, Hanif (b.1952): British novelist and screenwriter. He is able to combine sensitivity and honesty with *humor* when dealing with immigrant issues, sexuality, and the poverty and violence of life in London in the 1970s and 1980s. Notable works include MY BEAUTIFUL LAUNDRETTE (1986), SAMMY AND ROSIE GET LAID (1988), THE BUDDHA OF SUBURBIA (1990), LONDON KILLS ME (1991), GABRIEL'S GIFT (2001).

Kyd, Thomas (1558–94): Elizabethan English playwright, about whom little is known for certain. He was associated with *Marlowe*, and his notable works probably include THE SPANISH TRAGEDY (?1589), a classic *revenge tragedy*. He may have written a lost play entitled HAMLET, an *urtext* of which *Shakespeare* made use.

La Guma, Alex (1925–85): South African novelist. Many years of his life were spent under house arrest as a result of his strong political views against apartheid and this is conveyed through his writings, which depict a *realistic* and dark picture of the slums of South Africa. Notable works include A WALK IN THE NIGHT (1962), AND A THREEFOLD CORD (1964), THE STONE-COUNTRY (1967), IN THE FOG OF THE SEASON'S END (1972), TIME OF THE BUTCHERBIRD (1979).

Laing, Kojo (b.1946): Ghanaian novelist and poet who is an accomplished *modernist*. Influenced by *magic realism*, his writing often takes a positive approach to African matters. Notable works include SEARCH SWEET COUNTRY (1986), WOMAN OF THE AEROPLANES (1988), GODHORSE (1989), MAJOR GENTL AND THE ACHIMOTA WARS (1992).

Lake Poets (or Lake School): a term used, sometimes mockingly, by *Byron* and others to describe the group of poets and writers who lived in and were influenced by England's Lake District around the turn of the 19th century, including *Coleridge, Southey, Wordsworth,* and *De Quincey.*

Lamb, Charles (1775–1834): English essayist, poet, children's writer, and literary critic who was friends with *Coleridge, Southey, Hunt,* and *Wordsworth* and had an influence upon all of them. Notable works include TALES FROM SHAKESPEARE (1807), which he wrote in collaboration with his sister, Mary (1764–1847), THE ESSAYS OF ELIA (1820–23).

lament: a *poem* expressing deep sorrow for any kind of loss. See also *complaint, dirge, elegy, monody, threnody.*

Lamming, George (b.1927): Barbadian novelist, poet, essayist, and editor. His writings contain perceptive explorations of *themes* such as Caribbean identity and experience, colonialism, and West Indian views of Britain. Notable works include IN THE CASTLE OF MY SKIN (1953), THE EMIGRANTS (1954), OF AGE AND INNOCENCE (1958), WATER WITH BERRIES (1971), NATIVES OF MY PERSON (1972, regarded as his masterpiece).

lampoon: a *satirical* and often vulgar attack. It usually describes a piece of writing that *caricatures* or ridicules its target, e.g. *Dryden*'s attack on Thomas Shadwell (1642–92) in ABSALOM AND ACHITOPHEL, *Pope*'s attack on Hervey in EPISTLE TO ARBUTHNOT (1735). See also *burlesque.*

Langland, William (?1332–90): English cleric and poet, generally believed to be the *author* of PIERS PLOWMAN, a religious *allegory* that shows concern with the ordinary person and with contemporary corruption of the church. It is considered one of the first major *poems* in English.

Larkin, Philip (1922–85): English poet, novelist, and essayist. *Yeats* and *Hardy* were early influences on his *poetry*. A foremost member of *the Movement*, he disliked *modernism,* and his pessimistic yet *witty verse* has been regarded as perfectly defining the situation of a certain kind of solitary individual within his age. Notable works include A GIRL IN WINTER (1947), THE LESS DECEIVED (1955), THE WHITSUN WEDDINGS (1964), HIGH WINDOWS (1974).

Laurence, Margaret (1926–87): Canadian novelist and *short story* writer. Some of her writing concerns the lives of women in the *context* of Canadian small-town life. Notable works include THIS SIDE JORDAN (1960), THE STONE ANGEL (1964), A JEST OF GOD (1966), A BIRD IN THE HOUSE (1970), THE DIVINERS (1974).

Lawrence, D.H. (1885–1930): English novelist, *short story* and travel writer, poet, critic, and playwright. Much of his work explores his cultural surroundings (see also *regional novel*), reflected through political, sexual, and social relations, and he incorporates many autobiographical elements into his *fiction*. Extending the boundaries of *narrative prose*, he is stylistically innovative, moving from the ordinary to the highly imaginative in his quest to explore the psychology of the individual. Controversial in his lifetime, his critical standing has varied since from those who see him as crucial in the 20th century *canon* to feminist critics who consider him to be *phallocentric*. Notable works include LOVE POEMS (1913), SONS AND LOVERS (1913), THE RAINBOW (1915), WOMEN IN LOVE (1920), ENGLAND, MY ENGLAND (1922), STUDIES IN CLASSIC AMERICAN LITERATURE (1923), LADY CHATTERLEY'S LOVER (privately printed 1928; not published in England until 1960).

Lawson, Henry (1867–1922): Australian poet and *short story* writer who drew upon his sometimes harsh experiences in the New South Wales outback. He is known especially for his vigorous and colloquial bush *poem*s. His short stories came to characterize much of late 19th century Australian experience. Notable works include SHORT STORIES IN PROSE AND VERSE (1894), JOE WILSON AND HIS MATES (1901).

lay: a short medieval *narrative poem*, e.g. *Chaucer*'s THE FRANKLIN'S TALE (?1387), *Walter Scott*'s LAY OF THE LAST MINSTREL (1805), LAYS OF ANCIENT ROME (1842) by Thomas Macauley (1800–59).

Layton, Irving (b.1912): Canadian poet and essayist who is strongly outspoken on a wide range of social and political issues. Notable works include HERE AND NOW (1945), THE BULL CALF AND OTHER POEMS (1956), COLLECTED POEMS (1971), TAKING SIDES: COLLECTED SOCIAL AND POLITICAL WRITINGS (1977), A WILD PECULIAR JOY: SELECTED POEMS 1945–82 (1982).

Leavis, F.R. (1895–1978): English scholar and literary critic whose writings on *literature*, although controversial in his day, remain among the most influential of the 20th century. He founded and edited the literary *review* SCRUTINY (1932–53) and became a director of studies at Cambridge University. Notable works include NEW BEARINGS IN ENGLISH POETRY (1932), THE GREAT TRADITION (1948), THE COMMON PURSUIT (1952), ENGLISH LITERATURE IN OUR TIME AND THE UNIVERSITY (1969).

Leavisite: a traditional approach to English *literature* derived from the thinking and writing of the Cambridge critic *F.R. Leavis* and his wife Queenie (1906–81), two early graduates of the new Cambridge University English course. They held that:
- there is an accepted *canon* of great English literature – Leavis identifies *Austen, George Eliot, Henry James*, and *Conrad* in THE GREAT TRADITION as the great writers
- a *text* has an intrinsic artistic worth for all time, its *context* being irrelevant

- a text can and should be studied objectively, an individual reader's individual response being irrelevant. The word "I" therefore has no place in a critical *essay*
- yet, perhaps paradoxically, a reader should respond with a natural sensibility to a text so that what is read will have a civilizing effect upon her/him
- *close reading* of the text is essential.

These views dominated the teaching of literature in England at all levels until two-thirds of the way through the 20th century, and are still influential. See *literary/critical theory*.

Le Carré, John (b.1931): English novelist. The complex plots and grim detail of his highly regarded *spy stories* transcend the limitations of the *genre* and give *realistic* insights into the international tensions of the cold war before the fall of communism. Notable works include CALL FOR THE DEAD (1961), THE SPY WHO CAME IN FROM THE COLD (1963), THE LOOKING-GLASS WAR (1965), TINKER, TAILOR, SOLDIER, SPY (1974), THE HONOURABLE SCHOOLBOY (1977), THE NIGHT MANAGER (1993), THE CONSTANT GARDENER (2001).

Lee, Harper (b.1926): American novelist whose only *novel*, TO KILL A MOCKINGBIRD (1960), tells the story of racism in Alabama through the eyes of a six-year-old white girl. The novel, which won a *Pulitzer Prize*, has become a *classic* of American *fiction*.

Lee, Laurie (1912–97): English poet, autobiographer, and essayist. In all of his writings he shows his love of the countryside of his Gloucestershire youth and elsewhere. Notable works include MY MANY-COATED MAN (1955), CIDER WITH ROSIE (1959), AS I WALKED OUT ONE MIDSUMMER MORNING (1969).

leitmotif, a term derived from opera, is often used interchangeably with *theme* and *motif*, although unlike the latter leitmotif refers to recurrence within a single work. Some critics confine the meaning to either:

- a recurrent image, e.g. blindness in *Shakespeare*'s KING LEAR
- a recurrent pattern of words or repeated phrase, such as frequently happens in works by, for instance, *Faulkner, Joyce,* and *Woolf.*

Lessing, Doris (b.1919): British novelist, poet, *short story* and travel writer. Her radical, feminist politics are expressed through her experimental *narrative form* and *style*, and she frequently delves into the *psychological*, drawing on her personal experiences to voice her views on society and in particular social prejudices. Notable works include THE GRASS IS SINGING (1950), THIS WAS THE OLD CHIEF'S COUNTRY (1951), THE GOLDEN NOTEBOOK (1962), THE SUMMER BEFORE THE DARK (1973), MEMOIRS OF A SURVIVOR (1974), THE FIFTH CHILD (1988), LOVE, AGAIN (1996).

level stress occurs when *stress* falls evenly on two concurrent syllables, as in "dome-head" or "home run." In *verse* a *spondee* sometimes results.

Lewis, Alun (1915–44): Welsh poet and *short story* writer. His writings are formed from personal experiences of growing up in a poor mining village in the 1930s Depression and his time spent as a soldier. He explores feelings of isolation and expresses an understanding for the struggles of Welsh communities. Notable works include RAIDERS' DAWN (1942), THE LAST INSPECTION (1942), HA! HA! AMONG THE TRUMPETS (1945), IN THE GREEN TREE (1948).

Lewis, M.G. (1775–1818): English novelist, poet, and playwright. He was inspired by German *Romanticism,* and his best-known work is his *gothic novel* THE MONK (1796) – hence his nickname "Monk" Lewis. Some influence on *Walter Scott's poetry* has been noted.

Lewis, Sinclair (1885–1951): American novelist. His prolific output covers a range of subjects and covers such *themes* as the need for political and social change, race relations, Native American struggles, small-town American life, and fear of fascism. His *novels* changed complacent attitudes toward the American way of life. Notable works include MAIN STREET (1920), BABBITT (1922), ARROWSMITH (1925), ELMER GANTRY (1927), ANN VICKERS (1933), IT CAN'T HAPPEN HERE (1935), THE GOD-SEEKER (1949).

lexicon: literally a dictionary of some kind; however, the word has come to be applied to the characteristic stock of words or *diction* used by a particular writer.

liberal humanism: a traditional approach to *literature* that suggests that great literature explores a fixed and constant human nature. This, broadly speaking, is the *Leavisite* approach. It rejects various theoretical and/or political ways of reading the *text.*

light comedy is a term used to denote relatively undemanding lighthearted plays. Most (but not all) of *Coward's comedies* have been so described.

light ending is another term for *weak ending.*

light stress is when, in *verse,* a *stress* is required on a syllable not normally stressed in everyday speech.

limited point of view: see *narrator/narrative voice.*

line: a unit in *poetry,* the length of which (except in *free verse*) is determined by the *meter* – e.g. *pentameter* has five feet in a line.

linguistics: the scientific study of most aspects of language including etymology, morphology, phonetics, *semantics,* and syntax.

linked sonnet: see *sonnet.*

literary/critical theory: terms to describe the various approaches to *literature* that evolved as a reaction to the notion that there is one objective view of literature and culture. Among influential theories of the later 20th century are:

- *structuralism*
- *poststructuralism* and *deconstruction*
- *postmodernism*
- *feminist criticism*
- *historicism/new historicism*
- *cultural materialism*
- *Marxist criticism*
- *colonial/postcolonial criticism*

See *Leavisite.*

literati: a term, often used pejoratively, for those who know a great deal about *literature.*

literature is a general term used to describe anything written in any *genre* that reaches a certain undefined standard of artistic merit.

litotes: a *figure of speech*, often involving a negative, whereby an understatement is used to emphasize an opposite quality (e.g. "not good" implying "rather bad"). Often used both in all kinds of *literature* and everyday speech, and sometimes a part of *irony*. The opposite of *hyperbole*. See *negation*.

Lively, Penelope (b.1933): British novelist, children's and *short story* writer, and screenwriter. She is often concerned with the haunting impact of the past upon the present, drawing her *character*s with *humor* and sensitivity. Notable works include THE GHOST OF THOMAS KEMPE (1973), THE ROAD TO LICHFIELD (1977), MOON TIGER (1987).

Liverpool poets: the name given to English modern poets *Henri, McGough*, and *Patten* who, influenced by the 1960s Liverpool pop culture (including the Beatles), set out to popularize *poetry* and revive live performances. Two *anthologies* of their work, THE LIVERPOOL SCENE (1967) and THE MERSEY SOUND (1967), sold very well. NEW VOLUME (1983) contains a *selection* of their poetry written during the 1970s and early 1980s.

Livings, Henry (b.1929): English playwright. His plays are entertainingly anarchic and antiauthoritarian, eccentric in *style*, and sometimes feature a working-class *antihero*. Notable works include NIL CARBORUNDUM (1962), KELLY'S EYE (1963), EH? (1964).

local color: a term used of the depiction in *fiction* of the details of a region or place, often rural (e.g. customs, dress, flora and fauna). Writers preoccupied with this (e.g. *Hardy*'s Wessex or *Twain*'s Mississippi region) are sometimes called "local colorists." The term is occasionally unfairly used in the pejorative sense to indicate writings that are confined in their interest and lack universal appeal or applicability. Some critics believe that "local color" merely refers to decorative detail, and that the term "regionalism" should be applied when such detail is intrinsic and essential to a work.

Lochhead, Liz (b.1947): Scottish poet, playwright, and translator. Her technically skillful *verse*, which she often performs (see *performance poets*), uses Glasgow dialect to *dramatic* effect. Notable works include MEMO FOR SPRING (1972), BLOOD AND ICE (1982, play), DREAMING FRANKENSTEIN, AND COLLECTED POEMS (1984).

Lodge, David (b.1935): English novelist, literary critic, and essayist. His literary sympathies embrace both *traditional* approaches and modern *literary theory*, and he is best known for his *campus novel*s. Notable works include THE LANGUAGE OF FICTION (1966), CHANGING PLACES (1975, a campus novel), HOW FAR CAN YOU GO? (1980, published in the US as SOULS AND BODIES, 1982), WORKING WITH STRUCTURALISM (1981), WRITE ON: OCCASIONAL ESSAYS (1986), NICE WORK (1988), THE ART OF FICTION (1992), THINKS... (2001).

London, Jack (1876–1916): American novelist, *short story* and travel writer, essayist, and playwright. A self-proclaimed socialist who was yet fascinated by the values of individualism, he had varying success in balancing these contradictory impulses in his extensive output. His most famous work is THE CALL OF THE WILD (1903), a *tale* of a dog who overcomes the odds to become leader of the pack. Other notable works include WHITE FANG (1906), THE IRON HEEL (1908), THE MUTINY OF THE "ELSINORE" (1914).

Longfellow, Henry Wadsworth (1807–82): American poet, essayist, and translator. He sought to establish through his *poetry* an American mythology to match what he found in his reading of European *literature*, and in his day he rivaled *Tennyson* in popularity with English-speaking readers. Notable works include VOICES OF THE NIGHT (1839), EVANGELINE (1847), THE SONG OF HIAWATHA (1855), THE COURTSHIP OF MILES STANDISH (1858), TALES OF A WAYSIDE INN (1863), CHRISTUS (1872).

love poetry deals with the emotions and virtues of love rather than the physical side (which is defined as "erotic *poetry*"). In *Renaissance* times an ability to write a reasonable *poem* to one's mistress was considered to be an important accomplishment for a courtier: Ophelia describes Hamlet as a poet, and in *Shakespeare*'s AS YOU LIKE IT, Orlando goes around the forest hanging on the trees love poems to Rosalind. Among many poets who have written love poems, often *sonnets* and sometimes whole sequences, are *Chaucer, Wyatt, Surrey, Marlowe, Spenser,* Shakespeare, *Donne, Herrick, Burns, Keats, Byron, Tennyson, Dickinson, Elizabeth Barrett Browning, Dante Gabriel Rossetti, Christina Rossetti, Housman, Yeats, Hardy, Edward Thomas, Brooke, Auden, Betjeman, Cope, Duffy.*

Lovelace, Richard (1618–58): English *Cavalier* poet whose reputation rests upon a few stylish *lyric poems*. Notable works include "To Althea, from Prison" (?1642), LUCASTA: EPODES, ODES, SONNETS, SONGS, ETC. (1649).

low comedy is a term sometimes applied to unsophisticated *drama* that aims to make the audience laugh by very simple means such as rude jokes or slapstick. There are examples throughout all periods from ancient Greek drama to the present day.

Lowell, James Russell (1819–91): American poet, essayist, and editor. Although not as widely read today as his contemporaries *Longfellow* and *Whittier*, he is a major figure in 19th century American *poetry*. His most important work is THE CATHEDRAL (1870), a long *poem* that grapples with the issue of religious faith. Other notable works include A FABLE FOR CRITICS (1848), ODE RECITED AT THE COMMEMORATION OF THE LIVING AND DEAD SOLDIERS OF HARVARD UNIVERSITY (1865).

Lowell, Robert (1917–77): American poet and translator. His work often concerns his New England background, but not exclusively so, much falling under the label of *confessional poetry*. Notable works include LORD WEARY'S CASTLE (1946), POEMS, 1938–1949 (1950), LIFE STUDIES (1959), FOR THE UNION DEAD (1964), NEAR THE OCEAN (1967), THE DOLPHIN (1973).

Luthuli, Albert (?1898–1967): South African antiapartheid political activist, best known for his *autobiography* LET MY PEOPLE GO (1962).

Lydgate, John (?1370–1449): prolific English poet, influenced by *Chaucer*, whose contemporaries rated him on a par with Chaucer and *Gower*. Lydgate remained popular until the 17th century, but his *meter, style, verse form,* liking for *cliché,* and lengthy *text*s have left him largely unread since. Notable works include THE TROY BOOK (1412–21).

Lyly, John (*c.*1554–1606): English playwright and writer of *prose romance*s. His EUPHUES: OR, THE ANATOMY OF WIT (1578), written in elegant and elaborate prose, set a fashion for a *style* of prose writing that became known as *euphuism* (not to be confused with "euphemism"). Other notable works include CAMPASPE (1584) and ENDYMION: THE MAN IN THE MOON (1591).

lyric: a broad term covering relatively short poetic *forms* such as the *elegy, ode,* and *sonnet*. The word comes from the Greek word for a *song* to be accompanied by the lyre; the subject matter is personal and often concerns love expressed through a *persona*. The *genre* has been popular through the ages in many cultures, and was increasingly used in *Renaissance* England, first by *Wyatt* and *Surrey*, then by *Sidney, Shakespeare, Spenser, Jonson,* and the *Elizabethans*, and then with more complex undertones by *Donne, Herbert, Marvell,* and other *metaphysical* poets. The genre has remained popular through the ages (with such as *Coleridge* and *Wordsworth* during the *Romantic period*, and *Tennyson* during the 19th century) and many 20th century poets can be classed as lyric poets.

Macaulay, Rose (1881–1958): English novelist, essayist and travel writer whose *historical novels* are sharply perceptive, sometimes *satirical*, yet compassionate in their view of human nature. Notable works include THE WORLD MY WILDERNESS (1950), THE TOWERS OF TREBIZOND (1956).

Macbeth, George (1932–92): Scottish poet and novelist. In the 1950s he was a major figure in a writers' critical club called "the Group" (later to become the Writers' Workshop), participated in *performance poetry* in the 1960s, and produced *poetry* and arts programs for television. His work is always inventive, his *themes* often gruesome and morbid. Notable works include THE BROKEN PLACES (1963), THE COLOUR OF BLOOD (1967), COLLECTED POEMS 1958–1970 (1971), THE SAMURAI (1975), THE SEVEN WITCHES (1978), ANATOMY OF A DIVORCE (1988), TRESPASSING: POEMS FROM IRELAND (1991).

MacCaig, Norman (1910–96): Scottish poet. Considered to be one of Scotland's foremost poets, over the years he moved from traditional to freer *verse forms*. Edinburgh and the mountains of the West Highlands have inspired much of his writing (see *topographical poetry*). Notable works include FAR CRY (1943), THE INWARD EYE (1946), RIDING LIGHTS (1955), RINGS ON A TREE (1968), THE EQUAL SKIES (1980), VOICE-OVER (1988), COLLECTED POEMS (1985, revised 1990).

MacInnes, Colin (1914–76): English novelist, journalist, and essayist. Describing himself as an "anarchist sympathizer," he writes vividly, among other things, about the lives of young blacks in Notting Hill at the time when London is beginning to become a multiracial society. Notable works include ABSOLUTE BEGINNERS (1959).

MacLaverty, Bernard (b.1942): Irish novelist and *short story* writer. His books are often about loneliness, and he writes in a clear, unfussy, economic *prose style*. In CAL (1983) he conveys the human impact of the violence in Northern Ireland in a matter-of-fact yet tender way. Other notable works include SECRETS AND OTHER STORIES (1977), LAMB (1980), WALKING THE DOG AND OTHER SHORT STORIES (1994).

MacLeish, Archibald (1892–1982): American poet, playwright, and essayist. Influenced by *Pound* and *T.S. Eliot*, his early work explores intellectual and traditional ideas. Later he became interested in American political and social perceptions of itself and others, and its reactions to world events and social developments such as World War II and communism. He led an active public and academic life. Notable works include THE POT OF EARTH (1925), NOBODADDY (1926), ACTFIVE (1948), J.B. (1958), POETRY AND EXPERIENCE (1961), A CONTINUING JOURNEY (1968), RIDERS ON THE EARTH (1978).

MacLeod, Alistair (b.1936): Canadian *short story* writer and novelist. His works are often located in rural Nova Scotia, his treatment of the sometimes doomed struggles of men and women, young and old, are haunting and compassionate. Notable works include AS BIRDS BRING FORTH THE SUN AND OTHER STORIES (1986), THE LOST SALT GIFT OF BLOOD (1988), NO GREAT MISCHIEF (2000).

MacNeice, Louis (1907–63): British poet. Associated with *Spender, Day Lewis*, and *Auden*, he collaborated with the last on LETTERS FROM ICELAND (1937). He became an excellent writer of feature programs and radio plays. His *poetry* displays delicacy of touch and deft use of such *devices* as *assonance, internal rhyme, half rhyme*, and *ballad*-like repetition, and he wrote some distinctive *love poetry*. Notable works include BLIND FIREWORKS (1929), THE DARK TOWER (1947, radio play), SOLSTICES (1961), THE BURNING PERCH (1963), COLLECTED POEMS (1966).

magic realism is a term used to denote *fiction* that combines *realism* with the outlandish and the *fantastic*, thus reminding the reader that all *narratives* are inventions. Although the roots of magic realism go as far back as the *gothic novel*, the term is frequently applied to modern British novelists, e.g. *Rushdie, Angela Carter, Fowles, Winterson*. Important non-English experimenters include the German Günter Grass (b.1927), especially in THE TIN DRUM (1959) and the Colombian novelist Gabriel García Márquez (b.1928) in ONE HUNDRED YEARS OF SOLITUDE (1967).

Mahapatra, Jayanta (b.1928): Indian poet. Drawing on the *imagery* of his Indian surroundings and writing in both English and Oriya, his *poetry* is both loving and critical. Notable works include CLOSE THE SKY, TEN BY TEN (1971), THE FALSE START (1980), LIFE SIGNS (1983), SELECTED POEMS (1987).

Mailer, Norman (b.1923): American novelist, journalist, essayist, and literary critic. His writings have ranged widely in subject matter and *style*, and he has always been controversial, adopting staunchly personal stances in his criticism of society. During the 1960s he became disillusioned with leftwing politics and became a leading member of the *new journalism* movement which, broadly speaking, defended the merging of fact and *fiction* (see *faction*). His *novels* sometimes explore the subconscious. Notable works include THE NAKED AND THE DEAD (1948), THE ARMIES OF THE NIGHT (1968), OF A FIRE ON THE MOON (1971), THE EXECUTIONER'S SONG (1979), since which his work has been less well received. THE GOSPEL ACCORDING TO THE SUN (1997) is an interesting supposed *autobiography* of Christ.

Mais, Roger (1905–55): Jamaican novelist, poet, playwright, and journalist. His work is based on his interest in the black working class and the dreadful conditions of their slums and prisons during British colonial rule. His writing often displays strong biblical *rhythms* and *allusions*. Notable works include THE HILLS WERE JOYFUL TOGETHER (1953), BROTHER MAN (1954).

Malamud, Bernard (1914–86): American novelist and *short story* writer who characteristically explores Jewish experience. Born of immigrant Russian parents, he is one of the most widely read chroniclers of Jewish life in 20th century America. Notable works include THE NATURAL (1952), THE ASSISTANT (1957), A NEW LIFE (1961), THE FIXER (1967).

Malan, Rian (b.1954): South African journalist and autobiographer. Notable works include the semiautobiographical MY TRAITOR'S HEART (1990) which he subtitles A SOUTH AFRICAN EXPLORES THE MADNESS IN COUNTRY, IN HIS TRIBE [that is, the Afrikaaners] AND HIMSELF and in which with a reporter's eye he remorselessly examines the *paradox* of being a white liberal Afrikaaner in the land of apartheid.

malapropism: a misuse of long words, named after *Sheridan*'s *character* Mrs.

Malaprop (from the French "mal à propos," "not to the purpose"), who repeatedly misapplies long words in an attempt to sound impressive, e.g. "...she should have a supercilious [instead of 'superficial'] knowledge... that she might reprehend [comprehend]... I don't think that there is a superstitious [superfluous] article in it..." This kind of comic mistake, and the type of character who makes it, have a long English *tradition*, from Dogberry in *Shakespeare*'s MUCH ADO ABOUT NOTHING to characters in modern television situation comedy.

Malory, Thomas (?1408–?71): English writer, said to be the *author* of the famous *prose* version of *Arthurian legends*, LE MORTE D'ARTHUR (?1470). It was probably written in Newgate Prison, and was one of the first *texts* to be printed in English by *Caxton*. Some scholars have disputed the claim that Malory was the author.

Malouf, David (b.1934): Australian novelist, poet, and *short story* writer. He has moved between Australia and Europe, and the range of subject matter and interests in his writings draw upon this. Notable works include BICYCLE AND OTHER POEMS (1970), AN IMAGINARY LIFE (1978), WILD LEMONS (1980), REMEMBERING BABYLON (1993).

Mamet, David (b.1947): American playwright and essayist. A prolific writer of plays and screenplays, he is a leading light in contemporary American theater, much of his *drama* displaying discontent with contemporary American ways of life. Influenced by and intensely interested in the Russian playwright and *short story* writer Anton Chekhov (1860–1904), he tends to focus upon *character* rather than *plot*, and his *style* has been compared with that of *Pinter*. Notable works include SEXUAL PERVERSITY IN CHICAGO (1974), AMERICAN BUFFALO (1975), GLENGARRY GLEN ROSS (1983), HOUSE OF GAMES (1987), OLEANNA (1992), THE CRYPTOGRAM (1994).

manner is a term used to describe the characteristic *form* and *style* of a writer or piece of writing.

mannerism: a distinctive, repetitive (and sometimes irritating) feature of a writer's *style*. The word is used when describing art and architecture, most particularly of certain recurrent Italian features of the 16th century.

Mansfield, Katherine (1888–1923): New Zealand *short story* writer who is considered to be one of the finest writers in the *genre*. Her intelligent, well-shaped stories often draw on her New Zealand childhood, a focus partly developed by the trauma of her brother's death in World War I. Associated with the *Bloomsbury group* and influenced by Anton Chekhov (1860–1904), she shows in her writing a sense of the fragility of life, which came to be underlined by her own failing health. Notable works include "Prelude" (1918, published in BLISS, 1920), THE GARDEN PARTY (1922), THE DOVE'S NEST (1923), SOMETHING CHILDISH (1924).

marginalia: annotation written in the margins of books and manuscripts, ranging from those added by great writers in books they have owned to the notes of students who are preparing for an examination.

Marlowe, Christopher (1564–93): English playwright and poet. His colorful reputation is variously that of athiest, blasphemer, government spy, homosexual, and freethinker, and he clearly enjoyed dramatizing unconventional *characters* who defy secular, political, moral, and/or religious authority such as the title characters in

TAMBURLAINE (?1587), EDWARD II (?1592), and DOCTOR FAUSTUS (1594), the last of which uses the *morality play tradition* but subverts it by having Faustus condemned to hell at the end. Educated at Cambridge University, he was influenced by his study of classical writers such as Virgil and Ovid, but his plays move on from the traditional *form* of *Senecan tragedy* to something much more lively, partly through his development of *blank verse* (called "Marlowe's mighty line" by *Jonson*) which he made much more flexible than previous users such as *Norton* and *Sackville* in GORODUC. A friend of *Kyd*, he is generally regarded as the greatest contributor to *Elizabethan drama* before *Shakespeare* – Shakespeare's own early history plays such as the three parts of HENRY VI (?1589–92) were influenced by him. Other notable works include THE JEW OF MALTA (?1589), HERO AND LEANDER (1598), "The Passionate Shepherd to His Love" (1599).

Marston, John (1576–1634): English playwright and poet. His capabilities ranged from *comedy* through biting *satire* to *revenge tragedy*. In the 1590s he competed and disputed with *Jonson*, but later collaborated with him and *Chapman* on EASTWARD HO (1605). Other notable works include ANTONIO AND MELLIDA (1600), ANTONIO'S REVENGE (1600), THE MALCONTENT (?1602, whose main *character* is cast in the same melancholic, disaffected mold as Hamlet), THE DUTCH COURTESAN (?1604).

martian poetry is the name given to a kind of *verse* popular in Britain, in the late 1970s and 1980s, which observes human affairs as if seen through the eyes of a *persona* from space. The name derives from A MARTIAN SENDS A POSTCARD HOME (1979) by Craig Raine (b.1944).

Marvell, Andrew (1621–78): English poet and essayist. Influenced by *Donne* and his use of poetic *conceits*, he was friends with *Milton* and *Lovelace* (who, unlike Marvell, was a Royalist). Nowadays he is best known as a *metaphysical* and *pastoral* poet, but he was not known as a poet in his day. He was discovered by *Lamb* (in the 19th century he became known as "the green poet"), reappraised by *T.S. Eliot*, and is now admired for his arrestingly direct treatment of common poetic subject matter, e.g. the *carpe diem* lyric "To His Coy Mistress" (?1653). In his time he was known as the *author* of *ironic* and *witty* political and religious *satires*, a good example of which is "Last Instructions to a Painter" (1667), and he was a Member of Parliament for almost 20 years. Other notable works include "An Horatian Ode upon Cromwell's Return from Ireland" (1650), THE FIRST ANNIVERSARY (1665), MISCELLANEOUS POEMS (1681).

Marxist criticism is rooted in the cultural theories of Karl Marx (1818–83) and Friedrich Engels (1820–95). One of its basic beliefs is that all *literature* is culture-bound, and that the economic, political, and other *contexts* within which a *text* is produced are vital to its understanding and *interpretation*. Much Marxist criticism is devoted to assessing a text's level of *realism*, and exposing the unconscious *subtext*. The development of *structuralism* and *poststructuralism* has done much to stimulate Marxist criticism. See also *deconstruction*, *postmodernism*.

masculine ending, or "hard ending," occurs when a line of *verse* ends on a stressed syllable, as with most iambic verse. Trochaic verse (see *meter*) also often drops the final unstressed syllable in the line. For instance:

- "Alas! so all things now do hold their peace" (iambic, from *Wyatt's* "A Complaint by Night")

- "Lord, what fools these mortals be!" (trochaic, from *Shakespeare*'s A MIDSUMMER NIGHT'S DREAM).

See *weak ending*.

masculine rhyme is monosyllabic rhyming on the final stressed syllable of consecutive lines (as in bark/lark), e.g.

> Sweet Auburn! loveliest village of the plain
> Where health and plenty cheer'd the labouring swain
> > (from *Goldsmith*'s THE DESERTED VILLAGE)

It is the most common type of rhyming in English *poetry*.

Masefield, John (1878–1967): English poet, playwright, journalist, and children's *story* writer. His earlier *verse* is distinctive for *realism* of *character* and *setting* (often the sea), later work for lyrical rural evocations. His prolific output made *poetry* popular, and he was *poet laureate* from 1930 to 1967. Notable works include SALT-WATER BALLADS (1902, containing perhaps his best-known *poem* "I Must Go Down to the Sea Again"), BALLADS AND POEMS (1910), COLLECTED POEMS (1923), SARD HARKER (1924), THE MIDNIGHT FOLK (1927), THE BOX OF DELIGHTS (1935), DEAD NED (1938), LIVE AND KICKING NED (1939).

masque: a late 16th/early 17th century courtly entertainment involving such features as *poetry, song*, mime, and dancing within a dramatic framework. The *plot*s tended to be loosely constructed around a central *allegory* or mythological subject. Often elaborate costumes and masks were worn by the actors, and there were spectacular stage effects. At the end, the courtly audience joined in a dance with the actors. *Jonson* and the architect Inigo Jones (1573–1652) collaborated on masques, *Milton* wrote COMUS for performance in Ludlow Castle in 1634, and *Shakespeare* incorporated elements of masque into LOVE'S LABOUR'S LOST (?1594) and THE TEMPEST. See *antimasque*.

Massinger, Philip (1583–1640): English playwright who worked for *The King*'s *Men* from 1613 until his death. Capable of sharp *satire*, he collaborated with *Dekker, Fletcher*, and Nathan Field (1587–?1620). Notable works of which he was sole *author* include A NEW WAY TO PAY OLD DEBTS (?1625), THE ROMAN ACTOR (1626), THE CITY MADAM (?1632).

Masters, Edgar Lee (1868–1950): American poet, playwright, novelist, and biographer, chiefly known for the *verse collection* SPOON RIVER ANTHOLOGY (1915, revised 1916). In this quirky and hugely popular collection Masters presented a series of epitaphs, or tomb inscriptions, for a variety of imaginary *character*s from the fictitious community of "Spoon River" in the American midwest. Despite a prolific output in both *poetry* and *prose*, Masters was never to repeat the critical and popular success he achieved with his Spoon River *poem*s.

Masters, Olga (1919–86): Australian novelist, journalist, and *short story* writer. Narrow-mindedness and private pain often feature in her writing. Notable works include THE HOME GIRLS (1982), AMY'S CHILDREN (1987).

Matura, Mustapha (b.1939): Trinidadian playwright who emigrated to Britain in 1961. Humorous and *satirical*, his plays often focus upon the impact on the individual of the demise of indigenous Caribbean cultures. Notable works include AS TIME

GOES BY (1971), PLAY MAS (1974), NICE RUM AND COLA AND WELCOME HOME JACKO (1980), INDEPENDENCE AND MEETINGS (1982), THE PLAYBOY OF THE WEST INDIES (1984, based on *Synge's* THE PLAYBOY OF THE WESTERN WORLD).

Maugham, Somerset (1874–1965): English novelist, *short story* writer, and playwright. Much of his writing has been popular, but his short stories are most admired. Critics have remarked upon his *narrative* skill and shrewd observation, and several of his *novels* may be classed as examples of the *roman à clef*. He considered himself to be a leading "second-rater." Notable works include LIZA OF LAMBETH (1897), LADY FREDERICK (1907), OF HUMAN BONDAGE (1915), THE MOON AND SIXPENCE (1919), CAKES AND ALE (1930), THE SUMMING UP (1938), CREATURES OF CIRCUMSTANCES (1947).

maxim: a short, neatly expressed statement or *proverb* about human behavior. In some languages (e.g. French) there are books of maxims, but examples in English are scattered through various kinds of *literature*, e.g. in the writings of, among others, *Bacon, Blake, Coleridge, Johnson, Pope, Shaw*. They are common in English *drama*, for instance:

> The great are like the base, nay, they are the same,
> When they seek shameful ways to avoid shame
> > (*Webster*, THE DUCHESS OF MALFI)
>
> Experience is the name everyone gives to their mistakes
> > (*Wilde*, LADY WINDERMERE'S FAN)

Mayhew, Henry (1812–87): English journalist, playwright, novelist, and *short story* writer. He is best remembered for his investigations into the plight of the London poor, which did much to affect the public conscience and stimulate reform. His LONDON LABOUR AND THE LONDON POOR (a series of articles published as a book in 1851) is very useful background material for the study of contemporary *authors* such as *Dickens*. Other notable works include THE CRIMINAL PRISONS OF LONDON AND SCENES OF PRISON LIFE (1862).

McCullers, Carson (1917–67): American novelist, *short story* writer, and playwright. Her work is sometimes labeled "southern *gothic*" because of its use of lonely and eccentric *characters*, and its frequent location in her home state of Georgia. But her themes of love, loneliness, and selfhood are universal, and her sensitive treatment of race is widely admired. Notable works include THE HEART IS A LONELY HUNTER (1940), THE MEMBER OF THE WEDDING (1946), THE BALLAD OF THE SAD CAFÉ (1951).

McEwan, Ian (b.1948): novelist, *short story* writer, and screenwriter. His subject matter is characteristically disturbing and sometimes shocking, and it is conveyed with great clarity of *style*. Notable works include FIRST LOVE, LAST RITES (1975), THE CEMENT GARDEN (1978), THE CHILD IN TIME (1987), BLACK DOGS (1992), ENDURING LOVE (1997), AMSTERDAM (1998).

McGonagall, William (?1830–1902) Scottish poet. Most of his work is *doggerel*, characterized by lines of wildly irregular length and awkward *rhymes*. He is often deemed to be the worst poet of all time, but he also has his supporters. Notable works include POETIC GEMS (1890), his best-known *poem* probably being "The Tay Bridge Disaster."

McGough, Roger (b.1937): English poet and playwright, and one of the three

Liverpool poets. Among other things his writing is distinguished by sharp *wit*, *humor*, clever word play and *puns*. Notable works include SELECTED POEMS 1967–1987 (1989).

McGrath, John (b.1935): English playwright and director. Stemming from an interest in working-class theater, his plays often have an emphasis on local communities. Notable works include EVENTS WHILE GUARDING THE BOFORS GUN (1966), THE CHEVIOT, THE STAG AND THE BLACK, BLACK OIL (1973), LITTLE RED HEN (1975), A GOOD NIGHT OUT (1981).

meaning is what a writer intends to say.

measure is another word for *meter*.

mechanic form is where a writer determines the *form* of a work according to a predetermined set of *rules*, as opposed to *organic form* where the form is allowed to arise naturally from the subject matter and *theme*. It has been observed that the classical French *dramatists* of the 17th century constructed their plays according to mechanic form, and looked down upon *Shakespeare*'s preference for organic form, which they considered careless and shapeless. See also *unities, dramatic*.

medievalism, in a literary sense, is an emphasis on the *style*, subject matter, ways of thinking, and/or any other aspect of the Middles Ages (approximately AD800–1450). In particular, *Romanticism* and the associated revival of interest in the *gothic* saw a resurgence of medievalism, above all in much of *Keats*'s *poetry*. Others who have shown an interest in the medieval include *Spenser, Coleridge, Walter Scott, Tennyson*.

Medwall, Henry (*c*.1462–1502): English playwright. Only two works survive: NATURE (printed in ?1530), a *morality play;* and FULGENS AND LUCRECE (printed ?1515), first performed in about 1497 and thought to be the earliest known secular play (that is, a *drama* not on a scriptural or explicitly moral subject) in English.

meiosis is a deliberate understatement such as "rather good," and is often a part of *irony*. See also *litotes*.

melodrama was originally a play with a musical accompaniment that often reinforced the emotional aspect of the *drama;* the term came to refer to plays in which *characters* are two dimensional or *flat* – typically *villains, heroes*, or *heroines* – and the *action* bold, sentimental, and far-fetched, with sensational thrill and stage effects being more important than credibility. The *genre* reached a height of popularity during the *Victorian age* with plays such as LADY AUDLEY'S SECRET (1862) by Mary Braddon (1837–1915). Victorian melodramas are occasionally staged today, often for amusement in the *context* of a modern audience that will receive them very differently from their original audiences. The popularity of melodrama has continued through the movies (cowboy and horror films) and television (various soap operas).

melodramatic is a term used to denote any *drama* that has the characteristics of *melodrama*, and it is usually applied with a derogatory sense, implying that the drama is of a poor standard.

Melville, Herman (1819–91): American novelist, poet, and *short story* writer. His experiences at sea led him to write his early sea *tales*, which proved popular. The greatness of MOBY-DICK (1851) was recognized by the discerning, but the book was not widely esteemed at the time. During the 20th century Melville's reputation grew, and recently MOBY-DICK has been described as "the closest approach the United

States has had to a national *prose epic.*" His *metaphysical themes* and *psychological* insights were ahead of his time. Other notable works include TYPEE (1846), MARDI (1849), BILLY BUDD (written *c.*1886–91, published 1924).

memoir: an account by a writer of events and people encountered during a certain period in her or his life, rather than a work focusing upon the writer's own developing self. Therefore it does not set out to be a comprehensive *autobiography,* and good examples are *Graves's* GOODBYE TO ALL THAT and *Sassoon's* MEMOIRS OF A FOX-HUNTING MAN, both memoirs of the writer's experiences in World War I. See also *diary.*

memoir-novel: a kind of *novel* that by convention is written as if a true *memoir,* yet is *fiction,* e.g. *Defoe's* ROBINSON CRUSOE, *Smollett's* RODERICK RANDOM, *Ishiguro's* THE REMAINS OF THE DAY.

Meredith, George (1828–1909): English novelist, poet, critic, and journalist who is loosely associated with the *Pre-Raphaelites.* His *novels* are intelligent and *witty,* acute in their portrayal of *character,* especially female, and showing a mastery of *narrative* skill. His standing was high until the mid-20th century, but his writing is not very accessible to today's readers. Notable works include THE ORDEAL OF RICHARD FEVEREL (1859), MODERN LOVE (1862), THE EGOIST (1879), THE TRAGIC COMEDIANS (1880), POEMS AND LYRICS OF THE JOY OF EARTH (1883), DIANA OF THE CROSSWAYS (1885), ON THE IDEA OF COMEDY AND THE USES OF THE COMIC SPIRIT (1897).

merismus: a *rhetorical device* whereby a subject is divided into subcategories, e.g. in *Shakespeare's* MACBETH Malcolm refers to

> the king-becoming graces,
> As justice, verity, temperance, stableness,
> Bounty, perseverance, mercy, lowliness,
> Devotion, patience, courage, fortitude   (act IV, scene 3)

metacriticism is critical writing about literary *criticism,* e.g. a book that explores *structuralism.*

metadrama/metatheater: terms to describe a play or aspect of a play that deals with the nature of *drama.* It could be said, for example, that various aspects of *Shakespeare's* HAMLET are metadrama.

metafiction/metanovel: terms to describe *novels* about novels or novel-writing in which the *author* departs from *realism* and deliberately highlights an awareness that writer and reader are together creating the *fiction.* Examples include *Sterne's* TRISTRAM SHANDY, *Lessing's* THE GOLDEN NOTEBOOK, and *Fowles's* THE FRENCH LIEUTENANT'S WOMAN, with its alternative endings. See *antinovel, narrative.*

metaphor, like a *simile,* is a comparison between two things not usually compared in order to illuminate or provoke thought in the reader through the striking nature of the comparison. However, whereas a simile says that something is "like" something else, a metaphor describes something in terms of something else, e.g. "The road snaked its way up the mountain-side." In *Theroux's* THE GREAT RAILWAY BAZAAR the writer describes hearing "the smashing of paper parcels being stuffed into corners," arresting the reader by giving to paper a quality not usually associated with it. Metaphors help the reader to see objects and ideas in a fresh light, for instance:

In the lower sky
Television aerials, Chinese characters

(from Dunn's "On the Roofs of Terry Street")

See *implicit metaphor, tenor and vehicle.*

metaphysical is a term now mainly used to define a group of 17th century poets including *Donne* (who is usually credited with setting the trend), *Herbert,* and *Marvell* whose *poetry* contains common elements, such as:

- striking *imagery* and comparisons, often drawn from the new scientific and geographic discoveries of the day
- an interlinking of the physical and the philosophical
- complex thought and *themes*
- *witty conceits*
- *paradoxes*
- colloquially direct language (as opposed the formal fluency of much *Elizabethan lyric love poetry*)
- economical, tightly packed expression
- a strong sense of mortality
- flexibility of *rhythm* and *meter.*

The term is more widely applied to matters of philosophy (in Greek it means "after physics": in his academy *Plato* playfully used the term for the philosophy classes he ran after his physics classes).

meter is, in *poetry,* the regular use of a dominant unit of *rhythm,* known as a "foot." The following terms are used to describe the number of feet in a *verse* line:

- monometer – a single foot (very rare), e.g.
  I'm made
  A shade
  And laid
  I'th'grave
  There have
  My cave
  (Herrick's "Upon His Departure Hence," 1648)
- dimeter – two feet (rare), e.g.
  Their's not to / reason why
  Their's but to / do and die
  (Tennyson's "The Charge of the Light Brigade," 1855)
- trimeter – three feet, e.g.
  I look / into / my glass
  And view / my wast/ing skin
  (Hardy's "I Look into My Glass," 1898)
- tetrameter – four feet, e.g.
  The Assy/rian came down / like a wolf / on the fold
  (Byron's "The Destruction of Sennacherib," 1815)
- pentameter – five feet, e.g.
  He nev/er lift/ed up / anoth/er stone
  (Wordsworth's "Michael," 1800)

- hexameter – six feet (sometimes known as an *alexandrine*), e.g.
  I will / arise / and go / now, and go / to Inn/isfree
  And a small / cabin / build there, / a hive / for the hon/ey-bee
  (*Yeats*'s "The Lake Isle of Innesfree," 1892)

- heptameter – seven feet, e.g.
  I went / into / a pub/lic-'ouse / to get / a pint / o' beer
  (*Kipling*'s "Tommy," 1890)

- octameter – eight feet, e.g.
  There beneath the Roman ruin where the purple flowers grow
  Came that 'Ave Atque Vale' of the poet's hopeless woe
  (Tennyson's "Frater Ave Atque Vale," 1880)

The most common metrical feet in English poetry are:

- iambic (an unstressed syllable followed by a stressed, which tends to give a relatively stately rhythm). This is the most common of all, and is employed in the majority of English poetry and *dramatic* verse, such as Wordsworth's poetry and *Shakespeare*'s plays, e.g.
  He név/er líft/ed úp / anóth/er stóne
  (from Wordsworth's "Michael," 1800)

- trochaic (a stressed syllable followed by an unstressed, which tends to give a relatively bouncy rhythm), as in *Longfellow*'s THE SONG OF HIAWATHA (that is, the reverse of an *iamb*). Whole *poems* written in *trochees* are rare in English, one of the best-known being Longfellow's HIAWATHA where the insistent trochees create the aural effect of the Native American drumbeat. Another example is in Shakespeare's A MIDSUMMER NIGHT'S DREAM where Puck's trochees emphasize his bouncy, mischievous *character*, e.g.
  Thróugh the / fórest/ háve I / góne
  Bút Ath/énian / fóund I / nóne...
  This example shows how the final unstressed syllable of trochaic lines is often omitted.

- anapestic (two unstressed syllables followed by a stressed), e.g.
  The Assý/rian came dówn / like a wólf / on the fóld

- dactylic (one stressed syllable followed by two unstressed), e.g.
  Théirs not to / máke reply
  Théirs not to / réason why
  Théirs but to / dó and die

- spondaic (two stressed syllables), which can only be an occasional foot, e.g. in the fourth foot of:
  And às / she dìed / so mùst / wè dìe / oursèlves
  (*Robert Browning*'s "The Bishop Orders His Tomb at Saint Praxed's Church," 1845)

Whole poems cannot be written in spondees, as it is of course impossible to stress every single syllable in a poem!

- pyrrhic (two unstressed syllables) which, again, can only be an occasional foot, e.g.
  To a / grèen thòught / in a / grèen shàde
  (from *Marvell*'s "The Garden," 1681)

In this example the first and third feet are pyrrhics, the second and third are spondees. See *stress*.

method refers to the way in which a writer goes about communicating his *content* to the reader.

metonymy means, literally, "change of name," and is a *figure of speech* whereby the name of something is substituted by a feature associated with it, e.g. "The Crown [for King or Queen] has decreed..."; "When one sees Marlowe [meaning the plays written by Marlowe] on stage..."; "The stage [for acting on the stage] is a great profession." Similar to *synecdoche*.

Michaels, Anne (b.1958): Canadian poet and novelist. She has been praised for her language, which is rich yet clear, and for the density of her *imagery*. Notable works include THE WEIGHT OF ORANGES (1985), MINER'S POND (1991), FUGITIVE PIECES (1996).

Middle English period: generally considered to cover *literature* written in England between approximately 1066 (the Norman Conquest) and 1500.

Middleton, Thomas (1580–1627): English playwright who collaborated with many of his contemporaries including, probably, *Shakespeare*. His versatility extended to the writing of *pageants* and *masques* for special occasions. Notable works include his *tragedies* WOMEN BEWARE WOMEN (?1620) and THE CHANGELING (1622), written in collaboration with *Rowley*. Some scholars ascribe THE REVENGER'S TRAGEDY (1607) to him rather than *Tourneur*.

miles gloriosus: Latin name for a boasting, swaggering self-glorifying soldier who was a stereotype in Greek and Roman *comedy*. He remained a popular stage figure, and elements of his *character* are to be found in *Udall*'s RALPH ROISTER DOISTER and *Shakespeare*'s characters Falstaff and Pistol.

Millay, Edna St. Vincent (1892–1950): American poet, playwright, and essayist. She achieved fame while still a college student with the *poem* "Renascence" (1912) and subsequently became part of a Greenwich Village intellectual set that included *Stevens, Hart Crane*, and *O'Neill*. Her *poetry* is intensely personal in subject matter, and frequently uses traditional *forms*, but at the same time her outlook is *modernist* and feminist. Notable works include A FEW FIGS FROM THISTLES (1920), THE HARP WEAVER AND OTHER POEMS (1923), COLLECTED SONNETS (1941), COLLECTED LYRICS (1943).

Miller, Arthur (b.1915): American playwright and essayist. Influenced by *Ibsen*, he is interested in family conflict, which is sometimes precipitated by the false values of contemporary society and often unfolds like a Greek *drama*, his *character*s usually experiencing an *anagnorisis*. Plays such as THE PRICE (1968) have done much to broaden the notion of *tragedy*. Regarded as one of America's leading *dramatist*s, he has written many notable works including ALL MY SONS (1947), DEATH OF A SALESMAN (1949), THE CRUCIBLE (1953), A VIEW FROM THE BRIDGE (1955), THEATRE ESSAYS (1978), PLAYING FOR TIME (1980, television play), BROKEN GLASS (1994).

Milton, John (1608–74): English poet, playwright, pamphleteer, and translator. Regarded as one of the finest poets and *prose* writers of any age, he is particularly admired for his use of *blank verse*. In his middle years he was distracted from writing *poetry* by his strongly held political views concerning civil and religious liberties, becoming a staunch supporter of the parliamentarians and later the Commonwealth against the monarchy. During this time he wrote some of the finest prose *polemics* in the *English language.* After the onset of blindness his friend *Marvell* assisted him. Following the restoration of the monarchy in 1660, and consequent harassment and the public burning of his works, a quieter life gave him time to return to *literature,* whereupon he completed his masterpiece PARADISE LOST (1667), which *Dryden* described as one of the "most noble and sublime *poems* that this age or nation has produced." His reputation gained steadily after his death and, notwithstanding the attacks of critics such as *Johnson, T.S. Eliot,* and *Leavis,* he is established as preeminent among English poets. The *Romantics* in particular applauded his radical politics and his creation of a great English *epic* in PARADISE LOST. Other notable works include "On the Morning of Christ's Nativity" (written 1629, published 1645), "L'Allegro" and "Il Penseroso" (both written *c.*1631, published 1645), COMUS (1637), "Lycidas" (written 1637, published 1645), AREOPAGITICA (1644), PARADISE REGAINED (1671), SAMSON AGONISTES (1671).

Miltonic sonnet: see *sonnet.*

mimesis: see *imitation.*

minimalism/minimalist: general terms used to describe things presented in their barest possible essentials, as in some of *Beckett's* plays, *Carver's short stories,* or in this *poem* by *William Carlos Williams:*

> I have eaten
> the plums
> that were in
> the icebox
> and which
> you were probably
> saving
> for breakfast
> Forgive me
> they were delicious
> so sweet
> and so cold

("This is Just to Say," 1934)

miracle plays: see *mystery plays.*

Mistry, Rohinton (b.1952): Indian novelist and *short story* writer. One of his major concerns is the problem of personal identity within society and history. Notable works include TALES FROM FIROZSHA BAAG (1987), SUCH A LONG JOURNEY (1991).

Mitchell, Adrian (b.1932): English poet, novelist, and playwright. Since the 1960s his writing has been mainly entertaining, *witty,* and leftwing, and he tends to use a *free verse form* which is characteristic of *underground literature.* Notable works include OUT LOUD (1968), FOR BEAUTY DOUGLAS: COLLECTED POEMS (1982), ALL SHOOK UP: POEMS 1997–2000 (2001).

mock epic: a *poem* of *epic form* that treats the ordinary or trivial in the grand, elevated language of the epic, e.g. *Dryden*'s MAC FLECKNOE, or *Pope*'s THE RAPE OF THE LOCK, which uses a *mock heroic style* in order to ridicule the behavior of the upper classes in Queen Anne's days. See *burlesque*.

mock heroic is a term applied when a trivial subject is dealt with in an apparently heroic *manner* or lofty *style*, creating the effect of mocking the subject. It was especially popular in *Augustan* and 18th century *literature*. It is a feature of the *mock epic* and other poetic and literary *forms*, e.g. *Gray*'s poem "Ode on the Death of a Favourite Cat, Drowned in a Tub of Gold Fishes," or *Fielding*'s play TOM THUMB (1730), or the description of the battle in the churchyard in his *novel* TOM JONES. See *burlesque*.

mode: the *style*, *manner*, or *method* employed by a writer in communicating her or his subject matter to the reader. The term is similar in *meaning* to *form*, but is sometimes confused with *genre*. For instance, one might read something from the *science fiction* genre, written in a comic mode.

modern period: generally considered to cover *literature* written since 1914 (the outbreak of World War I).

modernism/modernist: terms used to describe a European and American movement in all the arts with roots in the 19th century and lasting through much of the 20th century. As with *Romanticism*, the movement:

- was about breaking away from old rules, *conventions* and *traditions*
- experimented with *form* and *style*
- had no definite start or ending, but, according to most critics, reached its height in the 1920s.

Among other things modernism embraced the *avant-garde, free verse, formalism, existentialism, expressionism, surrealism, symbolism, naturalism,* and *theater of the absurd,* and points the way toward *structuralism.* Important modernist works in English include *Joyce*'s ULYSSES, *T.S. Eliot*'s THE WASTE LAND, *Woolf*'s JACOB'S ROOM, *Pound*'s CANTOS, the *poetry* of *Yeats*; and among other important modernist thinkers are Friedrich Nietzsche (1844–1900), Karl Marx (1818–83), Sigmund Freud (1856–1939). See *postmodernism.*

moment: a less formal word for *epiphany*, used by *Percy Shelley* in his "A Defence of Poetry" (written 1821, published 1840). See also *spots of time.*

monodrama is a play with only one *character*, e.g. *Beckett*'s KRAPP'S LAST TAPE. *Tennyson* described his dramatic *monolog* "Maud" thus. The term could also be applied to a "one man show" (or, more correctly, one person show) such as Howard Burnham's (b.1946) LEWIS CARROLL (1984), or *Ackroyd*'s THE MYSTERY OF CHARLES DICKENS (2000).

monody: a mourning *ode*, originally said or sung by an individual, e.g. *Arnold*'s "Thyrsis, A Monody" (1866) in memory of the poet *Clough,* and in his introduction to "Lycidas" *Milton* describes his *poem* as a monody. See *complaint, dirge, elegy, threnody.*

monolog is a term that may refer to:

- a *monodrama*
- a *poem* in the *form* of a dramatic monolog where the poet speaks through a

persona, e.g. "My Last Duchess" and several other poems by *Robert Browning*. *Tennyson, Hardy, Kipling, Yeats, T.S. Eliot, Pound, Frost*, and others all exploit this form. See *stream of consciousness*

- a *soliloquy*.

monometer: see *meter*.

mood is the *atmosphere* that prevails in a work, or part of a work – often early on when the *tone* establishes an expectation in the reader or audience as to the future course of events. For instance, in the opening 40 lines or so of *Shakespeare*'s HAMLET the mood is established by such factors as the unease of the sentinels (manifested by the tenseness of their *dialog*), the time of night, the cold, their apprehension about the Ghost, and by its actual reappearance. See *ambience*.

Moore, Marianne (1887–1972): American poet, considered one of the outstanding woman poets of the United States in the 20th century. Her work is characterized by its intelligence, precise use of language, and highly individual *style* of irregular, *prose*-like lines of *free verse*. Her most famous *poem* is "Poetry" (1921). Other notable works include "The Steeple-Jack" (1935, revised 1961), "A Grave" (1924, revised 1935), "The Mind is an Enchanting Thing" (1944), all included in THE COMPLETE POEMS (1967).

moral: in literary terms, a lesson that may be learned from a piece of writing. For instance, it may be said that the moral of *Coleridge*'s "The Rime of the Ancient Mariner" is that, in *Blake*'s words, "every thing that lives is holy."

morality plays flourished during the mid-15th and first half of the 16th centuries, typically involving an *allegorical* struggle between *character*s representing vices and virtues over the soul of a figure called variously Man, Everyman, Mankind, or similar, who stands as one person representing all humanity. After much temptation the virtues always win. In many ways the plays show the struggle between good and evil that is characteristic of most *drama*. Two of the best plays in this *genre* are MANKIND (?1465) and EVERYMAN (?1500). Performances were sometimes given by traveling troupes who may be regarded as the first professional actors, and who set up stages in town squares, inn yards, or in the great halls of gentry or noblemen. THE CASTLE OF PERSEVERANCE (?1425) was an exception, requiring an elaborate circular earthwork within which the play was performed. *Elizabethan* playwrights use the *tradition*, e.g. *Shakespeare*'s Falstaff represents a kind of "vice" who tempts in the HENRY IV plays; and *Marlowe* subverts the tradition by having the vices (in the shape of Mephistopheles) win the soul of his main character in DOCTOR FAUSTUS. See also *Medwall*.

More, Sir Thomas (1478–1535): English writer, critic, and patron of the arts. A friend of Erasmus (1466–1536), Holbein (1497–1543), and many others of cultural importance, he is a key figure in *humanist Renaissance* thinking. He held high office under Henry VIII, became Lord Chancellor, refused to support the King's break from the church in Rome, was condemned as a traitor and beheaded. Notable works include UTOPIA (1516 in Latin, English translation 1551). *Shakespeare* probably contributed to the play SIR THOMAS MORE (?1594), and *Bolt*'s A MAN FOR ALL SEASONS (1960) is a notable treatment of the latter part of his life.

Morgan, Sally (b.1951): Australian novelist, biographer, playwright, and artist. Her work is greatly influenced by her Aboriginal heritage which she did not know she had until her mother told her when she was 15. Notable works include MY PLACE (1987), THE STORY OF JACK MCPHEE (1989), SISTER GIRL (1992).

Morris, Mervyn (b.1937): Jamaican poet and editor. His concerns are both for the social fabric and for the private and personal. He has experimented with conventional *verse forms*, and some of his short *poems* are strikingly powerful. Notable works include THE POND (1973), ON HOLY WEEK (1976), SHADOWBOXING (1979), EXAMINATION CENTRE (1992).

Morrison, Toni (b.1931): American novelist. She blends folktale, history, and *myth* in powerful, realistic, and consciously political stories of African-American people living in a white society, and focuses on the position of black women within society as a whole. Notable works include THE BLUEST EYE (1970), SULA (1974), SONG OF SOLOMON (1977), TAR BABY (1981), BELOVED (1987).

Mortimer, John (b.1923): English novelist, playwright, screenwriter, and *short story* writer. Capable of both cool and warm *humor*, he created the popular fictional *character* Horace Rumpole, an eccentric British barrister, or lawyer. Notable works include WHAT SHALL WE TELL CAROLINE? (1958), COME AS YOU ARE (1970), RUMPOLE OF THE BAILEY (1978), PARADISE POSTPONED (1985).

motif: a recurring element in *literature*, such as a *character, device,* emotion, or occurrence. It may be an aspect of a *theme* (with which the term is sometimes regarded as interchangeable). For instance:

- the malcontent is a recurrent motif in *Jacobean drama*
- *carpe diem* is a recurrent device in much literature
- jealousy is a motif in *Shakespeare*'s OTHELLO
- the course of true love not running smooth is a frequent occurrence in *comedy.*

See *leitmotif.*

Motion, Andrew (b.1952): English poet, novelist, and biographer. His lyrical *poetry* shows the influence of *Edward Thomas* and *Larkin,* with whom he worked at Hull University in the north of England. He was appointed *poet laureate* in 1999 after the death of *Hughes.* Notable works include THE PLEASURE STEAMERS (1978), SECRET NARRATIVES (1983), DANGEROUS PLAY (1984), LOVE IN A LIFE (1991). He has also written biographies of Larkin and *Keats.*

Movement, the: a term used in the 1950s to describe a looseknit group of writers including *Kingsley Amis, Davie, Enright, Gunn, Jennings,* and *Larkin.* Their work was typically *witty, ironic,* sardonic, and intellectual, and they aimed at a high degree of skilled craftsmanship in their writing. The key publication containing their work is NEW LINES (1956) edited by Robert Conquest (b.1917).

Mphalele, Es'kia (b.1919): South African novelist, essayist, and *short story* writer. He writes with sharp *narrative* skill about such matters as oppression, dispossession and poverty, exile, and corruption in African politics. Notable works include the autobiographical DOWN SECOND AVENUE (1959), THE AFRICAN IMAGE (1962, revised 1974), THE WANDERERS (1971).

Muir, Edwin (1887–1959): Scottish poet, novelist, translator, critic and autobiographer. Mainly traditional in *form* and *manner*, he yet approaches his subject matter in radical, *allegorical*, and/or philosophical ways. His experiences of travel and of undergoing psychoanalysis combine to produce *poem*s that tell of dream journeys with an underlying feeling of menace. He and his wife collaborated on significant translations of the Czech writer Franz Kafka (1883–1924). Other notable works include FIRST POEMS (1925), CHORUS OF THE NEWLY DEAD (1926), THE LABYRINTH (1949), "The Horses" (1952).

Muldoon, Paul (b.1951): Irish poet and playwright. His *poetry* is refreshingly honest, imaginative, and innovative. His elegant handling of *form, meter,* and *rhyme* are supported by verbal ingenuity and *wit.* He is also capable of lyrical simplicity and emotional directness. He experiments with *narrative,* and displays a tension born of his Northern Ireland background. Notable works include NEW WEATHER (1973), MULES (1977), WHY BROWNLEE LEFT (1980), QUOOF (1983), MEETING THE BRITISH (1987), MADOC: A MYSTERY (1990), THE ANNALS OF CHILE (1995), HAY (1998), COLLECTED POEMS 1968–1998 (2001).

Mungoshi, Charles (b.1947): Zimbabwean novelist, *short story* writer, and poet. He is generally regarded as the most eminent Zimbabwean *author* writing in English and Shona, and his *stories* often evoke his country's landscape. There are aspects of political protest in his writing, especially in the *collection* of stories COMING OF THE DRY SEASON (1972), which was banned before independence. Notable works include WAITING FOR THE RAIN (1975), THE SETTING SUN AND THE ROLLING WORLD (1980).

Munro, Alice (b.1931): Canadian novelist and *short story* writer. She is widely regarded as highly accomplished in the latter *genre,* often using provincial Ontario for her fictionalized *setting*s. She combines the everyday and the extraordinary as two sides of the same coin. Notable works include LIVES OF GIRLS AND WOMEN (1971), WHO DO YOU THINK YOU ARE? (1978, published in the US as BEGGAR MAID), THE PROGRESS OF LOVE (1986).

Murdoch, Iris (1919–99): English novelist and philosopher. Her prolific output often contains philosophical *symbolism* and debate within the *novel form.* Her *charac*ters often undergo an *epiphany.* Notable works include UNDER THE NET (1954), THE SANDCASTLE (1957), THE BELL (1958), A SEVERED HEAD (1961), THE ITALIAN GIRL (1964), THE SEA, THE SEA (1978), THE GOOD APPRENTICE (1986).

Murphy, Dervla (b.1931): Irish travel writer who writes with compassion about those whom she encounters in her travels from Ireland to India and Africa. Notable works include FULL TILT: IRELAND TO INDIA BY BICYCLE (1965), TIBETAN FREEHOLD (1966), IN ETHIOPIA WITH A MULE (1968), THE IKIMWI ROAD: FROM KENYA TO ZIMBABWE (1993).

Murray, Les (b.1938): Australian poet. Always keen that *poetry* should reach a wider audience and not just intellectuals, he draws authoritatively upon Australian culture, folklore, and landscape. Notable works include THE ILEX TREE (1965, a collaborative work), THE WEATHERBOARD CATHEDRAL (1969), THE BOYS WHO STOLE THE FUNERAL (1980), DOG FOX FIELD (1990).

mystery plays are dramatizations of Old and New Testament *stories* from the

Creation through to the Last Judgment. Their origins may be traced to 10th century Easter plays in Latin. Over the years the plays moved out of the churches into the churchyards, were developed in English, and were taken over by guilds of workers who often performed a play suitable to their craft (e.g. in one cycle NOAH'S FLOOD was performed by those who brought fresh water to the town, and in another THE CRUCIFIXION by the butchers). *Cycles* of plays developed in, among other places, the English cities of Chester, York, Coventry, and Wakefield. They were usually performed on Corpus Christi Day, and staging was either on fixed scaffolds in the town square, or on *pageant* carts that traveled around the streets performing each play at appointed stations before moving on. Performances died out during the 16th century. It is an attractive idea that a 22-year-old Warwickshire man called *William Shakespeare* might have been present at one of the last recorded performances in Coventry in 1586.

myth: originally meaning anything passed on by word of mouth, the term has assumed complex *meaning*s and *connotation*s. Among them are:

- a *story* from a religion that one no longer believes in; e.g. *Keats, Victorian* poets, and others make considerable use of classical mythology in their *poem*s
- a *tale* of supernatural beings
- a system or way of thinking devised by a writer; e.g. *Blake* developed his own mythology, a mixture of inherited myths, biblical stories, and his own *imagination*, as did *Yeats*, who made considerable use of Celtic legend
- an imagined territory within which a *narrative* occurs, e.g. *Faulkner*'s Yoknapatawpha County; or the *psychological* world created by *Melville* in MOBY-DICK
- a commonly held fallacy, usually one with a grain of truth, or at least a psychological truth, around which elaborate *fiction*s have been woven
- as used by *structuralist* critics, the system of *sign*s by which society expresses itself.

myth critics adopt a view that all *literature* is developed from *myth*s. The leading exponent of this attitude was the Canadian critic Northrop Frye (1912–91).

N

Nabokov, Vladimir (1899–1977): Russian-born American novelist, *short story* writer, translator, and poet. Much critical interest in his work has focused upon the influence of his Russian background upon his American writings, and he has been regarded by some as a postmodernist. Notable works include THE GIFT (in Russian, 1938; in English, 1963), THE EYE (in Russian as "The Spy," 1938; in English, 1965), LOLITA (1955), PALE FIRE (1962), LOOK AT THE HARLEQUINS! (1974).

Naipaul V.S. (b.1932): Trinidadian novelist, travel and *short story* writer of Indian descent. His *themes* include 20th century insecurity and the bad effects of colonialism; his *style* is often *witty* and sardonic. Notable works include THE MYSTIC MASSEUR (1957), MIGUEL STREET (1959), A HOUSE FOR MR. BISWAS (1961), THE MIMIC MEN (1967), IN A FREE STATE (1971), A BEND IN THE RIVER (1979), AMONG THE BELIEVERS (1981), FINDING THE CENTRE (1984), THE ENIGMA OF ARRIVAL (1987), HALF A LIFE (2001).

naïve narrator: see *narrator/narrative voice*.

Narayan, R.K. (1906–2001): Indian novelist and *short story* writer. An uncomplicated *diction* and clear *narrative prose style* both link him with the Indian storytelling *tradition* and make him appealing to Western readers. Notable works include SWAMI AND FRIENDS (1935), THE BACHELOR OF ARTS (1937), THE ENGLISH TEACHER (1945), WAITING FOR MAHATMA (1955), THE PAINTER OF SIGNS (1976).

narrative is a piece of *prose* or *poetry* that tells a *story*. In *drama* the narrative evolves through the *action*.

narrative verse describes a *poem* that tells a *story*. There are three main types: *ballad*, *epic*, and *romance*. *Verse* rather than *prose* was the common method of telling a story before the 18th century. Examples are *Chaucer's* THE CANTERBURY TALES, *Spenser's* THE FAERIE QUEENE, *Milton's* PARADISE LOST, *Wordsworth's* THE PRELUDE, *Larkin's* THE WHITSUN WEDDINGS, *Keats's* "The Eve of St. Agnes," *Owen's* "Strange Meeting."

narrator/narrative voice: these terms refer to the *voice* from whose viewpoint or standpoint a *story* is told. Critics have identified various categories:

- first-person narrator, who adopts a *persona* in order to tell the story her/himself. Such a narrator may also be "unreliable" (see below)
- second-person narrator: this is a less frequently used *form* where the *author* addresses "you" as if you, the reader, are a part of the *action*
- third-person narrator, or omniscient narrator, where the story is told from a godlike or bird's eye view, seeing all
- unreliable (or "fallible") narrator, where the author makes clear by various means that the narrator's opinions do not coincide with the author's. *Henry James* often used this *technique*. Stevens, the central *character* in *Ishiguro's* THE REMAINS OF THE DAY, is an unreliable narrator because he suppresses and evades the truth about himself and others
- limited (or "restricted") point of view narrator, where the author shows the world from the limited perspective of only one or a few characters, e.g.

Talbot and Colley in *Golding*'s RITES OF PASSAGE, the former being particularly "unreliable"

- intrusive narrator. *Dickens* sometimes intervenes in the action to ensure that he hammers home a point to his reader
- impersonal narrator, where the author attempts to report events as objectively as possible, sometimes not even accessing characters' feelings, e.g. in some of *Hemingway*'s stories
- self-conscious narrator, where the writer reminds us that what we are reading is *fiction*, and thus dispels the reader's illusion, e.g. Tristram in *Sterne*'s TRISTRAM SHANDY, or Nellie Dean in *Emily Brontë*'s WUTHERING HEIGHTS
- naïve narrator, such as Gulliver in *Jonathan Swift*'s GULLIVER'S TRAVELS, who is naïvely impressed by what he sees in the countries he visits, and through whose naïvety the reader is expected to see the truth of things (thus giving rise to *irony*).

Of the above, first and third-person narrator are by far the most common. A third-person narrator is not always as impartial as appears at first sight, and a reader must be alert to such *devices* as an intrusive adverb by which an author seeks to guide a reader into an opinion. For instance, " 'I remember being so proud,' he said pathetically" (from *Lessing*'s THE HABIT OF LOVING, 1957). The insertion of "pathetically" gives an authorial bias that the reader cannot ignore. Sometimes an author moves between both modes of narration, moving inside and outside a character's head in a mixture of third and first-person narrative known as free indirect style or free indirect discourse. For instance, "Tom sat opposite him... It crossed Tom's mind to steal the green ring... It would be easy..." (from *Highsmith*'s THE TALENTED MR. RIPLEY). Here the narrative moves from objective fact, to reported thought, to being inside a character's head. See *showing and telling*.

Nash, Ogden (1902–71): American poet, lyricist, and children's writer, chiefly known for his playful, *witty*, yet insightful light *verse*, which made a fine art out of deliberately bad poetic constructions. Notable works include FREE WHEELING (1931), HARD LINES (1931), THE BAD PARENTS' GARDEN OF VERSE (1936), ONE TOUCH OF VENUS (1943, lyrics for musical), PARENTS KEEP OUT (1951), THE PRIVATE DINING ROOM (1953), A NASH OMNIBOOK (1967).

naturalism, in a literary sense, is the use of realistic *settings* and *characters* to convey philosophical truths. A development of *realism* and influenced by Charles Darwin's biological ideas, theories of naturalism were developed during the 19th century in Germany and France by writers such as Émile Zola (1840–1902), and affected English novelists such as *Hardy*. Sometimes naturalism is used in connection with the writings of those who see nature and natural beauty as fundamental, e.g. *Wordsworth*.

naturalistic drama, a development of *naturalism*, is a term used of *drama* that in its *setting* and all surface appearances tries to imitate real life. Naturalism should not be confused with *realism*, which refers to the *psychological* reality of what is being presented. Thus a *drawing room comedy* may be perfectly naturalistic, taking place in a setting that exactly replicates a house interior and with the language of the *characters* being true to life; but there may be little psychological realism in the characters' thinking and behavior.

near rhyme: see *half rhyme.*

negation is a way of expressing a situation by denying something else. For instance, Macbeth says "light thickens" in order to indicate gathering darkness; and in "Hyperion" *Keats* writes "No stir of air was there" to indicate stillness. See *litotes.*

negative capability is a phrase coined by *Keats* to indicate a state wherein a writer appreciates and accepts the beauty of things without endlessly striving to understand everything down to the last detail, essentially suppressing his own intellect and enter- ing into an imaginative appreciation of most aspects of the surrounding world. He defined it as a literary quality "which *Shakespeare* possessed so enormously – I mean 'Negative Capability'; that is, when man is capable of being in uncertainties, myster- ies, doubts, without any irritable reaching after fact and reason ... with a great poet the sense of beauty over comes every other consideration." This appreciation of imaginative response before reason is a central aspect of *Romanticism.*

nemesis: punishment or retribution served on a tragic *hero* or *heroine.* The Greeks had a goddess Nemesis who was thought to hand out such punishment to those who ignored the gods' warnings, thus displaying *hubris.*

neoclassical period: covers *literature* written in England between 1660 (the restoration of the monarchy) and approximately 1780.

neoclassicism is a label applied to the *style* of certain *literature* and other arts (such as architecture) created during the *neoclassical period,* and is often contrasted with *Romanticism.* Essentially, the neoclassicists valued reason, intellect, and a balanced outlook, distrusting the emotions. (Today we might say that they regarded the func- tions of the cognitive left-hand side of the brain above those of the affective right-hand side.) They looked back to the rational, intellectual worlds of ancient Greece and Rome as models of common sense and balance. Notable neoclassical writers include *Dryden, Jonathan Swift, Pope, Fielding, Goldsmith.*

neologism: a newly coined word (from the Greek for "new word"). Neologisms may be of various types, for instance

- a completely new word (e.g. "hassle," "hippie")
- a word derived from an existing prefix or root (e.g. "stereophonic," "cam- corder")
- an established word with a new *meaning* (e.g. "gay," "wicked")
- an acronym (e.g. "radar" from "radio detecting and ranging").

A language that opens its arms to new words is a healthy, vibrant language, and today's slang becomes tomorrow's accepted usage. *Shakespeare* seems to have invented, or at least brought into currency, numerous words; for example, the first recorded use of words such as "accommodation," "assassination," and "obscene" are in his plays.

new critics advocated *objective criticism,* affirming that the *text* alone matters, and that biographical, sociological, and other contextual information surrounding a text is irrelevant. Influenced by *Richards* and in turn influencing *Leavis,* the movement was primarily American, and UNDERSTANDING POETRY (1938) by Cleanth Brooks (1906–94) and *Warren* made new criticism the standard teaching approach in America for several decades. See *close reading, intrinsic attitude, Leavisite.*

new historicism: see *historicism*.

new journalism refers to a kind of writing that, very generally speaking, sought to explore contemporary reality by blurring the boundaries between fact and *fiction*, aiming toward journalism with literary *technique*. Dissatisfied with pure journalism as a means of expressing the enormity of contemporary events such as the Vietnam War, the new journalists emerged in America during the 1960s with the publication of such books as In Cold Blood (1965) by Truman Capote (1924–84) and *Wolfe's* The Kandy-Kolored Flake Streamline Baby. Other notable works in the new journalism mold might include *Mailer's* The Armies of the Night, Wolfe's The Electric Kool-Aid Acid Test, and Dispatches (1974) by Michael Herr (b.1940). Wolfe described the aims of the movement in New Journalism (1973). See *faction*.

Newgate fiction: an early *form* of *crime fiction* popular in England in the 1830s, e.g. Paul Clifford (1830) by Edward Bulwer-Lytton (1803–73). The Newgate Calendar or Malefactors Register gave a record of scandalous crimes committed between 1700–74 and from 1826 onward, which provided excellent original material on which to base *novels*, some of which we might now describe as *faction*. Dickens's depiction of the criminal world in Oliver Twist was something of a reaction against Newgate fiction.

newspeak: jargon or official language that deliberately sets out to obscure the plain truth. The term was invented by *Orwell* in his *novel* Nineteen Eighty-Four.

Ngugi wa Thiong'o (b.1938): Kenyan novelist, *short story* writer, playwright, and essayist. He writes in English and his native Kikuyu, and among his *themes* of social and political injustice is the cultural and political necessity that Africans should write in their local language. Notable works include Weep Not, Child (1964, the first *novel* in English by an East African writer), A Grain of Wheat (1967), Petals of Blood (1977), Devil on the Cross (1980).

Nicholson, Norman (1914–87): English poet, playwright, and critic. Influenced by *T.S. Eliot* and *Wordsworth*, much of his *poetry* is *topographical* and draws on the people, industry, and general *setting* of his native town of Millom, Cumbria, and the adjacent Lake District countryside. He writes with imaginative vision about man in his natural environment. Notable works Include The Pot Geranium (1950), A Local Habitation (1972), The Lakes (1977, revised version of Portrait of the Lakes, 1963), Sea to the West (1981), Collected Poems (1994).

Nobel Prize for Literature: an international prize awarded every year since 1901 by the Swedish Academy in Stockholm to the writer who, in the opinion of the award-ing committee, has "produced in the field of *literature* the most outstanding work of an idealistic tendency." Former winners include *Yeats* (1923), *T.S. Eliot* (1948), *Faulkner* (1949), *Hemingway* (1954), *Steinbeck* (1962), *Beckett* (1969), *Patrick White* (1973), *Bellow* (1976), *Golding* (1983), *Soyinka* (1986), *Walcott* (1992), *Morrison* (1993).

noble savage: a term for uncivilized, but "noble" man, based on the concept that in a primeval time man was more worthy and honorable than modern man, who has been corrupted by modern civilization. This man is embodied in *Behn's* Oroonoko. The notion of the noble savage, close to nature, was attractive to writers during the *Romantic period*. See also *primitivism*.

nom de plume: another term for *pseudonym,* meaning literally "pen name" in French.

nonfiction novel: see *faction, new journalism.*

Norton, Thomas (1532–84): English playwright and poet, best known for co-authorship with *Sackville* of GORBODUC (1562), sometimes considered to be the first proper English stage *tragedy.* The play is written in *blank verse,* but the lines are overly regular and heavily *end-stopped,* and the result is mechanical and plodding.

nouveau roman: an experimental *avant-garde* type of *novel* that emerged in France during the mid-20th century. Established *devices* such as *plot, characterization, action,* and *narrative* were rejected in favor of a disconnected observation of things. See *antinovel.*

novel: a continuous piece of fictional *prose,* longer than a *short story* or *novella* and anything from 60,000–200,000 or even more words. It characteristically consists of *characters* within a *plot* that tells a *story,* covering any subject from any angle, and may range from the amusing to the tragic, from the easily accessible *thriller* to the most complex and experimental work. *Boccaccio's* 14th century DECAMERON, although essentially a *cycle* of short stories, is sometimes regarded as the forerunner of the novel. As regards the first "true novel" in English, some say *Bunyan's* PILGRIM'S PROGRESS, while others point to *Defoe's* ROBINSON CRUSOE or MOLL FLANDERS (an early example of a *picaresque* novel) or *Richardson's* PAMELA (an early example of the *epistolary novel*). After the 18th century rise of the novel, the 19th century saw its heyday in England with novelists such as *Austen,* the *Brontë* sisters, *George Eliot,* and *Thackeray* producing novels for a vast and avid market of readers. The novels of *Dickens* and others were first published in installment *form* in *periodicals,* making them easily available to a wide public. In the United States, *sentimental novels* by *Stowe* and *Alcott* were bestsellers, while the darker novels of *Hawthorne* and *Melville* explored the potential of *symbolism.* Later in the 19th century, *Twain* brought a distinctly American flavor to the picaresque *tradition.* By the late 19th and early 20th centuries the *genre* had been further stretched with *Hardy's* English *regional novels* and *Henry James's* international novels. In the 20th century *Joyce* and *Woolf* pioneered *stream of consciousness, Faulkner* and others experimented with *narrative style,* and others still used *magic realism.* Despite increasing competition from media such as television the novel has remained a popular form as more styles emerge and the genre is continually reinvented. See *antinovel, campus novel, crime novel, detective fiction, fabulation, gothic fiction, metafiction, modernism, narrator/narrative voice, nouveau roman, novel of adventure, novel of ideas, novel of sensation, novel of the soil, novelette, police procedural, propaganda literature, roman à clef, roman-fleuve, science fiction.*

novel of adventure: ROBINSON CRUSOE by *Defoe* is an example of this *genre,* which includes much *desert island fiction* and *romance literature.* Among exponents of this type are John Buchan (1875–1940), Anthony Hope (1863–1933), *Arthur Conan Doyle,* Alistair MacLean (1922–87), Nevil Shute (1899–1960).

novel of ideas: a type of *fiction* in which *dialog* and erudite debate are foremost rather than storyline and *character* development. One notable exponent is *Huxley* in *novels* such as CROME YELLOW and POINT COUNTER POINT.

novel of sensation: a *form* of *novel* popular from about the 1860s in which events are sensational and *melodramatic*, often involving crime and undisclosed secrets. Notable examples include *Collins*'s THE WOMAN IN WHITE and Mary Braddon's LADY AUDLEY'S SECRET (1862). Such novels may be regarded as forerunners of the *thriller* and *detective fiction*. See also *crime novel, gothic fiction, Newgate fiction*.

novel of sensibility: see *sentimental novel*.

novel of the soil: a *novel* where a major *theme* is man's relationship with the natural forces of the earth, e.g. *Steinbeck*'s THE GRAPES OF WRATH, *Lawrence*'s THE RAINBOW. See also *rural novel*.

novelette: a *fiction* shorter than a *novel* and longer than a *short story*. It can be used as a demeaning term for such as trivial *romances*. See *novella*.

novella has a similar meaning to *novelette*, but without its pejorative *connotations*. Sometimes the *plot* is restricted to the development of a single event. Examples are *Conrad*'s TYPHOON (1902), *Lawrence*'s THE VIRGIN AND THE GYPSY (1930), *Hemingway*'s THE OLD MAN AND THE SEA (1952).

Nowlan, Alden (1933–93): Canadian poet. Influenced, among others, by *William Carlos Williams*, his *poetry* focuses on such matters as family relationships and the damaging effects of puritanism. Notable works include THE ROSE AND THE PURITAN (1958), THE THINGS WHICH ARE (1962), SMOKED GLASS (1977).

Nowra, Louis (b.1950): Australian playwright. His theatrical, nonnaturalistic plays often explore individuals isolated in their own, obsessional, worlds. Notable works include ALBERT NAMES EDWARD (1975), VISIONS (1978), SUMMER OF ALIENS (1992), RADIANCE (1993).

objective correlative: a term used by *T.S. Eliot* to explain the notion that in all art, and especially *poetry*, every emotion should be defined objectively in relation to a set of facts. The term was made popular by Eliot in his *essay* "Hamlet and His Problems" (1919), in which he stated that Hamlet's emotions are excessive given his situation, and thus unrealistic; but that Macbeth's and Lady Macbeth's are appropriate to their situation. Eliot's idea was viewed quite favorably in the first part of the 20th century, but is nowadays considered too scientifically prescriptive.

objective criticism, popular among the *new critics*, advances the critical view that a piece of *literature*, once created, exists as an object in its own right, free of the writer and the reader. Its value is intrinsic, and its *context* is irrelevant. Since the advent of more recent *literary theories* this approach has fallen out of favor. See *close reading, intrinsic attitude, Leavisite, Richards.*

objectivism is achieved, it is supposed, when in a fictional work a writer presents events and *character*s' feelings in a detached and noncommittal fashion. *Henry James*'s *novels* and *Larkin*'s *poetry* have been, to some extent, so described. Subjectivism occurs in works such as *autobiography*, or in *conversation* or *lyric poems* such as *Coleridge*'s "Frost at Midnight" or *Wordsworth*'s "Tintern Abbey," in which the "I" *persona* is associated with the poet. In truth, few works are either wholly objective or subjective, but combine the two. See *narrator/narrative voice.*

objectivity: the concept of an objective "truth" to be discovered about the *meaning* of a work of *literature*. This concept was important to the *Leavisite* school, but since the advent of more recent *literary theories* has grown out of fashion. See *subjectivity.*

obligatory scene: a scene that a playwright is obliged to include because the development of the *drama* leads an audience to look forward to it. For instance, in *Shakespeare*'s MACBETH it would be difficult to imagine the play without an eventual confrontation between Macbeth and MacDuff.

oblique rhyme: another term for *half rhyme.*

obscurity, in *literature*, is when a reader is challenged to understand a writer because of such features as difficult language, strange sentence constructions, complex *verse forms*, use of foreign words, or multiple *allusion*. The term is often used to imply needless difficulty, inability to write clearly, or just incompetence; but sometimes the nature of a piece of writing demands treatment that is at first difficult for the reader but ultimately rewarding. *Johnson* disliked the *metaphysical* poets for their obscurity, *T.S. Eliot* was accused of it in THE WASTE LAND, as was *Joyce* in FINNEGANS WAKE.

O'Casey, Sean (1880–1964): Irish playwright and autobiographer. As a young man he developed socialist and republican sympathies. *Realism* and *tragicomedy* were hallmarks of his early plays, which dealt with such matters as poverty, patriotism, and survival. Later plays, beginning with THE SILVER TASSIE (1928), which was rejected by the Abbey Theatre, Dublin, and caused his rift with *Yeats*, are more *expressionist*. His six-volume *autobiography* has been much admired. Other notable works include THE SHADOW OF A GUNMAN (1923), JUNO AND THE PAYCOCK (1924), THE PLOUGH AND THE STARS (1926), WITHIN THE GATES (1933), THE STAR TURNS RED (1940).

occasional verse is *verse* written for a particular occasion, e.g. *Marvell's* "An Horatian Ode upon Cromwell's Return from Ireland," *Tennyson's* "The Charge of the Light Brigade." The *poet laureate* especially might be expected to write such *verse*, as in the latter example. See *elegy, ode.*

occupatio is a *rhetorical device*, much loved of politicians, whereby a subject is raised by stating that it should not be raised, e.g. "It is not appropriate to remind you that..."

O'Connor, Flannery (1925–64): American novelist and *short story* writer. With grim, *ironic humor* and in a clear, vivid *style* she deals with such subjects as religious fanaticism, spiritual poverty, and violence. Her writing has variously been described as poetic and *gothic*. Notable works include WISE BLOOD (1952), A GOOD MAN IS HARD TO FIND (1955), THE VIOLENT BEAR IT AWAY (1960).

octameter: see *meter.*

octave, or octet, is a *stanza* or section of *verse* containing eight lines, usually defined by a unit of *rhyme* pattern.

octosyllabic couplet: in *verse*, a pair of rhymed *tetrameters*, usually iambic but occasionally trochaic. Among others *Chaucer, Milton, Coleridge, Wordsworth*, and *Byron* used the *form*, and a good example is *Marvell's* "To His Coy Mistress." See *meter.*

ode: a kind of *lyric* in which the poet reflects on a particular subject in a serious *tone* and a lofty *style*. The original odes were written by the Greek poet Pindar as hymns of praise to winners of the Olympic Games and other sporting events. The *genre* was developed by the Latin poet Horace, and made popular in England by Abraham Cowley (1618–67), since when many poets have written odes including *Dryden* ("Song for St. Cecilia's Day," 1687), *Gray* ("Ode on a Distant Prospect of Eton College," 1747), *Coleridge* ("Dejection: An Ode"), *Wordsworth* ("Ode: Intimations of Immortality"), *Percy Shelley* ("Ode to the West Wind"), and of course, *Keats*, who wrote six famous odes.

Odets, Clifford (1906–63): American playwright and screenwriter. His first play, an *agitprop drama* called WAITING FOR LEFTY (1935), established him as a so-called "proletarian playwright," but he is essentially a writer of realistic plays with a tendency toward *sentimentality*, particularly in his later writing for Hollywood. Other notable works include AWAKE AND SING! (1935), PARADISE LOST (1935), GOLDEN BOY (1937), ROCKET TO THE MOON (1938), THE COUNTRY GIRL (1950).

Okara, Gabriel (b.1921): Nigerian poet and novelist. He is noted for his use of *oral tradition* in his writing, especially his *lyric poetry*. Notable works include THE VOICE (1964), THE FISHERMAN'S INVOCATION (1978).

Okpewho, Isidore (b.1941): Nigerian novelist and critic. His creative writing nearly always has a political agenda concerning his native land. Notable works include THE VICTIMS (1970), THE LAST DUTY (1976), MYTH IN AFRICA: A STUDY OF ITS AESTHETIC AND CULTURAL RELEVANCE (1983), TIDES (1993).

Okri, Ben (b.1959): Nigerian novelist, *short story* writer, and poet. His clear, concise *prose* conveys detailed observations of both individual and social responses to situations, often within the *context* of a strong sense of African place. Notable works include FLOWERS AND SHADOWS (1980), THE LANDSCAPES WITHIN (1981), INCIDENTS AT THE SHRINE (1986), STARS OF THE NEW CURFEW (1989), THE FAMISHED ROAD (1991), AN AFRICAN ELEGY (1992), DANGEROUS LOVE (1996).

Old English/Anglo-Saxon period: generally taken to refer to *literature* written and language spoken in England between approximately AD449 (the arrival of the first English-speaking tribes on the shores of Britain) and 1066 (the Norman Conquest).

Oliver, Mary (b.1935): American poet. Through sharp descriptions and straightforward language she explores the relationship between the individual and the natural world. Notable works include TWELVE MOONS (1979), AMERICAN PRIMITIVE (1983), HOUSE OF LIGHT (1990), THE CHANCE TO LOVE EVERYTHING (2000).

Olson, Charles (1910–70): American poet, critic, and influential leader of the "Black Mountain" school of *poetry*, originating at Black Mountain College in North Carolina where Olson was chancellor. He invented the term "Projective Verse" to describe his work, and believed that *form* should not dictate the construction of poetry – rather, *content* and free-flowing "perception" should be allowed precedence. Notable works include THE MAXIMUS POEMS (1960), THE ARCHAEOLOGIST OF MORNING (1971).

omniscient narrator: see *narrator/narrative voice*.

Ondaatje, Michael (b.1943): Canadian novelist and poet, born in Sri Lanka. His work is considered an important contribution to Canadian postmodernist writing. Much of his work explores the problems of an individual's past within a wider cultural history. His *poetry* is often dark and surreal, gaining the attention of the reader through arresting juxtapositions. In THE COLLECTED WORKS OF BILLY THE KID (1970) and RUNNING IN THE FAMILY (1982) he mixes *prose*, *verse*, and photographs. Other notable works include THE DAINTY MONSTERS (1967), THE MAN WITH SEVEN TOES (1969), RAT JELLY (1973), IN THE SKIN OF A LION (1987), THE CINNAMON PEELER (1990), THE ENGLISH PATIENT (1992).

one-act play: a *drama* played with no interval and usually of less than an hour's duration. Although the one-act play was once much more popular than it is today, some modern *dramatists* have excelled in the *genre*, e.g. *Pinter* with such plays as THE DUMB WAITER (1959) and LANDSCAPE (1968).

one-man show: (or, more correctly, one-person show) see *monodrama*.

O'Neill, Eugene (1888–1953): American playwright. Influenced by *Ibsen* and *Strindberg*, his powerfully theatrical plays, which through *expressionism* and a variety of other *styles* tackle subjects such as self-deception and self-destruction, have had great influence on American theater. Notable works include THE EMPEROR JONES (1920), ANNA CHRISTIE (1921), THE HAIRY APE (1922), ALL GOD'S CHILLUN GOT WINGS (1924), MOURNING BECOMES ELECTRA (1931), THE ICEMAN COMETH (1946), LONG DAY'S JOURNEY INTO NIGHT (1956).

onomatopoeia is a term used in both a narrow and a broad sense:

- the narrow sense confines the term to the use of words whose sound closely represents their *meaning*, e.g. "bang," "smack," "whisper"
- the broader definition allows the term to cover any way in which language closely suggests that which it denotes, extending beyond sound to, for instance, touch, appearance, or movement. In "Ode to Psyche" *Keats* describes the lovers as "couched," which gives a tactile sense of softness not possible had he simply written "lying." In his "Essay on Criticism" *Pope* talks of the sound echoing the sense (onomatopoeia is sometimes called "echoism") and gives as an example:

> When Ajax strives some rock's vast weight to throw
> The line too labors, and the words move slow

open couplet: a *couplet* in *verse* where the sense is not complete by the end of the second line, but carries over into the following lines, e.g.

> There anchoring, Peter chose from man to hide,
> There hang his head, and view the lazy tide
> In its hot slimy channel slowly glide;
>
> (from *Crabbe*'s THE BOROUGH)

open stage: any *form* of staging whereby the audience is not separated from the actors by a *proscenium arch*. Open staging has become increasingly popular again over the past century after a break of almost three centuries.

opera: a *drama* in which all the words are entirely, or almost entirely, sung. Potentially a very powerful *form* of drama, it has drawn few writers from other literary disciplines to be librettists, but opera has drawn much from *literature*, e.g. adaptations by the composer Benjamin Britten (1913–76) of *Melville*'s BILLY BUDD, *Henry James*'s THE TURN OF THE SCREW, and *Crabbe*'s story of Peter Grimes from THE BOROUGH.

oral literature/tradition: the composing and passing on of *stories* by word of mouth, often in poetic *form*. A tradition of creating *epics*, *ballads*, and *lyrics* (folk *songs*) has existed since primitive times, and is still practiced today in illiterate or semiliterate communities. The Anglo-Saxon epic BEOWULF has its origins in such a tradition.

oration: a speech delivered at a formal public occasion, e.g. Mark Antony's oration at Caesar's funeral in *Shakespeare*'s JULIUS CAESAR.

organic form is where the *form* of a work arises naturally out of the writer's subject and *theme*, growing and taking shape like a living organism, rather than being imposed by a set of rules as in *mechanic form*. It has been noted that, among others, *Shakespeare* and his fellow *dramatists*, as well as *Coleridge* and his fellow *Romantics*, favored organic form.

orientalism may loosely be described as Western writing on, and fascination with, things of the East. Such an interest began during the *Renaissance* and gathered pace in the 18th century, *Romantic* poets such as *Coleridge* and *Byron* often turning to oriental *themes* and *settings*. The rise of the British Empire stimulated *novels* located in the East, e.g. the work of *Kipling, Forster, Paul Scott, Farrell*; and also much *travel literature* by such as *Naipaul, Stark, Theroux, Thesiger*, William Dalrymple (b.1965).

originality is the discovery and use of innovative writing and the rejection of *imitation* or *convention*, whether of *form* or subject matter. Modern writers tend to consider originality to be more important than did earlier writers such as *Shakespeare* and *Milton*.

Orton, Joe (1933–67): English playwright and novelist. He explored violence, perversion, sex, and corruption, among other aspects of human behavior, to create sparkling, anarchic, deliberately tasteless and often farcical *black comedy*. Notable works include Entertaining Mr. Sloane (1964), Loot (1965), What the Butler Saw (1969).

Orwell, George (real name Eric Arthur Blair, 1903–50): English novelist, essayist, and journalist. In his clear and economic *style*, never using more words than necessary to convey his *meaning*, he writes of such matters as his deliberately chosen poverty in Paris and London, his observations of unemployment and his prophetic fears of the political manipulation of language (especially in his *essay* "Politics and the English Language," 1946). He is best known for Animal Farm (1945), an *allegory* on revolutions, and the grim Nineteen Eighty-Four (1949), both *satires* about totalitarianism and state control. Other notable works include Down and Out in Paris and London (1933), The Road to Wigan Pier (1937), Collected Essays, Journalism and Letters (1968).

Osborne, John (1929–94): English playwright and autobiographer. Leader of the so-called *angry young men*, he was still in his twenties when he wrote the landmark play Look Back in Anger (1956), which changed the direction of mainstream theater, moving it away from the *drawing room comedy* and the *well-made play* toward *kitchen sink drama*. Other notable works include The Entertainer (1957), Luther (1961), Inadmissable Evidence (1964), A Better Class of Person (1985), Déjà Vu (1992).

Osofisan, Femi (b.1946): Nigerian playwright and novelist. Influenced by *Soyinka*, he is interested in writing consciously politically plays in the widest sense. Notable works include A Restless Run of Locusts (1970), The Chattering and the Song (1974), Kolera Kolej (1975, *novel*), Yungba Yungba and the Dance Contest (1995).

Osundare, Niyi (b.1947): Nigerian poet. Using *oral* and literary *traditions*, lyricism and *satire*, his much acclaimed *poetry* shows concern for social justice. He is a well known *performance poet*. Notable works include Songs of the Market Place (1983), The Eye of the Earth (1986).

ottava rima: a *stanza* of eight ten-syllable *iambic* lines rhyming ababcc, pioneered by *Wyatt* who imported the *form* from Italy. It was used by *Keats* in "Isabella" and *Yeats* in "Sailing to Byzantium" (1928). It is sometimes known as a Byronic stanza because *Byron* used it with great success in his *narrative poem* Don Juan; he exploited the comic potential of the *rhyme scheme*, especially the final *rhyming couplet*, and the effect is enhanced by the *feminine endings* of the a and c *rhymes*.

Otway, Thomas (1652–85): English playwright and poet. Influenced by French playwrights, especially Jean Racine (1639–99), he wrote *drama* in both *blank verse* and *heroic couplets*, some of his tragic writing achieving a power not heard on stage since the *Jacobean age*. Notable works include Don Carlos (1676), The Orphan (1680), Venice Preserv'd (1682).

outsider: a term sometimes applied to writers such as *Kerouac*, or *characters* such as Holden Caulfield in *Salinger*'s THE CATCHER IN THE RYE, who are in some sense outsiders, detached from the society that surrounds them. The concept gained currency through THE OUTSIDER (1956) by Colin Wilson (b.1931).

Owen, Wilfred (1893–1918): English poet. Usually regarded as one of the finest of the *war poets*, he writes with passion and compassion, and with technical mastery over *meter*, *assonance*, and *rhyme*, of the futility of war and human suffering. Most of his best-known *poems* were written between the summer of 1917 and his death shortly before the November 1918 armistice. Notable works include "Dulce et Decorum Est," "Strange Meeting," "Futility," all in THE COMPLETE POEMS AND FRAGMENTS (1983). See *war literature*.

oxymoron: a *form* of verbal *paradox* wherein apparently contradictory words are combined with arresting effect, e.g. "loving hate" (from *Shakespeare*'s ROMEO AND JULIET) or "marriage hearse" (from *Blake*'s "London," 1794). See *antithesis*.

pageant: originally a cart or wagon upon which medieval *mystery plays* were performed, the word has come to refer to a sometimes spectacular *dramatic* presentation of historical events.

palilogy is the *rhetorical device* of deliberately repeating a word or words for emphatic effect. See *amplification, repetition.*

pamphlet: a short, unbound booklet, usually discussing a topical issue about which a writer feels strongly. The advantage of the pamphlet is that it is quite easy to produce and distribute, and is thus especially favored by *underground* writers, political dissidents, and revolutionaries. This means of communication has been used by many authors such as *Defoe, Dekker, Robert Greene, Milton, More, Percy Shelley, Jonathan Swift.*

panegyric: a speech or *poem* delivered in public, fervently praising someone or something, e.g. Mark Antony's funeral *oration* in praise of Caesar in *Shakespeare*'s JULIUS CAESAR.

panoramic method: another term for third-person narrative. See *narrator/narrative voice.*

paradox: a statement or situation that contains an apparent contradiction. *Wilde* uses paradox and *wit* to great effect in his plays, e.g. in his THE IMPORTANCE OF BEING EARNEST where Algernon, upon hearing that a certain Lady Harbury has been widowed, comments that he hears "her hair has turned quite gold from grief," paradoxically implying that her husband's death has had a rejuvenating effect upon her and her lifestyle. Other types of paradox can be dark, disturbing, or philosophical. *Shakespeare* used paradox to great effect in his SONNETS, which frequently reveal the puzzling contradictions of love, time, and human existence. See *antithesis, oxymoron.*

paraliterature is a name given to works such as certain mass-market *romance*s or *thriller*s that are not considered good enough to be called *literature.*

parallelism is where phrases or sentences of similar construction are set side by side in order to create an effect of balance or *antithesis*, e.g.

> I celebrate myself, and sing myself,
> And what assume you shall assume,
> For every atom belonging to me as good belongs to you.
>
> (*Whitman*'s "Song of Myself," 1881)

pararhyme: see *half rhyme.*

Park, Mungo (1771–1806): Scottish travel writer and explorer. A friend of *Walter Scott*, he determined in his travels the direction of the flow of the Niger, and his intrepid adventures became famous as a result of his graphic TRAVELS IN THE INTERIOR DISTRICTS OF AFRICA (1799).

Parkman, Francis (1823–93): American historian and travel writer who did much to chronicle the pioneering development of America by the French and English.

Notable works include THE CALIFORNIA AND OREGON TRAIL (1849), HISTORY OF THE CONSPIRACY OF THE PONTIAC (1851), A HALF-CENTURY OF CONFLICT (1892).

parody: the *imitation* of a particular *style* of writing or subject, usually for humorous effect. *Fielding*'s SHAMELA (1741) and JOSEPH ANDREWS are both parodies of *Richardson*'s novel PAMELA; *Austen*'s NORTHANGER ABBEY is a parody of the *gothic novel*; and *Gibbons*'s COLD COMFORT FARM parodies popular steamy rural *romances*, especially those of *Webb*. See *burlesque*.

passion play: a medieval religious *drama* representing Christ's crucifixion, usually performed on Good Friday, and sometimes incorporated into a cycle of *mystery plays*.

pastiche: a patchwork made up from bits and pieces of the work of a writer that constitutes a type of *imitation*, either as a tribute, an entertainment, or a *parody*.

pastoral, meaning "to do with shepherds," refers in a literary sense to the quality of a work that paints a pleasant, idealized view of life in the countryside. The ancient Greek and Roman writings of Theocritus (early 3rd century) and Virgil (70–19BC) respectively provided models for *Renaissance* pastoral *poems*, plays, and *prose romances* such as *Spenser*'s "Shepheardes Calendar," *Sidney*'s ARCADIA, ROSALYNDE (1590) by Thomas Lodge (1558–1625), *Marlowe*'s "The Passionate Shepherd to His Love." Pastorals have always been popular as escape *literature* for those living in town or at court, and *Shakespeare*'s AS YOU LIKE IT (based on ROSALYNDE) is so named because Shakespeare wished to portray elements of rural life as people liked to see them. Various *forms* of the pastoral remained popular in succeeding centuries through the writings of *Pope, Wordsworth, Blake, Clare*, and lesser writers, although there was an increasing tendency to portray country life with greater *realism*, as in *Crabbe*'s THE VILLAGE which sets out to portray aspects of rural life "As truth will paint it, and as bards will not." See also *topographical poetry*.

pastoral elegy: a *form* of *elegy* derived from classical writers that developed an elaborate set of *conventions* whereby, among other things, all nature is said to be involved in mourning someone, yet a springlike reawakening is promised, in part through the suggestion of the immortality of the dead one. Famous examples of this *genre* are *Milton*'s "Lycidas" and *Percy Shelley*'s ADONAIS.

pathetic: "worthy of *pathos*," "poignant," or "moving" are the true literary meanings of this word, which should not be used in the modern slang sense in writing about *literature*.

pathetic fallacy: a 19th century term for ascribing human qualities to nature. The most common example is the attribution of bad weather to a deliberate intention on the part of nature, as in *Hardy*'s THE RETURN OF THE NATIVE where the difficult conditions on Egdon Heath are for Eustacia Vye a result of deliberately hostile nature, whereas for the down-to-earth Thomasin they are merely the impartial actions of nature. *Shakespeare*'s King Lear admits the possibility of pathetic fallacy when, battered by the storm, he directly addresses the elements at the beginning of act III of KING LEAR.

pathos: an element in a work that evokes in an audience or reader feelings of grief, pity, and sorrow, e.g. the death of the Duchess in act IV, scene 2 of *Webster*'s THE DUCHESS OF MALFI, or the deaths of the children in *Hardy*'s JUDE THE OBSCURE.

Sometimes pathos has been overexploited, especially by novelists, a frequently cited example being the death of Little Nell in *Dickens*'s THE OLD CURIOSITY SHOP (1840–41).

Paton, Alan (1903–88): South African novelist, *short story* writer, biographer, and autobiographer. In CRY, THE BELOVED COUNTRY (1948) he brought the plight of black South Africans to the attention of the world, and much of his subsequent writing concerned the issue of apartheid. Other notable works include TOO LATE THE PHALAROPE (1953), DEBBIE GO HOME (1961, published in the United States in 1965 as TALES FROM A TROUBLED LAND).

Patten, Brian (b.1946): English poet and children's writer. One of the *Liverpool poets*, he ranges in his writing from *ironic* social criticism to tender lyrical *love poetry*. Notable works include GRINNING JACK (1990); GARGLING WITH JELLY (1988) and THAWING FROZEN FROGS (1990) are highly regarded *collections* of *poetry* for children.

pattern poetry is an early type of *concrete poetry* in the *form* of a *stanza* which creates a design or picture on the page, e.g. *Herbert*'s "Easter Wings" (1633).

Paulin, Tom (b.1949): Irish poet, literary critic, and playwright. His work is sometimes bleak, concerned with the sociopolitical situation in Northern Ireland. He often uses the Ulster dialect and urban *settings*. Notable works include A STATE OF JUSTICE (1977), THE STRANGE MUSEUM (1980), LIBERTY TREE (1983), IRELAND AND THE ENGLISH CRISIS (1984).

Peacock, Thomas Love (1785–1866): English satirist, poet, and essayist. Amusing, clever, and radical, he wrote *stories* and created *settings* that are sometimes *parodies* of the kind of *gothic romance* that was popular at the time. Notable works include HEADLONG HALL (1816), NIGHTMARE ABBEY (1818), MAID MARIAN (1822), CROTCHET CASTLE (1831), GRYLL GRANGE (1860–61).

penny dreadful was a name given in the late 19th century to a work of adventure, crime, action, and/or mystery not intended to be great *literature*. It was printed on and bound in paper and sold for a penny. See *detective fiction, melodrama, thriller*.

pentameter: see *meter*.

perfect rhyme, sometimes known as "full" or "true" *rhyme*, is rhyme in which the rhyming vowel and consonants are identical, but not the consonants preceding the vowel, as in launch/paunch.

performance poetry: *poetry* specifically written for public performance. See *Beat movement* writers, *Liverpool poets, Lochhead*.

performance poets: poets who do public readings of their own *poetry*, which may be *performance poetry*, but may originally have been written with the reader in mind.

period is a term used to categorize *literature* within a timescale. A period may refer to:

- a general span of time (e.g. *Renaissance*)
- the reign of a monarch (e.g. *Victorian*)
- a movement (e.g. *Romantic*).

All are very general terms and imposed retrospectively, originating before and spilling beyond any defined starting or ending date. Even terms such as Elizabethan are imprecise (see *Elizabethan drama*).

periodic essay: an *essay* published in a *periodical*.

periodical: a magazine or *journal* that appears at regular intervals, e.g. weekly or monthly.

peripeteia is a reversal in the *hero* or *heroine*'s fortunes – in *tragedy*, for the worse; in *comedy*, for the better. The term is usually applied to the former, as when in *Shakespeare*'s KING LEAR the King is reduced by the actions of his daughters to a pitiful figure out in a raging storm. See *Aristotle*.

periphrasis: the use of indirect, longwinded language, e.g. by Polonius in act II, scene 2 of *Shakespeare*'s HAMLET when he is trying to explain his theory regarding Hamlet's "madness" to the King and Queen.

peroration: the conclusion or winding up of an *oration* or highly formal piece of writing, often used to imply pomposity.

persona: originally referring to a mask worn by actors and changed in order to assume a different *character*, the term has come to mean the identity assumed by the writer of a *story* or *poem*. See *narrator/narrative voice*.

personification is the treating of an idea as if it were a person with human qualities; e.g. in "Composed upon Westminster Bridge, September 3, 1802" *Wordsworth* writes of London wearing "the beauty of the morn… like a garment"; and in the middle *stanza* of his "To Autumn" *Keats* deals with autumn as if the season were an aging man.

perspective: see *narrator/narrative voice*.

Petrarch (1304–74): Italian poet and *humanist*, and friend of *Boccaccio*, who was an enthusiastic student of ancient Greek and Latin *literature*, and whose inventive *verse* had a marked influence upon English *Renaissance* writers such as *Wyatt* and *Surrey*, especially as regards the *sonnet form* and *lyric love poetry*.

Petrarchan sonnet: see *sonnet*.

Petrarchism: any *imitation* of the *manner* of the Italian poet *Petrarch*. Among his English followers were *Wyatt, Surrey, Sidney, Spenser*, and *Shakespeare*.

phallocentric literature is a term from *feminist criticism* used to describe *literature* that is said to reinforce the notion of society organized according to masculine priorities.

Phillips, Caryl (b.1958): British playwright and novelist, born in St. Kitts. His tense, naturalistic plays tend to focus on Caribbean families in Britain and the West Indies. Notable works include STRANGE FRUIT (1980), WHERE THERE IS DARKNESS (1982), THE FINAL PASSAGE (1985), HIGHER GROUND (1989), PLAYING AWAY (1987), CROSSING THE RIVER (1993).

picaresque is a term given to a *narrative* that relates the adventures of a likable rogue ("picaro" is the Spanish for "rogue") whose *character* develops little during the course of his escapades. DON QUIXOTE (1605) by the Spaniard Miguel de Cervantes (1547–1616), although it does not conform in all respects and was not the first, is sometimes considered the father of the picaresque *novel*. The earliest example in English is THE UNFORTUNATE TRAVELLER (1594) by Thomas Nashe (1567–1601), and later notable examples that are either typically or partly picaresque include *Defoe*'s MOLL FLANDERS (a rare case where the leading figure is female), *Fielding*'s TOM JONES, *Smollett*'s RODERICK RANDOM, *Twain*'s THE ADVENTURES OF TOM SAWYER, *Bellow*'s THE ADVENTURES OF AUGIE MARCH. An example of picaresque narrative in *verse* is *Byron*'s DON JUAN.

picturesque: having the quality of a picture. In *literature*, seeking out beauty in nature, or the picturesque, became almost a cult in the 18th century, with many poets and other writers such as *Addison, Pope, Gray*, various *gothic* novelists, *Walter Scott*, and others incorporating picturesque descriptions into their work. This tendency is related to *Romanticism*, although some say that it is a superficial manifestation of the true Romantic's deeper responses to the power of nature. *Austen* in MANSFIELD PARK and *Peacock* in HEADLONG HALL make fun of it.

Pinter, Harold (b.1930): English playwright and screenwriter. Heavily influenced by *Beckett* and *theater of the absurd*, his plays consolidated a striking change in the direction of British *drama* in the 1950s. The histories and memories of his *characters* often play a key part in his plays, which sometimes contain a strong *subtext* of suppressed menace, and vary in their level of *realism*. Notable works include THE BIRTHDAY PARTY (1958), initially little appreciated but now often regarded as a minor *classic*, THE CARETAKER (1960), A SLIGHT ACHE (1961), THE HOMECOMING (1965), OLD TIMES (1971), NO MAN'S LAND (1975), BETRAYAL (1978).

Pirandello, Luigi (1867–1936): Italian playwright, *short story* writer, and novelist. He challenged theatrical *conventions* of *naturalism* and influenced many playwrights including *Beckett* and *O'Neill*. Notable works include RIGHT YOU ARE, IF YOU THINK SO (1917), SIX CHARACTERS IN SEARCH OF AN AUTHOR (1921), HENRY IV (1922).

pirate edition: an edition of a *text* that has been copied for profit, e.g. the so-called "bad" quarto of HAMLET, which was probably pirated by a member of *Shakespeare*'s own company so that the play could be performed elsewhere. There was at that time no copyright law to protect the *author*; nowadays such practice is illegal.

plagiarism is the unacknowledged and wholesale lifting of *text* from another source by a writer or student.

plaint: any poetic *lament*. See *complaint, elegy*.

Plath, Sylvia (1932–63): American poet and novelist. She separates herself from her *poetry* by the use of characteristically *ironic* and disturbing *tones* and undertones. Notable works include THE COLOSSUS (1960, the only work published before her suicide), the semiautobiographical *novel* THE BELL JAR (1963), ARIEL (1965), CROSSING THE WATER (1971), THE JOURNALS OF SYLVIA PLATH (1982).

Plato (?427–?347BC): ancient Greek philosopher and writer. His profound thoughts and platonic *themes* have had a significant influence on subsequent writers. Books 2, 3, and 10 of his THE REPUBLIC are good introductions to the nature of *literature*. Other notable works include EUTHYPHRO, PROTAGORAS, GORGIAS (thought to be his earliest works), CRITO, APOLOGY, PHAEDO (thought to have been written between 371–367BC), THE LAWS. The dates of most of his writings are uncertain.

plot: the writer's organization of a web of interconnected events in a play or *story* which build up the overall storyline. It is a more precise word than story because it denotes the deliberate organization of cause and effect of events within a scheme. *Forster*'s book ASPECTS OF THE NOVEL contains some useful definitions of the word "plot." See *subplot*.

pluralism/plurality: being numerous; in *literature*, a term conveying the idea that there are a multiplicity of ways of reading *texts*, and that there is no "correct" answer as to what a given text means. It is an essential awareness that students of literature must possess that different readers will read texts in different ways at different times, and that by taking into account varying perspectives a student may gain a wider understanding of what he or she reads. See also *deconstruction*.

pluralist criticism accepts a *plurality* of approach to *texts*. Deconstructuralists advocate this approach. Structuralist *criticism*, and attitudes that embrace a particular ideology, such as *Marxist criticism*, tend to disapprove. See *deconstruction, prescriptive criticism, structuralism*.

Poe, Edgar Allan (1809–49): American *short story* writer and poet, sometimes regarded as an archetypal *gothic* horror writer. By taking rationality to the extreme, his heavily paradoxical *style* often explores the beauty of the dead or dying and the deepest regions of human psychology, fear, and even split personalities. Poe's poetic philosophy was admired by the French writer Baudelaire (1821–67), and through him influenced the entire *symbolist movement*. Notable works include "The Fall of the House of Usher" (1839), "The Murders in the Rue Morgue" (1841), "The Black Cat" (1843), "The Pit and the Pendulum" (1843), THE RAVEN AND OTHER POEMS (1845).

poem: any composition that may be described as *poetry* or *verse*.

poesie is an archaic term for *poetry* or, more specifically, the act of creating poetry. *Keats* uses the term in this sense in "Ode to a Nightingale." *Wordsworth* defines the act of creating poetry as "emotion recollected in tranquillity."

poet laureate is a largely honorary post awarded in Britain in recognition of a poet's achievements. Originally the holder was required to write *occasional verse* for particular events such as a monarch's coronation but nowadays this requirement, like the stipend, is nominal. Among former holders are *Dryden* (1668–89), *Wordsworth* (1843–50), *Tennyson* (1850–92), and *Ted Hughes* (1984–99) and the current holder is *Motion* (1999–). Various American states appoint a poet laureate (the first to do so was California in 1915), and since 1986 there has been a national laureate. *Warren* was the first official US poet laureate; others include *Dove* (1993–95), Robert Pinsky (1997–2000), and *Billy Collins* (2001–).

poetaster: a derogatory word for an inferior poet.

poetic diction refers to a choice of words or language favored by poets at any particular time. The phrase is most often applied to the idea, common among the *neoclassical* poets of the 18th century, that *poetry* should be written in an artificially elevated language that should not be debased by the use of everyday words. In general, Latin-based words were preferred to direct Anglo-Saxon ones. *Gray* considered that "the language of the age is never the language of poetry." Examples of the poetic diction of this period are "feathered breed" for "birds," "finny tribe" for "fish," "milky race" for "cows," "purple groves pomaceous" for "orchards," "rich saponeaceous loam" for "good soil," and so forth. Some even considered it crude to use the word "ever" (always "e'er") or "over" ("o'er"). In the hands of the best poets of the period such as Gray or *Pope*, such poetic diction can be effective and very *witty*. However, it was such language against which *Wordsworth*, *Coleridge*, and other *Romantics* reacted, Wordsworth referring in his *preface* to the LYRICAL BALLADS to "the gaudiness and inane phraseology of many modern writers"; and elsewhere he declared his aim of writing in "the ordinary language of ordinary men." He did not always achieve his *naturalistic* aim (all art is, after all, by definition artificial); but his opinions have shaped the thinking of poets ever since.

poetic drama refers to any *drama* in which the *dialog* is written in *verse*, usually *blank verse*. *Elizabethan drama* is the most famous of the type. Thereafter there was some *closet drama* written in verse, but little of note until the 20th century when there was a brave attempt to revive popular interest in the *form* by, among others, *T.S. Eliot*, as in MURDER IN THE CATHEDRAL, and Christopher Fry (b.1907), as in THE LADY'S NOT FOR BURNING (1949).

poetic license is a term that covers:

- a taking of liberty with language and syntax by poets in order to create effects not strictly available according to the laws of *prose*
- mistakes, deliberate or through ignorance, made by writers in any medium that are trivial but still worry pedantic critics.

poetic prose: see *prose poem*.

poeticism is a term sometimes used pejoratively to denote the kind of artificial *poetic diction* against which *Wordsworth* reacted.

poetry is a term variously used to cover writing that:

- is written in any kind of *meter* (but this would not cover *free verse*)
- has any kind of pattern
- is written with a sense of the music of language, and not just for *meaning*.

Two definitions by famous poets are:

- "The spontaneous overflow of powerful feelings" (*Wordsworth*)
- "The best words in the best order" (*Coleridge*).

A lesser-known poet once described poetry as "words working overtime." The word poetry tends to be used for more significant (but not necessarily more serious) writing than *verse*.

point of attack: the point in a *story* or play where the main *action* commences.

point of reference: taken from art, this term has come to denote the perspective of a normal *character* in a world of excessive behavior. Kent in *Shakespeare's* KING LEAR may be regarded as such a figure.

point of view: see *narrator/narrative voice*.

polemic: a vigorously argued, nonobjective piece of writing on a controversial subject such as politics or religion, e.g. *Milton's* AREOPAGITICA. Other notable polemicists include *Jonathan Swift, Shaw*.

police procedural: a term for *realistic* crime *stories* in which the central figure is a professional police officer (rather than the clever amateur detective of *detective fiction* who often makes the police appear incompetent), e.g. *P.D. James*'s Dalgleish or Colin Dexter's (b.1930) Inspector Morse.

polyrhythmic refers to a *poem* which has various metrical patterns.

polysyndeton: the repeated use of conjunctions, as in *Hemingway*'s frequent use of "and" to string together phrases and clauses. The opposite of *asyndeton*.

Pope, Alexander (1688–1744): English poet, satirist, and critic. His lively, *witty*, and strictly metrical *verse* often focuses on the fashionable trends of his society and the landscape, and he is often cited as the most characteristic and best of neoclassical poets (see *neoclassicism*). Notable works include THE PASTORALS (1709), AN ESSAY ON CRITICISM (1711), THE RAPE OF THE LOCK (1712), THE DUNCIAD (1728), MORAL ESSAYS (1731–35).

popular novel: referring to any bestselling *novel*, the term often implies writing that is downmarket and not "real *literature*," yet many critically well-regarded writers such as *Le Carré* are also considered "popular."

pornography, in *literature*, is writing that is of an explicitly sexual nature and designed to arouse sexual appetite. The term is often used to refer to writing that is merely obscene and has no literary merit, but there is a long history going back to ancient times of quality pornographic writing, and the definition of what is and is not pornographic depends very much on the public taste of the time. The obscenity trial in England in 1960 that resulted in the final publication of *Lawrence*'s LADY CHATTERLEY'S LOVER (written 1928) is one example of a shift in such taste. Pornography is sometimes categorized into:

- erotica, concerning heterosexual activity
- exotica, covering a wide range of other sexual activities.

Porter, Katherine Anne (1890–1980): American novelist and *short story* writer, whose Southern heritage underlies almost all her work. She is widely acclaimed as a master of short *fiction*, with a pure, unadorned *style* and a gift for capturing moments that represent the essence of human experience. Her foray into longer fiction, the controversial *novel* SHIP OF FOOLS (1962), was not a critical success. Other notable works include FLOWERING JUDAS (1930), PALE HORSE, PALE RIDER (1939), THE LEANING TOWER (1944), COLLECTED STORIES (1965).

postcolonial criticism seeks to place the *literature* and experience of former colonies within their own cultural context, reevaluating them and separating them from the assumptions of the previously dominant Western cultural view, which saw such continents as Africa from the "colonizers'" perspective. Postcolonial criticism has emerged alongside other *literary theory* such as *structuralism, poststructuralism, postmodernism, feminist,* and *Marxist criticism.*

postcolonial literature (in English) is writing in English that originates in former colonies of Great Britain or America, usually (but not always) written by inhabitants of that colony after colonial times. A frequent mark of postcolonial language is the emergence of a variant *form* of the mother tongue (sometimes indicated by the use of lower case for english to distinguish it from the English of England). Some critics accept as "postcolonial" any *literature* written in English that emerges at any time from such colonies, whether before, during, or after colonial status. Such literature often concerns, explicitly or implicitly, the cultural, political, and social impact of colonization. The term is sometimes resented by those who regard the colonial period as a phase they wish to forget. *Ngugi* writes in his native Kikuyu whenever possible as an anti-imperialist statement; *Achebe* uses English in order to reach a global audience. Notable examples of postcolonial writers include:

- Achebe, *Coetzee, Gordimer,* Ngugi, *Okri, Soyinka* from Africa
- *Hulme, Mansfield, Stead, Patrick White* from Australasia
- *Naipaul, Walcott* from the Caribbean
- *Desai, Seth* from Asia.

See *Commonwealth literature.*

postcolonial realistic period: a title sometimes used to cover American *literature* written between approximately 1865 and 1900.

postmodernism, simply put, refers to that which follows *modernism.* In general terms it covers *literature* written since 1945 (the end of World War II). Postmodernism continued the antitradition stance of modernism, but after the confidence in progress that is a feature of modernism, postmodernism reflects the kind of insecurity, doubt, and occasional nihilism caused by such disturbing realities as Nazi atrocities, environmental pollution, and the threat of extinction under the shadow of the nuclear bomb. *Beckett's* writings are characteristic of this *mood. Feminist, Marxist,* and *psychoanalytic criticism* are all aspects of postmodernism, and it is closely related to *poststructuralism.* See also *literary/critical theory.* Examples of postmodernist texts include *Lessing's* CANOPUS IN ARGOS (1979), *Nabokov's* PALE FIRE (1962), *Pynchon's* V. (1963), IN COLD BLOOD (1966) by Truman Capote (1924–84), SLAUGHTERHOUSE-FIVE (1969) by Kurt Vonnegut (b.1922), ZEN AND THE ART OF MOTORCYCLE MAINTENANCE (1974) by Robert Pirsig (b.1928), and the *new journalism* of *Wolfe* and others.

poststructuralism is an element of *postmodernism* that covers a whole range of ideas, some developed from and some in conflict with *structuralism.* Some poststructuralists argue that every word a writer commits to paper is influenced by the historical, political, and social culture of which s/he is a part, and nothing can be evaluated for its own sake. The most important aspect of *poststructuralist criticism* is *deconstruction.* The chief proponent of poststructuralism is the Frenchman Jacques Derrida (b.1930). See *feminist criticism, Marxist criticism, psychoanalytic criticism.*

poststructuralist criticism, the main aspect of which is *deconstruction*, is based on, among other things, the notion that the *meaning* of any *text* is unstable, and that it can mean an almost infinite number of things according to the varying perceptions of different readers.

pot-boiler: a derogatory term for a work written merely to make money.

Pound, Ezra (1885–1972): American poet, critic, and translator. His *avant-garde* rhythmical and musical *verse*, which spans a wide range of cultural references, was influenced by *Robert Browning's dramatic monologs* and was greatly admired by *T.S. Eliot,* whose own verse owes much to Pound's advice. Notable works include PERSONAE (1909, based on the impression *Yeats* made on him), LUSTRA (1916), and, most importantly, THE CANTOS (from 1925).

Powell, Anthony (1905–2000): English novelist. By turns *witty* and *satirical,* light or black in his *humor,* his writings often capture a certain *zeitgeist* of England in the 20th century. Notable works include AFTERNOON MEN (1931), A DANCE TO THE MUSIC OF TIME (a sequence of 12 *novels,* 1951–75), TO KEEP THE BALL ROLLING (four volumes of *journals,* 1976–82), THE FISHER KING (1986).

practical criticism is a term used to describe the *close reading* of *texts* advocated by *Richards* and the *Leavisite* approach to literary studies.

preface: an introduction to a literary work, e.g. *Wordsworth*'s "advertisement" before his and *Coleridge*'s LYRICAL BALLADS, or *Shaw*'s prefaces to his plays.

Pre-Raphaelite period: generally considered to cover *literature* written in England between approximately 1848 and 1860. See *Pre-Raphaelites.*

Pre-Raphaelites: a group of young English artists who in 1848 rejected the current fashion in art, returning to the ideals of simplicity and truthfulness that they regarded as existing before the time of the artist Raphael (1483–1529) and the Italian *Renaissance.* This interest in *medievalism,* influenced by *Spenser* and further stimulated by the *poetry* of *Keats* and *Tennyson,* spread to writers such as *Dante Gabriel Rossetti* (an artist and poet), William Morris (1834–96), *Swinburne,* and *Christina Rossetti,* who focused upon sensuousness, *symbolism,* and religious meaning in a *style* partly reminiscent of the medieval period. Significant works produced under this influence include Christina Rossetti's GOBLIN MARKET (1862), Dante Gabriel Rossetti's "The Blessed Damozel" (1850), William Morris's THE EARTHLY PARADISE (1868–70).

prescriptive criticism occurs when a *text* is approached not with an open mind on the part of the reader, but with a bias that it should conform to certain rules or expectations. The opposite approach is *pluralist criticism.* All readers cannot to some extent help approaching a text with their own prejudices, even when trying to be pluralist. See also *reader-response theory.*

presupposition: a term for the notions and preconceptions about the nature of the world that a reader brings to a *text.*

Priestley, J.B. (1894–1984): English playwright, novelist, critic, and broadcaster. A committed socialist, he was a prolific writer on such subjects as the English social classes, his travels around England, and his fascination with ideas of time, all of which proved very popular with readers and the theater-going public of the day. His radio broadcasts did much to foster national morale during World War II. Notable works include THE GOOD COMPANIONS (1929), ANGEL PAVEMENT (1930), DANGEROUS CORNER (1932), TIME AND THE CONWAYS (1937), WHEN WE ARE MARRIED (1938), AN INSPECTOR CALLS (1945), SATURN OVER THE WATER (1961), ALL ENGLAND LISTENED (1968, radio talk).

primitivism, in a literary sense, is a term applied to writers in every age who value the so-called "natural" above the "artificial," and who look back to a golden age of the past when all was simple goodness. In the 18th century these ideas converged to form the cult of the "*noble savage*," an ideal of primitive man who was unsophisticated and nonintellectual, but had natural moral dignity. Many aspects of primitivism are present in *Romanticism.*

Pritchett, V.S. (1900–97): English novelist, critic, and *short story* writer. Drawing on his personal traveling experiences, his writing displays an acute sense of observation. Notable works include MARCHING SPAIN (1928), DEAD MAN LEADING (1937), THE SPANISH TEMPER (1954), A CARELESS WIDOW (1989).

problem play: a term applied to

- a *drama of ideas*
- plays that are difficult to place into traditional categories such as *tragedy, comedy, history,* and so forth, such as *Shakespeare's* MEASURE FOR MEASURE (?1604), TROILUS AND CRESSIDA (?1602) or ALL'S WELL THAT ENDS WELL (?1602).

prolepsis is another term for *flashforward.* See also *anachorism, analepsis, flashback, in media res.*

proletarian novel: a *novel* about working-class life, at times a kind of *thesis novel.* Some of *Sillitoe's* work may be so described.

prolog: either

- an introduction to a work that is an integral part of it, e.g. *Chaucer's* "General Prologue" to THE CANTERBURY TALES. In *drama* it tends to be in the *form* of a *chorus,* as in *Shakespeare's* HENRY V; or
- the name of the *character* who speaks the chorus.

See *epilog, induction.*

propaganda literature is a term that applies to any work such as a *thesis novel* or *thesis play* that sets out to advance a particular political, religious, or sociological belief. See also *agitprop.*

proposition: in *literature,* a section of a work where the writer explicitly or implicitly states a main aim or *theme,* e.g. the opening lines of *Milton's* PARADISE LOST.

proscenium arch: an architectural frame around the stage, behind which the actors perform, with the audience seated in front of it. Theaters were thus constructed between 1660 and the 1900s, although since the mid-20th century the fashion has been for a return to the *open stage* in order to bring the actors back into closer contact with the audience.

prose is the term used to describe language that seeks to communicate *meaning* without using any of the *devices* of *poetry.*

prose poem is a term given to *prose* that is close to *poetry* in its use of language, and employs *devices* such as *rhythm* and *imagery.* Writers as varied as *Ashbery, T.S. Eliot, Faulkner, Joyce, Laurie Lee, Robert Lowell, Wilde,* and *Woolf* have all been described as writers of poetic prose.

prosody is the study of the art and science of every aspect of *versification.*

protagonist: the main *character* in a *story.* See *antagonist.*

protest literature is a term sometimes used to cover any kind of writing from *ballad* to funeral *oration* in which *voices* protest against a situation, e.g. *Percy Shelley's* THE MASK OF ANARCHY or *Bennett's* address attacking the media at the funeral of the broadcaster Russell Harty.

Proulx, Annie (b.1935): American novelist, *short story* writer, and journalist. Her work has been variously described as postmodernist, feminist, accessible, popular, *witty*, and comic, displaying both a regional and wider sense of American identity. Notable works include HEARTSONGS AND OTHER STORIES (1988), POSTCARDS (1991), THE SHIPPING NEWS (1993). See *regional novel*.

proverb: a short, pithy, saying that neatly sums up a widely accepted truth, e.g. "Look before you leap." Proverbs are popular in all cultures in all ages, printed *collection*s ranging from THE BOOK OF PROVERBS in the Old Testament of the *Bible* to The OXFORD DICTIONARY OF ENGLISH PROVERBS (1935). See *maxim*.

pseudonym: a pen name or *nom de plume* adopted by an *author*, e.g. Karen Blixen wrote under the name *Isak Dinesen.*

pseudo-statement: a term invented by *Richards* to denote poetic truth, which is imaginative and not verifiable by scientific, objective, logical means. The idea that *poetry* can convey truths that cannot be tested by intellectual means is very old. Much *Romantic literature* is devoted to this notion, e.g. *Percy Shelley*'s "To a Skylark."

psychoanalytic criticism is an approach used by critics who consider a literary *text* as a product of a writer's psychology or as a way of analyzing the human mind in general. The theories of Sigmund Freud (1856–1939) are particularly important to such critics. See *postmodernism, poststructuralism, surrealism.*

psychological novel: a loose term used to cover the hundreds of *novel*s that are concerned with the psychological state of *character*s rather than with *action* and *plot*.

Ptolemaic system: the construct of beliefs based on the notion that the earth is the center of the universe and the sun, moon, stars, and planets revolve around it. Devised by Ptolemaeus, a Greek astronomer and geographer of the second century AD, this idea was not superseded until the *Copernican revolution* in the 16th century.

Pulitzer Prizes are American literary awards in various categories made every year by Columbia University since 1917. Winners include, in *poetry*: *Frost* (1924, 1931, 1937, 1943), *Robert Lowell* (1947, 1974), *Plath* (1982); in *drama*: *O'Neill* (1920, 1928, 1957), *Tennessee Williams* (1948, 1955), *Shepard* (1979); in *fiction*: *Steinbeck* (1940), *Faulkner* (1955, 1963), *Morrison* (1988).

pulp literature: cheaply produced *paraliterature* in book or magazine *form*, often including *pot-boiler*s and soft porn.

pun: a *witty* play upon words, where one word carries two or more *meaning*s within a sentence. All ages have enjoyed puns, good and bad, and they are a favorite element in many jokes. The *Elizabethan*s and *metaphysical* poets were particularly fond of employing them, e.g. Mercutio's dying pun in *Shakespeare*'s ROMEO AND JULIET, when he says that tomorrow he will be "a grave man," or the kind of wordplay that led *Johnson* to comment that a pun was the "fatal Cleopatra" for which Shakespeare was content to lose the world. See *ambiguity*.

Purdy, Al (b.1918): Canadian poet and novelist. Much of his writing is rooted in the landscape of rural Ontario and the impact it has upon the inhabitants' ways of thinking. Notable works include BEING ALIVE: POEMS 1958–78 (1978), COLLECTED POEMS (1986), THE WOMAN ON THE SHORE (1989).

purism: in *literature*, the insistence of absolute standards of "correctness" in writing. The main problems for purists are that:

- agreement on what is "correct" is difficult to establish
- language is always changing, and what was considered strange or slang yesterday is accepted usage today
- new ways of communicating such as emails are having an impact upon wider written usage.

"Appropriateness" is a much more useful notion than "correctness." The great strength of English, unlike perhaps French, is that it has always embraced new usage, with dictionaries tending to be descriptive rather than prescriptive.

purple prose: a term used to denote inappropriately ornate and overwritten *prose*.

Pynchon, Thomas (b.1937): American novelist and *short story* writer. His highly inventive, complex, *ironic*, and frequently baffling *style* has been called "cinematic," "absurdist," and "chaotic" – but it has assured him a place as a leading postmodernist author of the 20th century. His most famous work, considered his masterpiece, is GRAVITY'S RAINBOW (1973), which takes place in the final days of World War II. Other notable works include V. (1963), THE CRYING OF LOT 49 (1966), SLOW LEARNER (1984), VINELAND (1990).

pyrrhic: see *meter*.

quantity: in *verse*, the length of the sound of a syllable which affects a poet's choice of words. For instance, "bóók" is a long sound, "blàck" a short one.

quarto: page size formed by a printer's sheet being folded twice, thus creating four leaves, or eight pages. The quarto editions of *Shakespeare's* plays were printed in this size.

quatrain: a *stanza* or section of *verse* containing four lines, usually defined by a unit of *rhyme* pattern.

quintain: a *stanza* or section of *verse* containing five lines, usually defined by a unit of *rhyme* pattern.

quotation: the citing of a word, phrase or passage from a work.

quotation titles are titles of works that use phrases taken from earlier *literature*, e.g. *Faulkner's* THE SOUND AND THE FURY borrows a phrase from *Shakespeare's* MACBETH, and TENDER IS THE NIGHT by *F. Scott Fitzgerald* is a quotation from *Keats's* "Ode to a Nightingale."

Rabelaisian: reminiscent of the literary *style* of Rabelais (?1494–1553) – that is, writing that is by turns coarse, boisterous, *satirical*, extravagant, and obscene in one *tradition* of French writing of the day. The term is still applied to certain kinds of contemporary writing.

Ramanujam, A.K. (1929–93): Indian poet, scholar, and translator. In his *poetry* he handles his subjects with gentle, sensitive insight and clarity of expression, often drawing *inspiration* from the blend of his Indian roots and his long years in America. Notable works include THE STRIDERS (1966), RELATIONS (1972), SECOND SIGHT (1986).

Rao, Raja (b.1908): Indian novelist and *short story* writer. His work shows a strong awareness of the challenges of dealing with Indian *themes* and sensibilities through the medium of the *English language*, and some aspects of his writing anticipate *magic realism*. Notable works include KANTHAPURA (1938), THE SERPENT AND THE ROPE (1960), THE CAT AND SHAKESPEARE (1965), ON THE GANGA GHAT (1989).

Rattigan, Terence (1911–77): English playwright and screenwriter. A very popular playwright in his time, he is often regarded as a master of the *well-made play*. His work is marked by compassion for his *character*s. His avowed target audience of the middle-aged and middle-brow (whom he called "Aunt Edna") put him out of fashion during the ascendancy of the *angry young men* in England, but since his death his plays have regained much critical regard. Notable works include FRENCH WITHOUT TEARS (1936), THE WINSLOW BOY (1946), THE BROWNING VERSION (1948), THE DEEP BLUE SEA (1952), SEPARATE TABLES (1954), ROSS (1960).

reader-response theory is the name given to various different approaches to *literature* that focus upon the reader's relationship with the *text*, e.g. *psychoanalytic criticism* and *structuralism*. The reader's response to a text is seen as crucial in determining any *meaning* that may be arrived at: different individuals and, indeed, different communities will respond in different ways, all of them valid. See also *cultural materialism, hermeneutics, implied reader, new critics, reception theory.*

readerly/writerly: terms invented by Roland Barthes (1915–80) to determine whether a *text* is "readerly" – i.e. inviting the reader to be passive (as, for example, toward a *classic* realistic *novel*, which is unchallenging because reliant upon *convention* and a fixed, closed *meaning*); or "writerly" – i.e. requiring the reader to be active and work hard in order to respond and create meanings, almost "write" her/himself (as, for example, with *Joyce*'s ULYSSES and similar texts where there is a focus, sometimes selfconscious, on language, *structure*, the mechanics of the writing, and so forth). Barthes points out that any text can be made either readerly or writerly: it all depends on the reader's approach to it. See also *authorial intention, intentional fallacy, poststructuralism.*

realism has a range of possible definitions. Broadly speaking it can cover:

- writings from the 19th and 20th century that are concerned with focusing upon plain truths, often about the harsher aspects of life that had previously not been considered fit subject matter for *literature*

- insights into psychological truths, as distinct from *naturalism,* which is concerned with the accuracy of *setting* and other surface details
- both psychological insights and attention to accuracy concerning all facts and details
- a writer's concern with the here and now rather than escapist *fantasy*
- working-class realities in the struggle for power (see *Marxist criticism*)

realistic period: often used of American *literature* to define the period between approximately 1865 (the end of the Civil War) and 1900.

reception theory is an aspect of *reader-response theory* that considers the changing reactions of different generations of readers to a *text* and in relation to those of the present-day reader.

recognition: see *anagnorisis.*

recoil is when, in *tragedy,* the *protagonist* brings about her or his own downfall.

referential language is that which uses nonemotive, objective words in order to describe something with scientific precision. See *denotation,* and also *connotation.*

refrain: a line or lines repeated at regular points in a *poem,* often at the end of a *stanza,* sometimes with slight variations. Much used in *ballad*s.

regional novel: a *novel* in which the *setting* and society of a particular area is more than mere *local color,* but an important ingredient in the fabric of the work and core *theme*s. Among those who have made much use of regional aspects are *Gaskell, Hardy, Lawrence, Faulkner.*

regionalism: see *local color.*

relativism is the notion that two opposing judgments can be equally valid. For instance, a piece of writing may be considered to be good or bad according to the taste of either the individual reader or the times in which s/he lives.

Renaissance: a time of "rebirth" in learning following the Middle Ages, resulting in the growth and flourishing of art, architecture, science, philosophy, and *literature* such as had not been seen in Europe since classical times. Some regard 14th century Italy as the cradle of the Renaissance, which then spread across Western Europe to England during the ensuing 200 years. The revival saw the appearance of great thinkers, scholars, and writers, often *humanist*s, such as Erasmus (?1467–1536) and *More* who rekindled an interest in the achievements of Greece and Rome. Long-held beliefs about the nature of God, man, and the universe were challenged in many areas of learning: *Copernicus* and Galileo Galilei (1564–1642) overturned the *Ptolemaic* view of the universe which had placed the earth at the center; Martin Luther (1483–1546) and others led the Protestant Reformation against the domination of the Roman Catholic church; Columbus (1451–1505) "discovered" the New World (1492); and the arrival of printing facilitated the spread of new and influential ideas. Important Renaissance writers include *Dante, Petrarch, Boccaccio,* Cervantes (1547–1616), *Wyatt, Spenser, Sidney, Shakespeare, Bacon.* The word "renaissance" is sometimes used to denote any revival in the arts.

Renaissance (or **early modern) period:** generally considered to cover *literature* written in Europe between approximately 1500 and 1660.

repetend: a word or phrase that is repeated at irregular intervals in a *poem* (as opposed to the regularity of a *refrain*).

repetition of any kind, from individual sound through patterns of language to whole sections of *text*, and from *allusions* through to ideas, is a *device* frequently used in *literature*, especially *poetry*, and usually for emphasis. See *amplification, palilogy*.

resolution: the outcome of the *climax* of a play or *story*. See also *act, catastrophe, dénouement, plot*.

rest: a term borrowed from music, indicating a pause in the *meter* in place of an unstressed syllable.

Restoration comedy: a type of English *comedy* that dominated the stage between the restoration of the monarchy in 1660 and the appearance of *sentimental comedy* in the early 18th century. Also known as artificial comedy or *comedy of manners*, it was characterized variously by stylishness, *wit*, and bawdiness. The plays lacked the broad appeal of the *Elizabethan* theater, with audiences tending to be drawn from the upper classes and consisting of those who went to see portrayed on stage the ladies and galants from their own social circle. The usual subject matters were love, intrigue, social climbing, and marital infidelity. In performance the plays can be very funny, but were described by *Meredith* as "that weary feast where no love is." The most gifted playwrights in this *genre* were *Congreve, Etherege, Farquhar, Vanbrugh, Wycherley*.

Restoration period: generally considered to cover *literature* written in England between 1660 (the restoration of the monarchy under Charles II) until approximately 1700.

Restoration tragedy: a less enduring *genre* than *Restoration comedy*, and never reaching the heights of the *drama* of the *Elizabethan age*. Nonetheless there were some notable *tragedies* written during the *Restoration period* including *Dryden*'s *blank verse* ALL FOR LOVE and *Otway*'s VENICE PRESERV'D, both blank verse dramas. See *heroic drama/tragedy*.

revenge tragedy is a *genre* of *drama* that was very popular during the *Elizabethan* and *Jacobean ages*. Derived partly from the *tragedies* of the Greek playwright Aeschylus (525–456BC) and the Roman playwright Seneca (?4BC–AD65), the *plots* revolve around a *hero* (or sometimes *antihero*) who sets out to right a wrong, usually the murder of a close relative, and who succeeds at the end of the play but dies in the *catastrophe*. One key to the success of such plays is that the emotions of the audience are torn: they know that, morally, revenge is unacceptable and should be left to God; yet dramatically they wish to see the avenger "get his man" (or, in at least one instance, woman). The most famous play in this genre is *Shakespeare*'s HAMLET.

reversal: see *peripeteia*.

review is a journalistic term normally given to a brief survey of a book in a magazine or newspaper. It is also the name given to a *periodical* that specializes in such surveys and other critical or literary pieces of writing, e.g. CRITICAL QUARTERLY, QUARTERLY REVIEW.

revision: the act of altering or updating a *text*, or the revised text itself.

revisionism: the act of updating or altering *text* in order to distort history, which is Winston Smith's job in *Orwell*'s NINETEEN EIGHTY-FOUR.

Revolutionary age: a term sometimes used to cover American *literature* written between 1765 (the Stamp Act) and approximately 1790.

revue is a theatrical entertainment comprising a miscellany of short items such as sketches, *songs* and dance, sometimes with a unifying *theme* and often topical and/or *satirical*, e.g. *Coward*'s WORDS AND MUSIC (1932).

rhetoric is the art of using language to persuade, both written and, especially, in speech. *Aristotle* defined rhetoric as the art of "discovering all the available means of persuasion in any given case." The Roman Cicero (106–43BC) and others codified rhetoric into a series of *rules* which have changed little until relatively modern times, and which were divided into a logical sequence of five processes:

- *invention*, or the discovery of appropriate and relevant material
- disposition or arrangement; that is, the structured organization of that material
- *style*; that is, the manner appropriate to the situation or occasion (e.g. "grand," "neutral," or "plain")
- memory, or how to remember speeches
- delivery, or method for delivering speeches to maximum effect.

A certain amount of insincerity may often be apparent to the reader of, or listener to, rhetoric. For the more specific impact of rhetoric on writing see *rhetorical figures*.

rhetorical criticism is the name given to a way of looking at *literature* that focuses upon the *devices* used by a writer in *prose* or *poetry* to guide the responses of the reader. This critical approach grew during the 1960s and 1970s, much influenced by THE RHETORIC OF FICTION (1961) by the American scholar Wayne Booth (b.1921).

rhetorical figures: any artistic arrangement of words in order to create an emphasis or other effect, e.g. *antithesis, chiasmus, rhetorical question, zeugma*. It is important to note that this term only refers to a nonstandard rearrangement of words, be it grammar or syntax, and not to such *figures of speech* as *metaphor*, which alters the literal *meaning* of words.

rhetorical question: a question asked for effect, without expectation of an answer, e.g. "If Winter comes, can Spring be far behind?," the final line of *Percy Shelley*'s "Ode to the West Wind." It is a figurative *device* much loved of politicans ("Are we to accept this state of affairs?"). Sometimes the speaker or writer immediately offers an answer to the question, as when Falstaff in *Shakespeare*'s HENRY IV PART 1 asks "Can honour set to a leg? No. Or an arm? No. Or take away the grief of a wound? No."

Rhone, Trevor (b.1940): Jamaican playwright. Sometimes employing historical *allegory*, the social *criticism* of his plays is conveyed realistically and with *humor* about such topics as Jamaican life today, with a good ear for dialect and speech patterns. Notable works include SMILE ORANGE (1971), SCHOOL'S OUT (1975), OLD STORY TIME (1979), TWO CAN PLAY (1983).

rhyme, sometimes spelled "rime," is the use in *poetry* of repeated vowel sounds, and is sometimes wrongly taken as the main indicator that what one is reading is poetry rather than *prose*. There was little use of rhyme in Anglo-Saxon poetry, *alliteration* being the dominant poetic *device*. Rhyme is used mainly, but not exclusively, at line endings to repeat identical or similar accented sounds, e.g. sow/low, beast/feast, tougher/buffer. There are various types of rhyme according to the number of syllables in the rhyming word, such as *masculine rhyme, feminine rhyme, triple rhyme*; these classifications are nowadays infrequently used in English poetry, but more useful categories are *end rhyme, internal rhyme, eye rhyme, perfect rhyme, half rhyme* (or "near" rhyme).

rhyme royal: a *stanza* of seven ten-syllable *iambic* lines rhyming ababbcc, sometimes known as a Chaucerian stanza because *Chaucer* used it in TROILUS AND CRISEYDE, THE PARLEMENT OF FOULES, and several of THE CANTERBURY TALES. Others who have experimented with the *form* include *Wyatt*, Michael Drayton (1563–1631), *Spenser, Shakespeare*.

rhyme scheme is the term used to describe the pattern of *rhymes* in a *stanza*, usually indicated alphabetically, e.g. the rhyme scheme in *rhyme royal* is ababbcc.

rhyming couplets are pairs of rhyming *verse* lines (aabbcc...). See *alternate rhyme*.

Rhys, Jean (1890–1979): Dominican-born English novelist and *short story* writer. She is best known for her *novel* WIDE SARGASSO SEA (1966), an imagined "prequel" to *Charlotte Brontë*'s JANE EYRE that deals with the early life in the West Indies of the first Mrs. Rochester. Exploitation is a recurrent *theme* in her writing. Other notable works include SLEEP IT OFF LADY (1976).

rhythm is the sense of movement in a piece of writing created by various patterns of *stress* on the syllables. In *poetry* this is generated by the *meter*.

rhythmical pause: another term for a *caesura*.

Rich, Adrienne (b.1929): American poet, essayist, and critic. A radical feminist who is discontented with American politics, she often explores *themes* of selfhood with directness in her technically accomplished and prolific output. Her writing has been called *confessional poetry*. Notable works include THE DIAMOND CUTTERS (1955), SNAPSHOTS OF A DAUGHTER-IN-LAW (1963), NECESSITIES OF LIFE (1966), DIVING INTO THE WRECK (1973), ON LIES, SECRETS, AND SILENCE (1979), BLOOD, BREAD, AND POETRY (1986), AN ATLAS OF THE DIFFICULT WORLD (1991), ARTS OF THE POSSIBLE (2001).

Richards, I.A. (1893–1979): English literary critic who was one of the founders of the Cambridge University English *literature* course. His book PRACTICAL CRITICISM (1929) advocates precise *close reading* of the words on the page, divorced from considerations of history or *context*. Other notable works include THE PHILOSOPHY OF RHETORIC (1936). See *intrinsic attitude, Leavisite*.

Richardson, Samuel (1689–1761): English novelist who made a major contribution to the development of the *novel*, pioneering the *epistolary form*. PAMELA, OR VIRTUE REWARDED (1740–41) is generally considered to be the first modern exploration in a novel of the emotions and psychology of *character*s. His other notable works include CLARISSA (1747–48) and SIR CHARLES GRANDISON (1753–54).

riddle: a word puzzle ending with a question, the answer to which is an object, person, or idea. Riddles have been popular in all cultures, one of the most famous being the riddle of the Sphinx in *Sophocles*' OEDIPUS REX: "What goes on four legs in the morning, two legs in the afternoon, and three legs in the evening?" – the answer being man, who crawls on all fours early in life, on two legs in the prime of life, and on three (by using a stick) when old. Riddles were frequent in Anglo-Saxon *literature*, in which such objects as a shield or an onion were described in inventive ways so that listeners had to guess what was being described.

riding rhyme: see *heroic couplets*.

rime: an old spelling of *rhyme*.

rime riche, French for "rich rhyme," occurs when rhyming words are identical in sound, e.g. stair/stare, threw/through, and even identical in *form*, for instance, when rhyming still/still and playing upon two different meanings of the word.

rising action is when the *action* of a play is rising toward its *climax*. See *act*, *anabasis*.

rising rhythm, in which most English *verse* is written, occurs when the final syllable of each foot is stressed, as with iambic and anapestic meter. Trochaic and dactylic meter create falling rhythm. See *meter*.

Robinson Crusoe myth: the idea, often idealized, of being cast away on a desert island. Ever since *Defoe* drew on the experiences of Alexander Selkirk (1676–1721), writers and artists have elevated the castaway to *mythic* status through such works as *Cowper*'s poem "The Castaway," *Golding*'s LORD OF THE FLIES, and *Walcott*'s reworking of the Crusoe *story* in THE CASTAWAY.

Rochester, Earl of: see *Wilmot*.

rocking rhythm is a term used by *Hopkins* to indicate a metrical foot (see *meter*) containing three syllables, the first and third being stressed, the middle one unstressed, as in the first three words of his "The Wreck of the Deutschland":

> Bút he scóres...

rococo is an architectural term referring to elegant flourishes of decorative scroll-work. It is generally applied to writing that displays flourishes of verbal dexterity and *wit*, e.g. parts of *Pope*'s work, especially THE RAPE OF THE LOCK.

Roethke, Theodore (1908–63): American poet. Inspired by the locations and landscape of his Michigan childhood as a means of defining individual identity, he has written much *love poetry*. Notable works include OPEN HOUSE (1941), THE WAKING: POEMS 1933–1953 (1953), I AM! SAYS THE LAMB (1961), THE FAR FIELD (1964).

rogue literature is concerned with the criminal underworld, and was particularly popular in the 16th and 17th centuries, as in some of the writings of *Robert Greene* and *Dekker*.

roman à clef means, in French, "novel with a key," and refers to a *novel* wherein apparently fictitious *character*s are thinly disguised portrayals of a real people, e.g. *Coleridge*, *Byron*, and *Percy Shelley* in *Peacock*'s NIGHTMARE ABBEY (1818), *Lawrence* in *Huxley*'s POINT COUNTER POINT (1928). *Maugham* was notorious for failing sufficiently to disguise his models.

roman-fleuve: from the French meaning "river novel," a term that refers to a *saga* concerning the doings of a set of *character*s over a long period of time, which can therefore run into several books or a series of *novels*. First appearing in France early in the 19th century, it has perhaps its most famous example in À LA RECHERCHE DU TEMPS PERDU (1913–27, translated as REMEMBRANCE OF THINGS PAST, 1922–31) by Marcel Proust (1871–1922). A typical instance in English *literature* is *Galsworthy*'s THE FORSYTE SAGA.

romance: an entertaining *story* written in *verse*, and later *prose*, about the world of *courtly love* and chivalry, e.g. *Arthurian* romances concerning the knights and ladies of King Arthur's court, and other stories of classical *heroes*. Such *tales* contrast with the *epic*, which is a story about war. Influenced by such *collections* as Richard Burton's (1821–90) translation of Oriental tales THE ARABIAN NIGHTS (1885–88), romances were not realistic stories but told of magical, almost fairytale worlds where knights perform such deeds as jousting in tournaments and battling with fantastical animals in order to save their ladies. Famous examples include the 14th century SIR GAWAIN AND THE GREEN KNIGHT in verse and *Malory*'s 15th century LE MORTE D'ARTHUR in prose. Later, the term "romance" was extended to cover any kind of adventure story, often involving love, but by no means always. *Burlesque* mock-romances then appeared, such as *Beaumont*'s comedy THE KNIGHT OF THE BURNING PESTLE, where the "hero" is a grocer's apprentice, *Fielding*'s *parody* JOSEPH ANDREWS, and *Samuel Butler*'s *mock heroic* HUDIBRAS. Interest in chivalric romance reemerged with such works as *Spenser*'s THE FAERIE QUEENE, and later with *Keats*'s "The Eve of St. Agnes" and *Tennyson*'s IDYLLS OF THE KING.

romantic comedy denotes a kind of *drama* in which love is the main *theme* and where, after difficulties along the way, the lovers are united. The *genre* developed in popularity during *Elizabethan* times, *Shakespeare*'s AS YOU LIKE IT and A MIDSUMMER NIGHT'S DREAM being typical examples, and has remained so ever since.

romantic irony is a *device* whereby a writer builds up the illusion of reality in order to shatter it deliberately by intruding into the work as a *self-conscious narrator*, making the reader aware of the created *fiction* by commenting, often humorously, upon such matters as the *character*s and the problems of where next to take the *narrative*, e.g. *Sterne* in TRISTRAM SHANDY, *Byron* in DON JUAN.

Romantic period: generally considered to cover *literature* written in Europe between approximately 1780 and 1830. In America the term is often used to refer to the period approximately from 1828 to 1865 (alternative terms being the *American renaissance* or the *age of transcendentalism*). See *Romanticism*.

Romanticism is a term applied to a European-wide revolution in *literature* and other arts covering approximately the period 1780 to 1840. Romantics reacted against *neoclassicism*, 18th century rationalism, and the praise of pure intellect, choosing instead to celebrate the importance of feelings and the *imagination*. Among many other things, Romantics were variously interested in:

- nature-worship, especially of wild, lonely places
- primitivism
- *medievalism*, and the *gothic*
- Oriental, alien, or vanished cultures
- the supernatural, bizarre, or nightmarish
- idealism

- political and social revolution
- opposition to established institutions such as the monarchy and the church
- physical sensations and passion
- the notion of *carpe diem*
- above all, the importance of the individual creating his or her own relationship with the world.

The French writer Jean-Jacques Rousseau (1712–78) is generally regarded as the father of Romanticism. The most widely read English Romantic writers are *Wordsworth, Coleridge, Keats, Mary* and *Percy Shelley,* and *Byron.* The most widely read European Romantic writers are Goethe, Schiller, Kant, Hegel, Hugo, Gautier, Dumas père, and Stendhal. Among American writers in the Romantic *tradition* are *Poe, Emerson, Thoreau, Hawthorne, Melville, Longfellow,* and *Whitman.* In music the best-known composers are Berlioz, Mendelssohn, Schumann and, above all, Beethoven; and in painting Corot, Delacroix, Ingres, and Millet. It is appropriate to write of the Romantic movement or writers with a capital "R" in order to distinguish them from romantic writers who are concerned with sentimental love stories. At its best Romanticism is a celebration, a life-enhancing hymn of praise to the beautiful things in the world. The hippie movement of the 1960s could be described as a neo-Romantic movement, and there have been and still are other manifestations of new Romanticism. We are all, in a sense, post-Romantics.

Rose Theatre: an Elizabethan theater built by *Henslowe* and John Cholmley (?1550–?95) near the River Thames at *Bankside* in the Southwark area of London, close to the Bear Garden and the *Globe Theatre.* The theater features in the 1999 film SHAKESPEARE IN LOVE.

Rosenberg, Isaac (1890–1918): English poet and artist, who was killed in World War I. His *poetry* is characteristically *realistic,* sharp in its *imagery* and technically inventive. Notable works include NIGHT AND DAY (1912), YOUTH (1915), MOSES (1916, play), POEMS (1922, published posthumously).

Rossetti, Christina (1830–94): English poet. Of Italian parentage and sister to the artist *Dante Gabriel Rossetti,* she is famous in two artistic respects: as a poet and as a model for the painters of the *Pre-Raphaelite* Brotherhood. She wrote *ballads,* hymns, carols, and children's *verse,* all of which showed her intense regard for detail, her depth of emotion, and her ability to use *symbolism* to great effect. Notable works include GOBLIN MARKET (1862).

Rossetti, Dante Gabriel (1828–82): English poet and translator. He was the brother of *Christina Rossetti,* and the leading light of the *Pre-Raphaelite* Brotherhood as a painter and a *lyric* poet. He translated works by various European writers, notably the lyrics of *Dante.* His own *poetry* contains detail of great depth, color, mysticism, and *fantasy,* his best-known including "The Blessed Damozel" (1850), THE HOUSE OF LIFE (1870, revised 1881), "Sister Helen" (1870), "Troy Town" (1870).

Roth, Philip (b.1933): American novelist and playwright. His frequently comic, incisive *novels* mainly concern the American Jewish community. Notable works include GOODBYE COLUMBUS (1959), PORTNOY'S COMPLAINT (1969, controversial because of its sexual subject matter), ZUCKERMAN BOUND (1979–85), SABBATH'S THEATER (1995).

Rotimi, Ola (b.1938): Nigerian playwright. His historical *tragedies* often contain social and political comment upon contemporary Africa. Notable works include OUR HUSBAND HAS GONE MAD AGAIN (1966), THE GODS ARE NOT TO BLAME (1968), KURUNMI (1969), HOLDING TALKS (1970), HOPES OF THE LIVING-DEAD (1985).

round characters, as defined by *Forster* in ASPECTS OF THE NOVEL, are *characters* who are rounded, three-dimensional, and develop during the course of a *story*. He cites Becky Sharp from *Thackeray's* VANITY FAIR as an example. See *flat characters*.

roundel: an eleven-line *poem* in three *stanzas* with the opening words of the poem repeated as a *refrain* at the end of the first and third stanzas, thus: abaR(refrain), bab, abaR. The *form* was developed by *Swinburne* and published in his A CENTURY OF ROUNDELS (1883).

Rowley, William (?1585–?1637): English playwright. As an actor he played fat clowns, but he is best known as collaborator with *Middleton* on A FAIR QUARREL (?1616), and especially THE CHANGELING (1622), and with *Dekker* and *John Ford* on THE WITCH OF EDMONTON (1621). He also wrote a few *citizen comedies* and other plays on his own. His plays remained popular during the 17th century.

Roy, Gabrielle (1909–83): Canadian novelist. Her writing gives a realistic view of life from rural Manitoba to urban Quebec. Notable works include THE TIN FLUTE (1946), ALEXANDRE CHENEVERT (1954), THE ROAD PAST ALTAMOUNT (1966), CHILDREN OF MY HEART (1977).

rules, in a literary sense, are a set of *conventions* and precepts, developed by custom, which sometimes goes back to classical times (see *classic*), laying down how *novels*, *poems*, plays, and so forth should be constructed. For instance, over time rules have evolved that a novel should tell a *story* in a logical sequence, a *sonnet* should have 14 lines, and a play should observe the *dramatic unities*. A sonnet would not be a sonnet unless it consisted of 14 lines. However, in *Renaissance* times and later, English playwrights such as *Shakespeare* often disregarded the rules of the dramatic unities that the French playwrights held dear in order to have more freedom in composition.

run-on lines: another term for *enjambment*.

Runyon, Damon (1884–1946): American *short story* writer and journalist whose books include GUYS AND DOLLS (1932) in which Runyon brings to life *characters* of Broadway such as Nicely Niceley Johnson and Harry the Horse. He writes in the present tense and uses much Broadway slang which gives his work a great sense of vibrancy. The *style* is so individual that it is given the name Runyonese.

rural novel: a term sometimes used to define a subgenre (see *genre*) of *stories* set in the countryside, and occasionally containing elements of the *pastoral*, such as *Hardy's* Wessex *novels* or *Webb's* PRECIOUS BANE, and *Gibbons's* parody thereof in COLD COMFORT FARM. See also *novel of the soil*.

Rushdie, Salman (b.1947): Anglo-Indian novelist, *short story* and travel writer. His bilingual, postcolonial upbringing informs his work, much of which is characteristic of *magic realism*. The publication of THE SATANIC VERSES (1988) resulted in a charge of blasphemy against the Islamic religion, followed by a "fatwa" (death sentence) imposed upon him by Ayatollah Khomeini (1902–89) of Iran, after which Rushdie went into hiding. Other notable works include MIDNIGHT'S CHILDREN (1981), SHAME (1983), HAROUN AND THE SEA OF STORIES (1990), EAST, WEST (1994), THE MOOR'S LAST SIGH (1995).

Ruskin, John (1819–1900): English critic and scholar of wide-ranging interests extending from art, art history, and architecture, to social reform and politics, ornithology, geology, and botany. He had an impact on nearly every sphere of cultural activity in England, including *literature*. His MODERN PAINTERS (1843–60) helped to define *Romanticism*, and his love of *gothic* architecture did much to further contemporary interest in *medievalism*. Other notable works include THE SEVEN LAMPS OF ARCHITECTURE (1849), THE STONES OF VENICE (1851–53, including a famous *essay* entitled "The Nature of the Gothic").

Russell, Willy (b.1947): English playwright and screenwriter who in much of his work writes with energy and *wit* about *character*s and their struggles in his native city of Liverpool. Notable works include BREEZEBLOCK PARK (1975), EDUCATING RITA (1980), BLOOD BROTHERS (1981, revised 1983), SHIRLEY VALENTINE (1986).

S

Sackville, Thomas (1536–1608): English playwright and poet. His best-known work is the *tragedy* GORBODUC (1562), which he wrote with *Norton* and which some claim to be the first English tragedy. In some respects the plot foreshadows *Shakespeare*'s KING LEAR.

Sackville-West, Vita (1892–1962): English poet, novelist, and biographer. A close friend of *Woolf*, she favored topics such as travel, gardening, history, and literary topics. Notable works include THE LAND (1926), THE EDWARDIANS (1930), ALL PASSION SPENT (1931), COLLECTED POEMS (1933).

saga: a medieval Norse *narrative*, originally oral but often later written down, about kings and other *hero*es. Sagas have had some influence on later writings, for example *Longfellow*'s SAGA OF KING OLAF (1863). More generally a saga has come to mean a long and detailed *story*.

saga novel: a long *novel*, sometimes one of a series, usually concerning a family, e.g. *Galsworthy*'s FORSYTE novels. See *roman-fleuve*.

Salinger, J.D. (b.1919): American novelist and *short story* writer. He is best known for THE CATCHER IN THE RYE (1951), whose *narrator*, the teenaged social outcast Holden Caulfield, has seemed to speak directly to successive generations of young readers. Salinger has a good ear for the freewheeling conversational *style* of his *character*s. Other notable works include FRANNY AND ZOOEY (1961).

Sandburg, Carl (1878–1967): American poet, children's writer, and biographer. He is one of America's most beloved *author*s, whose popular children's *stories* and highly regarded *biographies* (especially of Lincoln) are today more critically respected than his accessible, but occasionally sentimental, *poetry*. His best-known poem is "Chicago" (1914), a *free-verse* celebration of the city and its people in the manner of *Whitman*. Notable works include CHICAGO POEMS (1916), THE PEOPLE, YES (1936), ABRAHAM LINCOLN (1926–39), HARVEST POEMS (1960), and the children's *collection* ROOTABAGA STORIES (1922).

Sapphic ode: a very complicated metrical poetic *form* named after the ancient Greek poetess Sappho (7th century BC). Various English poets such as *Sidney, Cowper, Southey, Tennyson, Swinburne, Pound* experimented with it.

Saro-Wiwa, Ken (1941–95): Nigerian novelist, playwright, poet, and journalist, who was outspoken in his opposition to the Nigerian military regime. Before his execution in 1995 for alleged involvement in the murders of four Ogoni chiefs, his work explored modern Nigerian culture, often using strong *satire*. Notable works include SONGS IN A TIME OF WAR (1985), SOZABOY (1985), PRISONERS OF JEBS (1988), ADAKU (1989).

Sassoon, Siegfried (1886–1967): English poet, playwright, and autobiographer. Best known for his antiwar *poetry*, he highlights the true horrors of war by using an unpatriotic, *ironic tone*. His later writings are more spiritual and autobiographical. Notable works include A SOLDIER'S DECLARATION (1917), MEMOIRS OF A FOX-HUNTING

MAN (1928), MEMOIRS OF AN INFANTRY OFFICER (1930), VIGILS (1935, revised edition), SIEGFRIED'S JOURNEY (1945). See *war literature*.

Satanic school is a term invented by *Southey* in his harsh attack on the life and morals of *Byron, Percy Shelley*, and possibly *Keats*, in the *preface* to A VISION OF JUDGEMENT.

satire, in *literature* or other arts, aims to make a moral point by mocking follies and vices, often through sometimes biting *humor*. Its *comedy* is not intended for mere entertainment, but for a purpose. The beginnings of satire may be traced to ancient Roman writers. Among others *Chaucer, Shakespeare, Jonson*, and *Donne* all employed satire, but the great age of English literary satire is generally considered to be the late 17th and 18th centuries, notably in the writings of *Dryden, Pope*, and *Jonathan Swift*. Later satirists include *Byron, Peacock, Shaw, Huxley, Orwell*, and *Waugh*. See *burlesque, irony*.

satirical comedy is a *form* of *comedy* whose aim is to highlight the follies and vices of society. Sometimes the *character*s are *grotesque* rather than gently amusing, as in *Jonson*'s THE ALCHEMIST and VOLPONE. Later examples of the *genre* include *Sheridan*'s THE SCHOOL FOR SCANDAL, *Bennett*'s FORTY YEARS ON, *Stoppard*'s JUMPERS, *Hare*'s TEETH 'N' SMILES, *Mamet*'s AMERICAN BUFFALO and GLENGARRY GLEN ROSS, *Churchill*'s SERIOUS MONEY.

scansion is the process of closely examining the *stress* pattern within each foot of each line of *verse*, and the overall *rhythm* and movement of the *poem* which is thereby created. See *meter*.

scene: the subdivision of an *act*, containing an *episode* normally separated in time sequence, and sometimes place, from the episode that follows. In *Elizabethan drama* a scene is normally deemed to have ended at a point when all the *character*s leave the stage, but act and scene divisions in editions of *Shakespeare* and his contemporaries have been supplied by later editors. Some modern plays consist of a continuous series of episodes with no breaks in the time sequence or scenery.

Schreiner, Olive (1855–1920): South African novelist who broke *conventions* through her pioneering feminist writing, influencing such writers as *Brittain*. Her evocative descriptions of the African landscape are haunting, but the sermonizing tone of much of her writing can be alienating for the modern reader. Notable works include THE STORY OF AN AFRICAN FARM (1883), DREAMS (1890), AN ENGLISH-SOUTH AFRICAN'S VIEW OF THE SITUATION (1899), WOMAN AND LABOUR (1911), FROM MAN TO MAN (1926).

science fiction is a type of *fantasy literature*, usually in the *form* of a *short story* or *novel*, which creates an alternative society based on the imagined technology of the future (and sometimes the past) and frequently involves such elements as space travel, alien beings, and supernatural forces. Science fiction stretches the *imagination* by rooting the *fantastic* in reality. *Mary Shelley*'s FRANKENSTEIN is sometimes described as the key work in the development of the *genre*, with later writers including *Wells, Huxley, Orwell, Burgess, Wyndham*, Isaac Asimov (1920–92), Ray Bradbury (b.1920), Arthur C. Clarke (b.1917), Brian Aldiss (b.1925), and Frank Herbert (1920–86). The genre is often not regarded as "serious" literature.

Scott, Dennis (1939–91): Jamaican poet and playwright. His *poems* often adopt several intimate *voices*, all of which tend to focus on the self. A recurring interest in his work is humorous behavior in relation to racial and political oppression. Notable works include UNCLE TIME (1973), DOG (1981), DREADWALK (1982).

Scott, Paul (1920–78): English novelist. Several years of living in India, Burma, and Malaya, and experiencing the difficulties of Anglo-Indian relationships leading up to independence, gave him *inspiration* and *settings* for his works, most famously THE RAJ QUARTET (1966–75), whose first volume is THE JEWEL IN THE CROWN (1966). Other notable works include BIRDS OF PARADISE (1962), STAYING ON (1977).

Scott, Walter (1771–1832): Scottish novelist, poet, playwright, and editor. His early work was nearly all *poetry, verse romances* on historical or legendary subjects such as THE LAY OF THE LAST MINSTREL (1805). Partly prompted by the success of *Byron's* CHILDE HAROLD'S PILGRIMAGE, which he regarded as superior to anything he could achieve in poetry, he turned to historical romances in *novel form*. The great popularity of WAVERLEY (1814) confirmed the decision, turning Scott into the most widely read novelist of his time. His descriptions of ruins and landscape helped to define *Romanticism*, and his *settings* stimulated interest in *mediaevalism* and the *historical novel*. His *characterization, humor*, handling of history, and concern with political and social change had an impact upon writers such as the *Brontës, George Eliot*, and *Gaskell*. Other notable works include GUY MANNERING (1815), OLD MORTALITY (1816), ROB ROY (1817), THE HEART OF MID-LOTHIAN (1818), THE BRIDE OF LAMMERMOOR (1819), IVANHOE (1819), PEVERIL OF THE PEAK (1823), QUENTIN DURWARD (1823), REDGAUNTLET (1824).

Scottish Chaucerians: a name given to group of Scottish poets of the late 15th and early 16th centuries, such as *Dunbar* and *Henryson*, whose work may have been influenced by *Chaucer*, particularly in the use of *rhyme royal*.

second-person narrator: see *narrator/narrative voice*.

selection: a term usually applied to a volume containing representative work of a single writer, often a poet, e.g. *Layton's* A WILD PECULIAR JOY: SELECTED POEMS 1945–82. See *collection, anthology*.

self-conscious narrator: see *narrator/narrative voice*.

self-reflexive writing is writing in which the *author*, often a *self-conscious narrator* and sometimes an autobiographer, incorporates into the *text* thoughts about the business of creating it, e.g. *Sterne's* TRISTRAM SHANDY, *Wordsworth's* THE PRELUDE.

semantics is the study of all aspects of words.

semiotics/semiology: the systematic study of all aspects of *signs*, including words.

Senecan style of writing is concise and economic, after the *style* of the Roman writer Seneca (?4BC–AD65). It may be regarded as the opposite of a *Ciceronian style*.

Senecan tragedy: the *closet drama* of Seneca, which had considerable influence on the *style* and subject matter of much *Elizabethan drama* in its use of such features as a five-*act structure, chorus*, the *revenge theme*, ghosts, messengers, sensational and often gory events (which the Elizabethans often showed on stage, whereas in Seneca they are reported events), *stichomythia*, grand (and sometimes tedious) speeches. Examples include *Norton* and *Sackville*'s GORBODUC, *Kyd*'s THE SPANISH TRAGEDY, *Shakespeare*'s TITUS ANDRONICUS (1594). Influences are also apparent in his HAMLET and in *Webster*'s THE DUCHESS OF MALFI.

Senior, Olive (b.1943): Jamaican essayist, *short story* writer, and poet, whose work frequently explores Jamaican political and social conditions. Notable works include THE MESSAGE IS CHANGE (1972), TALKING OF TREES (1985), SUMMER LIGHTNING (1986), WORKING MIRACLES (1991).

sense, in a particular meaning that developed in the 18th century, denotes a capacity for sound and intelligent judgment, which *Austen* contrasts with *sensibility* in SENSE AND SENSIBILITY.

sensibility is a term sometimes used to denote the ability to respond with feeling and *sympathy*, even *empathy*, to a *text* or other artistic *form*, especially in relation to:

- beauty
- the plight of others.

The term became popular in the late 18th century, and could refer to either the responses of the reader or those of *character*s in the book. See *sensibility, age of*.

sensibility, age of: a term that has been used to define a period of *literature* from 1744 (the death of *Pope*) until somewhere around 1784 (death of *Johnson*), 1789 (French Revolution), or as late as 1798 (publication of *Wordsworth* and *Coleridge*'s LYRICAL BALLADS). In general, this period sees a reaction against the cynicism of the *Restoration* and the writings of such as Thomas Hobbes (1588–1679), and the beginnings of the movement toward *Romanticism* and the elevation of feeling above *neoclassical* intellectualism and "correctness." Examples of relevant works are *Gray*'s "Elegy," *Sterne*'s A SENTIMENTAL JOURNEY, *Goldsmith*'s THE DESERTED VILLAGE, *Cowper*'s THE TASK. It was considered that to react with *sensibility* was proof of moral virtue in an individual; but this sometimes descended into *sentimentality*, *Sheridan* satirizing hypocritical sentiment in THE SCHOOL FOR SCANDAL, and *Austen* criticizing overdeveloped sensibility in SENSE AND SENSIBILITY. See *sense*.

sentimental comedy, in part a reaction against the perceived immorality of *Restoration comedy*, is a term used to denote the undemanding kind of play popular in the 18th century in which, typically, morally upstanding middle-class *hero*es and *heroine*s utter fine sentiments in the face of adversity prior to a contrived happy ending. Notable examples include *Steele*'s THE CONSCIOUS LOVERS, *Goldsmith*'s THE GOOD NATURED MAN, THE WEST INDIAN (1771) by Richard Cumberland (1732–1811). *Sheridan*'s hypocritical Joseph Surface in THE SCHOOL FOR SCANDAL is a *parody* of such heroes.

sentimental novel: in general terms, a type of popular *novel* that emphasizes personal emotions and moral *theme*s; in *literature* the term is especially applied to certain novels of *sensibility* written during the *age of sensibility* such as *Richardson*'s PAMELA or *Sterne*'s TRISTRAM SHANDY and A SENTIMENTAL JOURNEY. The ultimate excess of "sensibility" is seen in THE MAN OF FEELING (1771) by Henry MacKenzie (1745–1831), where the *hero* is of such extreme sensitivity (a term that later replaced sensibility) that he dies as a result of pent-up emotion leading to a declaration of love. After the *genre* waned, the popularity of such sentimental episodes continued, an example being the death of Little Nell in *Dickens's* THE OLD CURIOSITY SHOP (1841).

sentimentality is when *sensibility* descends into a mawkish self-indulgence in a *manner* which students nowadays describe as "cheesy."

Sepamla, Sipho (b.1932): South African poet and novelist. He strongly promotes the arts in South Africa to create political awareness. His *style* is both subtle and direct, often employing *irony*, and he uses his skill as a writer to voice his opinions on the political struggles of township life. Both THE SOWETO I LOVE (1977) and A RIDE IN THE WHIRLWIND (1981, banned at the time in South Africa) deal with the Soweto uprising of 1976. Other notable works include HURRY UP TO IT! (1975), THE ROOT IS ONE (1979), THIRD GENERATION (1986), FROM GORE TO SOWETO (1988).

septet: a *stanza* or section of *verse* containing seven lines, usually defined by a unit of *rhyme* pattern. See also *rhyme royal.*

sermon: an instructive talk on a moral or religious subject. *Renaissance* and *Victorian literature* in particular have many fine examples by such writers as *Donne* and Cardinal Newman (1801–90).

Serote, Mongane Wally (b.1944): South African poet and novelist. He was imprisoned in 1969 for nine months and released without charge, and his strongly political works protest with a bitter and angry creative *voice* against the sufferings of urban blacks. Notable works include YAKHAL'INKOMO (1972), TSETLO (1974, banned at the time in South Africa), NO BABY MUST WEEP (1975), TO EVERY BIRTH ITS BLOOD (1981), THE NIGHT KEEPS WINKING (1982).

serpentine verse is a line or *stanza* that begins and ends with the same word.

sestet: a *stanza* or section of *verse* containing six lines, usually defined by a unit of *rhyme* pattern.

sestina: a complicated and rare *verse form* consisting of six *stanzas* of six lines each followed by a three-line *envoi.* The same six end words are used throughout, but in a different order according to a set pattern. The form was devised by troubadour poets in 13th century France. English poets who have used it include *Sidney* (in ARCADIA), *Swinburne* (in COMPLAINT OF LISA, 1870), *Kipling, Pound* (in SESTINA: ALTAFORTE, 1909), *T.S. Eliot, Auden, Ashbery.* See *sestet.*

Seth, Vikram (b.1952): Indian poet, novelist, *short story* writer, and children's and travel writer. With *wit* and technical skill he explores a variety of cultures and *themes.* Notable works include THE GOLDEN GATE (1986), ALL YOU WHO SLEEP TONIGHT (1990), A SUITABLE BOY (1993).

setting: the location or period within which a *story* or play is placed. For instance, in *Hardy's* THE RETURN OF THE NATIVE, the setting of Egdon Heath is of prime importance in the fabric of the *novel* as a whole. In *drama*, setting includes any stage scenery.

Sexton, Anne (1928–74): American poet and children's writer. She is remembered as a writer of *confessional poetry* because of her intensely personal subject matter, especially with regard to women's experience. But she was also noted for her strong *imagery* and her ability to write effectively in both *free verse* and more traditional *forms*, showing adept use of *rhyme* and *meter*. Notable works include To BEDLAM AND PART WAY BACK (1960), LIVE OR DIE (1966), LOVE POEMS (1969), THE AWFUL ROWING TOWARD GOD (1975, published after her suicide).

Shaffer, Peter (b.1926): English playwright and novelist. His well-constructed *drama*s show compassionate philosophical and psychological insights into human yearnings. Notable works include FIVE FINGER EXERCISE (1958), THE ROYAL HUNT OF THE SUN (1964), BLACK COMEDY (1965), EQUUS (1973), AMADEUS (1979), THE GIFT OF GORGON (1992).

shaggy dog story: a long drawn-out joke, full of digressions, which usually has a laughably weak *climax*. *Heller*'s CATCH-22 has been described as a literary shaggy dog *story*.

Shakespeare, William (1564–1616): English poet and playwright, he probably thought of himself primarily as the former and would be surprised to find that his fame rests mainly upon the latter. He is capable of a range of *lyric poetry*, most notably in his SONNETS (published 1609, but almost certainly written in the 1590s) which cover such subjects, *themes*, and ideas as love, the effects of time, mortality, *carpe diem*, flattery, and the pride of the great and meretricious. As his playwrighting career progressed, he largely took on *Marlowe*'s mantle as the foremost developer of the *blank verse* line as a vehicle for the creation of powerful poetic *drama*. Shakespeare's combined skill with words (many of which he himself seems to have coined or at least brought into currency), poetic mastery, acceptance of the psychological complexities and contradictory nature of human beings, and intuitive understanding (what *Keats* later called *negative capability*), along with his complete grasp of the theater of his day, make him, in the eyes of many, the master playwright of all time. He has had an impact on all art *form*s: his works are constantly recycled, updated, and/or transposed into other media (film, *opera*, musical comedies, and so forth). The stream of Shakespearean criticism and scholarship began soon after his death and has never ceased, commentators including *Dryden, Johnson, Coleridge, Hazlitt, Bradley, Shaw, Granville-Barker*, and *Tillyard*. Attempts to edit and collate the various printed versions of his plays began early in the 18th century, editors including *Pope*, Johnson, *Boswell*, and *Kermode*. Notable works by Shakespeare include: *poem*s – VENUS AND ADONIS (1593), THE RAPE OF LUCRECE (1594); histories – HENRY IV, PARTS 1 AND 2 (?1596–98), HENRY V (1599); *comedies* – A MIDSUMMER NIGHT'S DREAM (?1596), MUCH ADO ABOUT NOTHING (?1598), AS YOU LIKE IT (?1599), TWELFTH NIGHT (?1601); *tragedies* – ROMEO AND JULIET (?1594), JULIUS CAESAR (1599), HAMLET (?1601), OTHELLO (?1603), KING LEAR (1605), ANTONY AND CLEOPATRA (?1606), MACBETH (1606); late plays, sometimes classed as romantic *tragicomedies* – THE TEMPEST (?1610), THE WINTER'S TALE (?1611). The first *collection* of his works is the 1623 Folio edition which *Jonson* prefaces by the claim that Shakespeare "was not of an age, but for all time."

Shakespearean sonnet: see *sonnet*.

Shavian: characteristic of the *manner, attitude*s, and/or subject matter of *Shaw*.

Shaw, George Bernard (1856–1950): Irish playwright, critic, and novelist. Influenced by *Ibsen*, his plays wittily and irreverently entice the audience to think about socialist issues such as equal opportunities. In order to reinforce his points he often wrote long *preface*s to his plays, and his *stage directions* are very detailed and demanding. He claimed that his *drama*, largely out of fashion nowadays, was superior to that of *Shakespeare*. Notable works include CANDIDA (1897), MRS. WARREN'S PROFESSION (1902), MAN AND SUPERMAN (1905), MAJOR BARBARA (1905), PYGMALION (1914), HEARTBREAK HOUSE (1920), SAINT JOAN (1923).

Shelley, Mary (1797–1851): English novelist, biographer, and editor. Time spent with her husband *Percy Shelley* and *Byron* in Switzerland and Italy influenced her choice of *settings*, especially in her best-known work, the *gothic novel* FRANKENSTEIN, OR THE MODERN PROMETHEUS (1818), begun in 1816 as part of a *ghost story* competition suggested by Byron. She often used the type of historical *themes* that were characteristic of *Romanticism*. Other notable works include THE LAST MAN (1826).

Shelley, Percy Bysshe (1792–1822): English poet, translator, and playwright. His highly imaginative writing was much inspired by political views: he exemplifies the radical intellectual aspects of *Romanticism*, opposing tyranny, oppression, and injustice wherever he came across it. "Freedom!" and "Liberty!" were his war cries, and his technically masterful *poetry* is characteristically exuberant, humorous, fiery, high-soaring, and visionary. He became friends with *Hunt, Keats, Hazlitt,* and *Peacock*. Notable works include QUEEN MAB (1813), "Ozymandias" (1818), THE CENCI (1819), THE MASK OF ANARCHY (written 1819, and published 1832; inspired by the Peterloo Massacre, where innocent protesters were killed by government cavalry), "The Cloud" (1820), "Ode to the West Wind" (1820), PROMETHEUS UNBOUND (1820), "To a Skylark" (1820), ADONAIS (1821), "A Defence of Poetry" (1821), "When the Lamp is Shattered" (1824).

Shepard, Sam (b.1943): American playwright, *short story* writer, and screenwriter. His *avant-garde* plays deal with popular culture surrounding family relations in America. Notable works include ICARUS'S MOTHER (1965), OPERATION SIDEWINDER (1970), MAD DOG BLUES (1971), THE TOOTH OF CRIME (1972), BURIED CHILD (1978), FOOL FOR LOVE (1983), A LIE OF THE MIND (1985).

Sheridan, Richard Brinsley (1751–1816): Irish playwright in the *comedy of manners tradition*. Notable works include THE RIVALS (1775, in which Mrs. Malaprop's misuse of language gave the word *malapropism* to the *English language*), THE SCHOOL FOR SCANDAL (1777), THE CRITIC (1779).

Sherriff, R.C. (1896–1975): English playwright and novelist whose best-known work is JOURNEY'S END (1928), a powerful play about the effects upon different soldiers of trench life during World War I. Laurence Olivier's performance of Stanhope in the original production helped to make him famous. Other notable works include BADGER'S GREEN (1930), THE WHITE CARNATION (1953).

Shields, Carol (b.1935): American-born Canadian poet and novelist. She is often compared with *Atwood*, and her *themes* are developed through the use of skillful postmodern *techniques* yet a direct and accessible *narrative style*. Notable works include HAPPENSTANCE: THE HUSBAND'S STORY (1980), HAPPENSTANCE: THE WIFE'S STORY (1982), THE REPUBLIC OF LOVE (1992), THE STONE DIARIES (1993).

short meter: a *quatrain*, usually iambic, composed of three trimeters and a third line that is a tetrameter, and rhyming abcb or abab (see *meter*). Much used in *songs*, especially hymns, e.g. *Herbert's* THE ELIXIR (1633):

A man who looks on glass,
On it may stay his eye,
Or, if he pleaseth, through it pass,
And then the heaven espy.

short novel: another term for *novella*.

short short stories: see *short story*.

short story: a brief work of *fiction* in which the basic elements are similar to the *novel*, but the writing is tighter in *form* and limited to fewer and sometimes only a single incident. Earlier forms were the *fable* and folktale, and relatively self-contained stories in the *Bible* such as Noah's Flood or Jonah and the Whale can be defined as short stories. *Poe* defined them as *prose* tales that could each be read at one sitting or in one-half to two hours (see *tale*). It is difficult to define when a short story becomes long enough to be classed as a *novella* – Dickens's A CHRISTMAS CAROL or *Henry James's* THE TURN OF THE SCREW are, at the least, very long short stories. Certain modern writers such as *Carver* have specialized in what are sometimes known as short short stories, unelaborated *anecdotes*, or *mood* pieces of a single page or less. Some critics divide short stories into two types:

- a traditional variety that is a tightly structured story with a twist at the end
- a modern variety that has less obvious form and aims to depict a mood and *atmosphere* rather than tell a clear story.

Short stories are a popular *genre* to this day in certain magazines, newspapers and *periodicals*. American writers seem to be particularly skillful at the form. Notable writers include *Poe, Hawthorne, Melville, Dickens, Hardy, Bierce, Twain, Harte, O. Henry, Conrad, Mansfield, Arthur Conan Doyle, Wells, Chesterton, Lawrence, F. Scott Fitzgerald, Faulkner, Runyon, Dinesen, Hemingway, Porter, Naipaul, Kingsley Amis, Theroux, Trevor, Angela Carter, Graham Swift*.

showing and telling: in a *narrative*, a writer is "showing" the *characters* when their *actions*, *dialog*, and thoughts are presented to the reader, who then has to make her or his judgment about those characters. "Telling" occurs when the *author* intervenes to tell the reader about the characters and thus influences the reader's opinions. It is sometimes considered a superior *technique* to "show," but some great writers tend to "tell." *Henry James* tends to "show"; *Austen*, to "tell." See *characterization*.

sibilance: *alliteration* of the letter "s" or "z." See *sigmatism* for an example.

Sidney, Philip (1554–86): English poet, literary critic, and *prose* writer. He came to be regarded as the idealized *Renaissance* courtier of the *Elizabethan age*, both in his life (and the noble manner of his death) and through the *style* and subject matter of his *poetry*. He experimented in a variety of *forms*, and English *literature* owes a considerable debt to him. Notable works include ARCADIA (1590, a prose *romance* seen by some as the ancestor of the English *novel*), ASTROPHEL AND STELLA (1591, the first English *sonnet cycle*), THE DEFENCE OF POESY (1595).

sight rhyme: see *eye rhyme*.

sigmatism: repeated use of the letter "s" in order to create *sibilance*, e.g.

> All shod with steel
> We hissed along the polished ice in games…
>
> (from *Wordsworth*'s THE PRELUDE)

sign: any *symbol*, such as a word, that stands for something. In the case of a word, the "signifier" is the word itself; the "signified" is the concept or *meaning* that it conveys.

signified: see *sign*.

signifier: see *sign*.

Silko, Leslie Marmon (b.1948): American novelist and screenwriter. Her writings are heavily based on her own experiences of growing up as half Native American and explore identity struggles that result from not fitting entirely into one culture. Notable works include LAGUNA WOMEN (1974), CEREMONY (1977), ALMANAC OF THE DEAD (1991), GARDENS IN THE DUNES (1999).

Sillitoe, Alan (b.1928): English novelist and poet. His writing, often of a political nature, is frequently set in or near his home town of Nottingham, and depicts working-class struggles within a modern industrial society. Notable works include SATURDAY NIGHT AND SUNDAY MORNING (1958), THE LONELINESS OF THE LONG-DISTANCE RUNNER (1959), A TREE ON FIRE (1967), LOST LOVES (1990).

silver-fork novel, or "fashionable *novel*," is a slightly mocking term for works written by *Frances Trollope* and others during the period 1810–50 that concern the manners and etiquette of the upper classes.

simile: a comparison between two things not usually compared in order to illuminate or provoke thought in the reader through the striking nature of the comparison. A simile is usually heralded by "as" or "like," e.g. "The road wound like a snake up the mountain-side." Similes have been common in both *poetry* and *prose* since the earliest *literature* in English. See *epic (or extended) simile, metaphor*.

sincerity: in discussions of *literature*, a term to describe its truthfulness, honesty, and integrity. The notion that to be sincere is central to good writing has long been a part of approaches to literature. With characteristic Victorian moral solemnity *Arnold* considered that literature could not be great unless it showed that "high seriousness which comes from absolute sincerity." *De Quincey* found *Pope* to be devoid of "a sincere thought or a sincere emotion." However, it is often impossible to be clear about the intentions of a writer, and most critical thinking today suggests that readers should stick to an objective assessment of what they see on the page, ignoring what the *author*'s intentions may or may not have been. See *intentional fallacy*.

Sinclair, Upton (1878–1968): American novelist, playwright, and essayist. A prolific writer in many *genres* and numerous subjects, he achieved fame and critical acclaim for a single work, THE JUNGLE (1906), a "muckraking" portrait of the Chicago slaughterhouses. Both hailed as a masterpiece and dismissed as mere *propaganda*, it resulted in immediate social legislation and became part of 20th century American history.

single rhyme is another term for *masculine rhyme*.

Skelton, John (?1460–1529): English poet and satirist. His *verse* conveys a lively picture of the political and social life of the time, and he was highly regarded by his contemporaries, the Dutch scholar Erasmus (?1467–1536) calling him "the light and glory of English letters." See *skeltonics*. Notable works include THE BOWGE OF COURT (1499), A BALLAD OF THE SCOTTISH KING (1513), MAGNYFYCENCE (written 1516), THE TUNNING OF ELINOR RUMMING (written ?1517).

skeltonics: fast-moving, helter-skelter *verse* in short lines with frequent rhyming effects and similar to *doggerel*. Named after such *poems* by *Skelton* as THE WORLD NOWADAYS (?1512) and COLIN CLOUTE (written ?1521–22).

sketch: a term used variously to describe:

- a short piece of *drama* to begin an entertainment, or a "curtain raiser," popular in late 19th and early 20th century
- an item within a *revue*, often *satirical* and topical
- a short piece of *prose*, e.g. *Dickens*'s SKETCHES BY BOZ (1836–37), sometimes amounting to a *short story*
- an article in a newspaper or magazine.

slant rhyme: another term for *half rhyme*.

Slessor, Kenneth (1901–71): Australian poet and journalist. His formal but imaginative *verse* frequently covers such subjects as war (he was the official war correspondent between 1940–44), friends, and sea *stories*. Notable works include EARTH-VISITORS (1926), DARLINGHURST NIGHTS AND MORNING GLORIES (1933), FIVE BELLS (1939).

slice of life, from the French "tranche de vie," is a term sometimes used to refer to writing that describes life in a realistic way, presenting the facts in a direct, raw, apparently unvarnished fashion. The term was applied to *novels* such as *Braine*'s ROOM AT THE TOP and *Sillitoe*'s SATURDAY NIGHT AND SUNDAY MORNING at around the same time as the phrase *kitchen sink drama* was applied to *drama*. "Slice of life" sometimes suggests that the work does not have a conventionally artistic shape, but aims to replicate real life in its seeming randomness.

Smart, Christopher (1722–71): English poet and playwright. Most of his work, written while imprisoned for debt or in hospital for insanity, contains elaborate religious language and praises the natural order of the divine world in an unusually prophetic and public *voice*, sometimes using the Old Testament *rhythms* of Hebrew *verse*. The celebratory nature of much of his *poetry* has sometimes caused him to be called an early *Romantic*. Notable works include A SONG TO DAVID (1763), JUBILATE AGNO (published 1939).

Smith, Stevie (1902–71): English poet and novelist. Her work is often illustrated with simple line drawings, and her humorous *style* takes her heavily autobiographical subjects from the absurd to the lighthearted to the serious and theological. Notable works include NOVEL ON YELLOW PAPER (1936), A GOOD TIME WAS HAD BY ALL (1937), NOT WAVING BUT DROWNING (1957).

Smollett, Tobias (1721–71): Scottish novelist, critic, poet, and playwright. His largely autobiographical works, not always successful with the reading public of his day, range from political *satires* to travel *journals*. His work is sometimes loosely referred to as *picaresque*. Notable works include RODERICK RANDOM (1748), THE REPRISAL (1757), THE EXPEDITION OF HUMPHRY CLINKER (1771).

Snyder, Gary (b.1930): American poet. His eight years spent in Japan studying Zen Buddhism are at the heart of his free, detailed, and philosophical *verse*, which is centrally concerned with ecology, spiritualism, and human culture in relation to everyday life. See *Beat movement*. Notable works include THE BACK COUNTRY (1967), REGARDING WAVE (1969), TURTLE ISLAND (1974), EARTH HOUSE HOLD (1969).

socialist realism is a stance based on the belief that *literature* (and other arts) should present the world from the Marxist viewpoint. See *Marxist criticism*.

society verse: see *vers de société*.

sociological novel: see *thesis novel*.

sociology of literature: an approach to *literature* based on the idea that all literary creations are the product of social, cultural, and historical *contexts*. See the various aspects listed under *literary/critical theory*.

Socrates (469–399BC): Greek philosopher. Although he himself wrote nothing down, his teachings on ethics have been handed on to us via *Plato, Aristotle*, and Xenophon (?420–?355BC), and have thereby had a considerable influence upon Western writers and thinkers. A key to his theories is that virtue is knowledge and wickedness is a result of ignorance.

Sofola, Zulu (b.1938): Nigerian *dramatist*. Ranging from the tragic to the comic, her combination of local dialects and standard English explores both Western and African cultures. Notable works include WEDLOCK OF THE GODS (1970), KING EMENE (1974), SONG OF A MAIDEN (1991).

soliloquy: a *device*, much used in the Elizabethan theater, whereby a *character* communicates thoughts directly to the audience by speaking aloud when no other character is present on the stage. It is a *convention* that the audience can accept the complete honesty of a character's thoughts so revealed, as there can be no motive for deception (unless the character is self-deceived). Hamlet's soliloquies are probably the most famous in English *literature*. See also *aside*.

solo play: see *monodrama*.

song: in a literary sense, a *lyric poem* written with the purpose of being set to music. Some of the best of these were written during the *Elizabethan age*. Songs appear in *Shakespeare*, and were included in *masques* in the early 1600s. After this time, "song" in a literary sense increasingly refers to a *verse* lyric *form* rather than indicating any intention that the words should be set to music. Other writers of songs include *Wyatt, Jonson, Donne, Milton, Dryden, Herrick, Goldsmith, Sheridan, Smart, Burns, Blake* (SONGS OF INNOCENCE AND OF EXPERIENCE), *Yeats, O'Casey, T.S. Eliot, Auden, Arden*. See *ballad*.

sonnet: a 14-line *lyric poem* composed in *iambic pentameter* and organized in one of several possible *rhyme schemes*:

- Petrarchan (or Italian) sonnet, developed by the Italian poet *Petrarch*, consisting of an *octave* (rhyming abbaabba) and a *sestet* (rhyming cdecde or cdcdcd). The octave tends to contain the posing of a situation or problem, the sestet its resolution
- Shakespearean (or English) sonnet, consisting of three *quatrains* (rhyming abab, cdcd, efef) and a concluding *couplet* (rhyming gg). The three

quatrains tend carefully to construct a situation or problem, climaxing in an underlining of it (or occasionally an undercutting of it) in the final couplet

- Spenserian sonnet, a slight variant of the Shakespearean sonnet with the interlinking rhyming pattern abab, bcbc, cdcd, ee (hence it is sometimes known as a "linked sonnet").

Wyatt and *Surrey* are credited with importing the sonnet *form* into England. After the Elizabethan heyday *Milton* revived it (although he dispensed with the Petrarchan turning point at the beginning of the sestet, within which his rhyme scheme was more flexible); and then the *Romantics* and 19th century poets rekindled an interest, notably *Wordsworth, Keats, Percy Shelley, Elizabeth Barrett Browning*, and *Christina Rossetti*, most of whom favored the Petrarchan form. Among other subjects Wordsworth wrote many sonnets on capital punishment. More recent sonneteers include *Yeats, Frost, Auden, Dylan Thomas*, and *Seth*. See also *meter*.

sonnet sequence: a series of *sonnets* on a *theme*, usually love, and addressed to a particular individual. Each *poem* is complete in itself. The most famous example is *Shakespeare's* SONNETS. Other notable sequences include *Sidney's* ASTROPHEL AND STELLA and *Spenser's* AMORETTI. An example on a theme other than love is *Donne's* HOLY SONNETS (1633). Notable later writers of sonnet sequences include *Wordsworth, Dante Gabriel Rossetti, Elizabeth Barrett Browning*, and *Dylan Thomas*.

Sophocles (496–406BC): Greek playwright, one of the three great Athenian writers of Greek *tragedy* (the other two being Aeschylus (525–456BC) and Euripedes (485–406BC)). Only seven of his hundred or so works survive, the best-known being OEDIPUS REX and ANTIGONE (together with OEDIPUS AT COLONUS making up the *trilogy* known as the Theban plays) which have had considerable influence over the centuries on writers as varied as *Milton, Dryden, Percy Shelley, Arnold, Swinburne, Yeats*, and *Heaney*.

sound poetry, fashionable in the 1960s and relevant mainly as *performance poetry*, sets no store by logical *meaning* and merely celebrates sounds for their own sake, e.g. by saying any single word in as many ways as possible.

source: a work from which another writer has made reasonable use (unlike *plagiarism*) in the development of the *plot, story*, or ideas of his own work. For instance, *Shakespeare* uses ROSALYNDE (1590) by Thomas Lodge (1558–1625) as a source for AS YOU LIKE IT, and he and other Elizabethan *dramatists* use Raphael Holinshed's (?1525–?80) CHRONICLES (1577) for their *history plays*.

Southey, Robert (1774–1843): English poet, historian, essayist, and biographer. A friend of *Coleridge*, he planned a "Pantisocratic" community in America with Coleridge which came to nothing. He was associated with the *Lake Poets*, although his poetic output is little akin to that of *Wordsworth* and Coleridge. However, like Wordsworth, he changed politically from radicalism to conservatism as he grew older, and this did not endear him to the younger generation of *Romantics*: he attacked them (especially *Byron* and *Percy Shelley*) and several writers in turn (especially Byron, *Hazlitt*, and *Peacock*) attacked him. He was *poet laureate* from 1813–43. Notable works include JOAN OF ARC (1796), A VISION OF JUDGEMENT (1821).

Soyinka, Wole (b.1934): Nigerian playwright, novelist, critic, screenwriter, and poet. He expresses his unease about a Nigeria under military rule by capturing a traditional African spirit through *comedy*, mime, and dance. Notable works include THE LION AND THE JEWEL (1959), A DANCE OF THE FORESTS (1960), KONGI'S HARVEST (1964), MADMEN AND SPECIALISTS (1970).

Spark, Muriel (b.1918): Scottish novelist, *short story* writer, poet, literary critic, and autobiographer. Her writing contains much black *humor* (see *black comedy*) and *irony*, and she often focuses upon the stranger aspects of human behavior with an elegance of *style*. Several of her *novels* are set in Italy, where she lived for a while. Notable works include THE BALLAD OF PECKHAM RYE (1960), THE PRIME OF MISS JEAN BRODIE (1961), THE GIRLS OF SLENDER MEANS (1963), THE MANDELBAUM GATE (1965), COLLECTED POEMS (1967), COLLECTED STORIES (1967).

Spender, Stephen (1909–95): English poet, playwright, and critic. Always a politically conscious writer, he was very concerned with using his work as a public *voice*, where he combines *realism* and idealism. Notable works include THE DESTRUCTIVE ELEMENT (1935), TRIAL OF A JUDGE (1938), POEMS OF DEDICATION (1946), and the *autobiography* WORLD WITHIN WORLD (1951).

Spenser, Edmund (*c*.1552–99): English poet. He admired *Chaucer*, and his use of an archaic medieval language adds charm to his great allegorical heroic *romance* THE FAERIE QUEENE (1590–96) but was criticized by *Sidney* and *Jonson*. THE SHEPHEARDES CALENDAR (1579) has been regarded as one of the best *pastoral* sequences in English. His *poetry* has been admired in all the ages that followed him, and he especially influenced *Milton*, who responded to his intellectual didacticism, and *Keats*, who like many of the *Romantic* poets loved his sensuousness and *medievalism*. Other notable works include AMORETTI (1595), COLIN CLOUT'S COME HOME AGAIN (1595), EPITHALAMIUM (1595), PROTHALAMIUM (1596).

Spenserian sonnet: see *sonnet.*

Spenserian stanza: a nine-line *iambic stanza* in which the first eight are *pentameter* and the final line a *hexameter* (or *alexandrine*), rhyming ababbcbcc. Devised by *Spenser* for THE FAERIE QUEENE, and in some ways a development of *ottava rima*, the *form* has been used to good effect by such as *Byron* in CHILDE HAROLD'S PILGRIMAGE, *Keats* in "The Eve of St. Agnes," *Percy Shelley* in ADONAIS, and *Tennyson* in "The Lotos-Eaters."

spondee: see *meter.*

spontaneity: in literary terms, a property of writing that is believed to be the result of *inspiration* rather than hard work. The *Romantics* regarded spontaneity highly: *Wordsworth* spoke of *poetry* as "the spontaneous overflow of powerful feelings"; *Keats* wrote that the creation of poetry should be "as natural as the leaves on a tree"; and *Percy Shelley* might have been thinking of the act of writing poetry when he called the song of the skylark "unpremeditated art." He rejected the idea that fine poetry was the result of "labour and study" whereas *Auden*, while accepting the notion of initial inspiration, considered that thereafter writing was "slogging away."

spots of time: *Wordsworth*'s term for a *moment* or *epiphany.*

sprung rhythm: a form of poetic *rhythm* pioneered by *Hopkins* whereby the metrical foot consists of one stressed syllable and any number of unstressed syllables, and a *verse* line contains a variable number of feet. See also *meter, rocking rhythm.*

spy story: a term to describe *fiction* concerning any kind of espionage. Although there were earlier *stories*, the popularity of the *genre* has its origin in *novels* such as Anthony Hope's (1863–1933) THE PRISONER OF ZENDA (1894), Baroness Orczy's (1865–1947) THE SCARLET PIMPERNEL (1905), and *Conrad's* THE SECRET AGENT (1907). World Wars I and II and the cold war of the 20th century encouraged the proliferation of spy stories, most famously those of Ian Fleming's (1908–64) James Bond and *Le Carré's* Smiley.

stage directions: instructions other than speech in the *text* of a play that indicate to actors or readers *setting*, movements, *tone* of voice, gestures, sounds, or other nonverbal instructions. In early plays these were nonexistent, and many in the texts of writers such as *Shakespeare* have been added by later editors. Some playwrights, such as *Shaw*, incorporated very full and precise stage directions that leave little to the imagination.

standpoint: see *narrator/narrative voice, showing and telling.*

stanza: a section of regular length in a *poem*, usually repeating the same metrical and rhyming pattern and number of lines. Sections of *poetry* of irregular length (as, for example, in *Wordsworth's* "Tintern Abbey") should be called "sections" or *verse paragraphs*, and not stanzas.

Stark, Freya (1893–1993): English travel writer. Her strong *style*, exploring landscapes and history, focuses on her many solitary travels, mainly to the Middle East. Notable works include BAGHDAD SKETCHES (1933), THE VALLEYS OF THE ASSASSINS (1934), A WINTER IN ARABIA (1940), TRAVELLER'S PRELUDE (1950).

Stead, Christina Ellen (1902–83): Australian novelist. Her extensive traveling around America and Europe is conveyed through the variety of *settings* of her work, which often explores her leftwing politics partly through autobiographical and psychological studies. Notable works include THE SALZBURG TALES (1934), THE MAN WHO LOVED CHILDREN (1940), DARK PLACES OF THE HEART (1966, published as COTTER'S ENGLAND, 1967).

Steele, Richard (1672–1729): Irish essayist and playwright. He wrote in several *periodicals* and papers such as THE GAZETTE, SPECTATOR, THEATRE, and THE TATLER (which he founded), often collaborating with *Addison*. His *dramas* pointed the way toward the *sentimental comedy* which became popular later in the 18th century. Notable works include THE FUNERAL (1701), THE IMPORTANCE OF DUNKIRK CONSIDER'D (1713), THE CONSCIOUS LOVERS (1722).

Steinbeck, John (1902–68): American novelist, playwright, and journalist. His *style* and subjects vary widely, but he is probably best remembered for his ability to explore the struggles of rural working life in his homeland, especially California, with striking *realism*. Notable works include TORTILLA FLAT (1935), OF MICE AND MEN (1937), THE GRAPES OF WRATH (1939), CANNERY ROW (1945), EAST OF EDEN (1952), THE WINTER OF OUR DISCONTENT (1961).

Sterne, Laurence (1713–68): English novelist. Made famous by the experimental novel TRISTRAM SHANDY (1759–67), he broke all *narrative conventions* and was a pioneering writer well ahead of his time. His *stream of consciousness technique*, later picked up by writers such as *Joyce*, denies the reader a comforting, reliable narrator (see *narrator/narrative voice*). This innovative shifting, fragmentary *style* always carries a unique shrewd *wit*, making Sterne's work comic yet thought-provoking throughout. Other notable works include THE SERMONS OF MR. YORICK (1760–69), A SENTIMENTAL JOURNEY THROUGH FRANCE AND ITALY (1768).

Stevens, Wallace (1879–1955): American poet. His writing explores the *Romantic* notion of the *imagination* against a more modern sense of reality through elaborate, *metaphoric*, and fanciful language. His later work was noticeably more abstract in *style*, but his essential belief in the power and endurance of *poetry* remained constant. Notable works include "Sunday Morning," published in HARMONIUM (1923), THREE TRAVELERS WATCH A SUNRISE (1920), IDEAS OF ORDER (1936), THE MAN WITH THE BLUE GUITAR AND OTHER POEMS (1937), PARTS OF A WORLD (1942), TRANSPORT TO SUMMER (1947).

Stevenson, Robert Louis (1850–94): Scottish novelist, playwright, essayist, and poet. His adventurous nature is reflected in his lighthearted storytelling, which often touches on a darker side through his admiration for morally dubious *character*s. Notable works include TREASURE ISLAND (1883), KIDNAPPED (1886), THE STRANGE CASE OF DR. JEKYLL AND MR. HYDE (1886), THE BLACK ARROW (1888).

stichomythia: alternate lines of *dialog* in *drama*, often using *antithesis* and/or repeated patterns. It is an excellent *device* for *argument* or building up tension. For example:

Queen Elizabeth:	Shall I be tempted of the devil thus?
King Richard:	Ay, if the devil tempt you to do good.
Queen Elizabeth:	Shall I forget myself to be myself?
King Richard:	Ay, if your self's remembrance wrong yourself.
Queen Elizabeth:	But thou didst kill my children.
King Richard:	But in your daughter's womb I bury them.

(from *Shakespeare*'s RICHARD III, ?1592)

stock characters/response/situations: these are terms for easily recognizable and accepted features:

- stock characters are jealous husbands (as Simkin in *Chaucer*'s THE REEVE'S TALE), ignorant country fellows (as William in *Shakespeare*'s AS YOU LIKE IT), swaggering soldiers (as Pistol in Shakespeare's HENRY V), and so forth
- stock responses are predictable reactions, such as when we are encouraged to hiss the *villain* (often another stock character)
- stock situations are familiar patterns in *literature* such as the eternal triangle (as in Chaucer's THE MERCHANT'S TALE) or confusion caused by identical twins (as in Shakespeare's THE COMEDY OF ERRORS, ?1594).

Stoppard, Tom (b.1937): Czech-born British playwright and screenwriter. Both his stage and television plays challenge and explore literary *convention*s, and ask philosophical questions through *puns* and *parody*. Some praise his plays for their verbal ingenuity and grand flights of intellectual daring; others complain that they display *style* but lack *content*. Notable works include ROSENCRANTZ AND GUILDENSTERN ARE

DEAD (1966), JUMPERS (1972), PROFESSIONAL FOUL (1977), NIGHT AND DAY (1978), THE REAL THING (1982), ARCADIA (1993), SHAKESPEARE IN LOVE (1999, film script).

storm of association: a term used by *Wordsworth* to describe the power of *inspiration* that drives a poet to write.

story: a sequence of events that does not become a *plot* until those events are structured into a *narrative.*

story-within-a-story: a term for a *story* that is a digression from the main *narrative*, e.g. "The Story of a Goblin Who Stole a Sexton," which is told to the assembled party on Christmas Eve in *Dickens's* THE PICKWICK PAPERS.

Stow, Randolph (b.1935): Australian novelist and poet. His work often involves journeys of self-discovery. Notable works include A HAUNTED LAND (1956), THE BYSTANDER (1957), THE MERRY-GO-ROUND IN THE SEA (1965), VISITANTS (1979), THE SUBURBS OF HELL (1984).

Stowe, Harriet Beecher (1811–96): American novelist and children's writer who created one of the largest publishing sensations of the 19th century with the best-selling UNCLE TOM'S CABIN (1852). The *novel* has been criticized as *sentimental* and patronizing in its portrayal of African-Americans, but few question the huge social impact of its antislavery message in the 19th century. Other notable works include SUNNY MEMORIES OF FOREIGN LANDS (1854), DRED: A TALE OF THE DISMAL SWAMP (1856), and MY WIFE AND I (1891), which argues for career freedom for women.

stream of consciousness is a *narrative technique* whereby a writer attempts to recreate in words the natural, freewheeling thought processes of a person's mind. Works such as *Sterne's* TRISTRAM SHANDY and *Coleridge's* "Frost at Midnight" are forerunners of the technique, but the term is generally associated with 20th century experiments in *novel form* in such works as *Joyce's* ULYSSES, *Woolf's* TO THE LIGHTHOUSE, and *Faulkner's* THE SOUND AND THE FURY. À LA RECHERCHE DU TEMPS PERDU (1913–27, translated as REMEMBRANCE OF THINGS PAST, 1922–31) by Marcel Proust (1871–1922) is probably the most famous European stream of consciousness novel. The *device* has become a common narrative *method.* See also *antinovel, interior monolog.*

stress refers to the syllables in words upon which emphasis naturally falls, the use of which is essential in developing *rhythm* in *poetry.* See *meter.*

Strindberg, August (1849–1912): Swedish playwright and novelist. His writings show his neurotic reactions to class, sex, and religion, and, later on, his search for salvation. He influenced, among others, *O'Neill* and the *theater of the absurd.* Notable works include THE FATHER (1887), MISS JULIE (1888), THE DANCE OF DEATH (1901), THE GHOST SONATA (1908).

structural irony is created when the *author* employs a structural *device* that creates *irony.* For instance, there may be a fallible or naïve narrator (see *narrator/narrative voice*) whose point of view is misguided, the knowing reader being aware of the writer's *intention* and thus of the irony.

structuralism, as a concept applied to *literary theory*, begins with the idea that no *text*, or aspect of the language of a text, has any existence or significance on its own, but only makes sense when considered as part of a whole language system.

Structuralists argue that, far from the traditional view that *literature* reflects reality, all writing is made up of a system of *signs*, *codes*, and *conventions*. Some structuralists go on to argue that there is no point of contact between the writer and reader (see *death of the author*), that the former creates a *persona* through which s/he writes the text, and that persona is as much a literary construction as the *characters* created in a *novel* or play. Structuralism emerged during the 1960s, the key advocate being the Frenchman Roland Barthes (1915–80), who argued that the author is never fully conscious of what s/he is doing. Structuralism has been superseded by the *post-structuralist* theories of *deconstruction*.

structure is the overall organization of a work. Some regard the word as interchangeable with the word *form*; others consider the latter to be confined to the shaping of parts within the structure of the whole. Many modern critics only use structure as a specialist word in connection with *literary/critical theory*. See *structuralism*.

style is a term to describe how a writer conveys subject matter, and covers every characteristic aspect of *manner* such as *attitude, diction, figurative language, form, imagery, narrative technique, structure*, syntax, and so forth. Writers who are typical of the style of a period or reminiscent of a previous writer's style may be given an *epithet* such as *Augustan* or Dickensian.

stylistics: the scientific analysis of written and spoken *style*.

stylometrics is computer-aided *stylistics*, by which means it is easier to detect, for instance, which of *Shakespeare's apocryphal* works are more or less likely to have been written by him.

Styron, William (b.1925): American novelist and *short story* writer. Influenced by *Faulkner*, he deals with sweeping *themes* of sin, guilt, evil, and redemption, but without the force and profundity of his great predecessor. Notable works include Lie Down in Darkness (1951), The Confessions of Nat Turner (1967), Sophie's Choice (1979).

subjectivity: of, or relating to, personal emotion rather than objective reasoning; in literary terms, it describes the idea that the perception and *interpretation* of every work of *literature*, indeed of all things abstract or concrete, is affected by the individual reader's experience of the world. See *objectivity*.

sublime: a term used to describe things (such as nature) that are exalted, awe-inspiring, or noble; it is also used to suggest various kinds of lofty literary excellence in *style* and/or subject matter. Many *Romantics* apply the term to the emotions evoked by the *gothic* and descriptions of the grandeur of nature. Some critics value *Chaucer* and *Shakespeare* for their ability to move between the sublime and the earthy.

subplot: a secondary *plot* in a play or *story* that in some way reflects, echoes, parallels, contrasts with, or in other ways enhances the main plot. The *device* was popular in *Elizabethan drama*. Examples are the Gloucester family subplot in relation to the Lear family main plot in *Shakespeare's* King Lear, the Falstaff scenes in his Henry IV plays, or *Rowley's* madhouse scenes in The Changeling. See *double plot*.

substitution, in *verse*, is the replacement of a regular foot with one of a different *meter*. The most common substitution in English verse is the use of a *trochee* at the beginning of an otherwise iambic line, as in *Surrey*'s

Cálm is / the séa / the wáves / work léss / and léss
(from the *sonnet* "Complaint by Night of the Lover Not Beloved")

subtext is, in general terms, the hidden agenda behind the surface of the *text*, what *Pinter* has called "the pressure behind the words." It is that which is implicit rather than explicit. It may take the *form* of a reader or member of an audience working out, or imagining, what lies behind words or *actions*. Some *Marxist* critics believe that *authors* themselves may be unaware of the subtext they are creating, often the result of the cultural, social, and political climate in which they are writing. See *literary/critical theory*.

subversion occurs when any *text* or idea sets out to undermine or subvert an established way of looking at things. For instance:

- *feminist criticism* aims to subvert what it sees as the traditionally *phallocentric* nature of *literature*
- whereas *Leavisites* argued that there is an established *canon* of great literature, and that the function of the literary critic is to pursue and interpret the true *meaning* of each text, structuralists and *poststructuralists* subvert this idea by arguing that the established canon is merely an accident of history, that any one text can be read in an almost infinite number of valid ways, that *authorial intention* is irrelevant, and that anyway true meaning is impossible to establish.

There are many other kinds of political, social, and cultural subversion. Most begin by being *avant-garde*, then themselves become an established way of looking at things, and are then subverted by new approaches to literature. See also *alternative literature*, *underground literature*.

succès d'estime: a work that is praised by the critics but not popular with the public at large. e.g. *Hulme*'s THE BONE PEOPLE.

suggestion is the stimulation of ideas, feelings, impulses, and/or meanings beyond the surface *meaning* through such *techniques* as *allegory, association, symbolism*. See also *connotation, subjectivity*.

surprise (ending): a turn in the *tale*, which the direction of events or *conventions* of a *story* has not led us to expect. It is a *paradox* that in the case of traditional kinds of *short story* a surprise ending is expected. In an effective story the exact nature of such a twist in the tale should not be foreseen by the reader, but should in retrospect be perceived as prepared for by the *author*. See *suspense*.

surrealism refers to a movement in art and *literature* that explored "beyond the real" in order to depict the workings of the unconscious mind. Influenced by the writings of Freud (1856–1939), key artists were Giorgio de Chirico (1888–1978), René Magritte (1898–1967), and Salvador Dali (1904–89), and key writers were mainly French. The movement has had a lasting and important impact upon all the arts. American writers such as *William Burroughs* in *prose*, *Albee* in *drama*, and *Ashbery* in *poetry* have experimented with surrealism. See *expressionism; absurd, theater and literature of the*.

Surrey, Henry Howard, Earl of (?1517–47): English poet and translator. Often linked with *Wyatt* as an early experimenter with the *Petrarchan sonnet* in English, he helped to adapt it into what became known as the *Shakespearean sonnet*. He is credited with introducing *blank verse* into English *poetry*. Notable works include "Complaint by Night of the Lover Not Beloved" (1557), "So Cruel Prison" (1557).

suspense: a lack of certainty as to what is going to happen in a *story*, and an eagerness to know what will happen. An interplay between suspense and *surprise* is an important element in many stories.

suspension of disbelief occurs when a reader or member of an audience knows that, however natural they may seem, the *setting* and/or events of a book or play are not "real," and that the perceived reality thereof depends upon going along with the writer in an imaginative act of willing acceptance. *Shakespeare*'s Chorus at the beginning of HENRY V urges us to do just this. *Coleridge* coined the phrase "willing suspension of disbelief" in BIOGRAPHIA LITERARIA.

Sutherland, Efua (b.1924): Ghanaian playwright and children's writer. Her writing is mainly concerned with the attempt to merge traditional and contemporary social cultures. Notable works include THE ROADMAKERS (1961), EDUFA (1962), FORIWA (1962), THE MARRIAGE OF ANANSEWA (1971).

Swift, Graham (b.1949): English novelist and *short story* writer. Much of his work deals with the personal history and memories of his *character*s, and shows elements of *magic realism*. He creates and sustains complex psychological states, and is skilled in evoking a sense of place and *atmosphere*, such as in WATERLAND (1983). Other notable works include THE SWEET SHOP OWNER (1980), SHUTTLECOCK (1981), LEARNING TO SWIM (1982), LAST ORDERS (1996).

Swift, Jonathan (1667–1745): Irish-born English satirist, essayist, and poet. *Congreve* was a schoolfellow, *Dryden* a cousin, *Addison*, *Pope*, and *Steele* friends. His prolific output is very varied: he wrote on political and religious matters, and attacked social and intellectual abuses, injustices, and stupidity of all kinds, often with great satirical *wit*, and became a noted Irish patriot. His works were disliked in the 18th and 19th centuries by writers such as *Johnson* and *Thackeray* for what was regarded as his harsh, coarse misanthropy; but the 20th century saw a revival of interest in his common sense, intelligence, and sharply observed *satire*. Notable works include A TALE OF A TUB (1704), THE BATTLE OF THE BOOKS (1704), GULLIVER'S TRAVELS (1726), A MODEST PROPOSAL (1729).

Swinburne, Algernon Charles (1837–1909): English poet, playwright, novelist, and critic. Influenced by *Dante Gabriel Rossetti* and *Whitman*, and by both classical and *romantic traditions*, he has a command over a great range of poetic *forms*. He was a part of the aesthetic movement (see *aestheticism*), and his writings were often highly individualistic and offended Victorian sensibilities. Notable works include ATALANTA IN CALYDON (1865), POEMS AND BALLADS (1866), POEMS AND BALLADS: SECOND SERIES (1878).

syllabic verse is *meter* that is measured by the number of syllables in the line, regardless of the *stress* pattern.

syllepsis is an alternative term for *zeugma*.

symbol: a kind of *metaphor* where something stands for something else. For instance:

- in *Blake*'s *poem* "The Sick Rose" (1794) the rose is an *emblem* that stands for perishable loveliness and love as embodied by the woman's body
- *Coleridge* wrote of objects in the outside world, especially in nature, as symbols of what he was feeling
- in THE GLASS MENAGERIE by *Tennessee Williams* the collection of glass animals is symbolic of Laura's state of mind.

symbolism: the use of *symbols* in a persistent, planned way in *literature*. Several of the English *Romantic* writers such as *Blake* and *Percy Shelley* make much use of recurrent symbols in their *poetry*, and symbolism was also prominent in the *prose* writings of various 19th century American *authors* such as *Hawthorne, Melville, Emerson,* and *Poe*.

symbolist movement: a term that specifically defines a group of French 19th century writers including Charles Baudelaire (1821–67), Arthur Rimbaud (1854–91), Paul Verlaine (1844–96), Stéphane Mallarmé (1842–98), and Paul Valéry (1871–1945) who believed in the intrinsic value of the *symbol* itself, and aimed to create a meaningful *aesthetic* experience through the suggestive and evocative use of words. They had a considerable influence upon later writers in English such as *Yeats, T.S. Eliot, Pound, Joyce,* and *Faulkner*.

sympathy is a term used in *literature* to indicate feelings of understanding that a reader or audience has toward the situation of a *character*, while remaining detached. See *empathy*.

synaeresis: the combining of two separate vowels to create a single syllable as in "seest" for "see-est." The *technique* is common in *poetry* in order to preserve the regular *meter* of a line. See *elision*.

synaesthesia is the mixing of two or more senses within one image, common in writers such as *Keats*, who frequently use sensuous *imagery* – e.g. in "Ode to a Nightingale" he implies all five senses in describing wine as:

> Tasting of Flora and the country green,
> Dance, and Provençal song, and sunburnt mirth…

and later in the *poem* he describes sight in terms of touch:

> But here there is no light,
> Save what from heaven is with the breezes blown…

In *Spender*'s "Seascape" (1946) he writes of the sea as "burning music for the eyes."

syncope: the reduction of a word by skipping over letters, as in "o'er" for "over." See *elision*.

synecdoche: a *figure of speech* in which a part stands for a whole; e.g. in LYCIDAS, Milton refers to the unseeing and greedy clergy as "blind mouths." The *device* is often used in everyday speech. See *metonymy*.

Synge, J.M. (1871–1909): Irish playwright. Influenced by *Yeats*, he spent much time gathering background material about Irish peasant life, language, and landscape for his plays, which are a curious mixture of lyrical depictions of illusion and harsh reality. Notable works include RIDERS TO THE SEA (1904), THE PLAYBOY OF THE WESTERN WORLD (1907), DEIRDRE OF THE SORROWS (1910).

systrophe: a *rhetorical device* by which something is defined by an accumulation of phrases or by *repetition*, e.g. Macbeth's *apostrophe* to Sleep:

> ...the innocent sleep,
> Sleep that knits up the ravell'd sleave of care
> The death of each day's life, sore labour's bath,
> Balm of hurt minds, great nature's second course,
> Chief nourisher in life's feast, ...

(from Shakespeare's MACBETH, act II, scene 3)

tale: a type of *short story* or short *narrative poem* that concentrates more on *action* and incident than on *atmosphere* and *character*. It often draws upon an *oral* rather than a literary *tradition*. Among others, *Conrad* and *Faulkner* have been noted writers of tales. See also *yarn*.

tapinosis is a figurative *device* that ridicules something by ludicrously exaggerating it, as in the following extract from a description of a game of cards:

> An Ace of Hearts steps forth: the King unseen
> Lurked in her hand, and mourned his captive Queen.
> He springs to vengeance with an eager pace,
> And falls like thunder on the prostrate Ace.
> (from *Pope*'s The Rape of the Lock)

See *hyperbole*.

taste, in a literary sense, has come to refer to subjective preferences for certain kinds of *literature*, often influenced by fashion. In the 18th century the word denoted objective aesthetic and critical judgment concerning what was defined as good or bad literature (and many at that time considered that *Shakespeare*'s plays lacked taste). See also *aesthetics, objectivity, subjectivity.*

Tate, Allen (1899–1979): American poet, novelist, editor, and literary critic. Originally one of the "Fugitive" poets (after the Nashville literary magazine of that name) and a defender of the ideas espoused by the *new critics*, he became a leading intellectual voice on the American literary scene. In both his *poetry* and his *criticism* he argued for the importance of *tradition*. Notable works include the *poems* "Ode to the Confederate Dead" (1926), "The Mediterranean" (1937), and the *collections* Collected Essays (1959), Essays of Four Decades (1969).

Taylor, Edward (?1642–1729): English-born American colonial poet and Puritan minister. Influenced by the English *metaphysical* poets, many of whom used the *techniques* of simple language and *witty metaphor* to express religious *themes*, he wrote devotional *poems* like "Huswifery," "Upon a Spider Catching a Fly," and "Meditation" (all written in the early 1680s). None of Taylor's *verse* was published in his lifetime, and his work was not discovered until 1937. Collected Poems was published in 1939.

technique is the particular craft and *method* employed by a writer. It is often not appropriate to separate technique from *content*, as what a writer wishes to say will largely dictate technique (although some *devices* are purely decorative). For example, *Percy Shelley*'s colorful and soaring *imagery* in "To a Skylark" is integral to the *meaning* of the *poem*.

telling: see *showing and telling*.

Tennyson, Alfred Lord (1809–92): English poet and playwright. As an undergraduate at Cambridge he formed a close relationship with Arthur Henry Hallam, whose early death in 1833 so affected Tennyson that, after a 17-year gestation period, he published the series of moving *poems* In Memoriam (1850), probably the longest *elegy* in the English language. His technically masterful poems range from the melancholy, solitary, and lyrical to the confident, moral, *epic*, and even imperialist. He was *poet laureate* from 1850–92. Notable works include POEMS (1832, including "The Lady of Shalott," "The Lotos-Eaters," and "Ulysses"), THE PRINCESS (1847), MAUD AND OTHER POEMS (1855, including "The Charge of the Light Brigade"), IDYLLS OF THE KING (1859–85), DEMETER AND OTHER POEMS (1889, including "Crossing the Bar").

tenor and vehicle: a description for *metaphor*, in which the tenor is the subject and the vehicle is the metaphoric image that conveys the subject. For example, in "the high, steep mountain of Achievement," "Achievement" is the tenor and "the high, steep mountain" is the vehicle. The terms were coined by *Richards* in THE PHILOSOPHY OF RHETORIC.

tension in *literature* occurs when any kind of conflict is created in the reader or audience. It may be, for example, between the literal and metaphorical, or the emotional and the intellectual. An instance of the latter might be in *Shakespeare's* HAMLET where emotionally and dramatically an audience might wish to see Hamlet take *revenge*, at the same time intellectually knowing that revenge is wrong in the eyes of the law and God; thus tension is created. One might also talk of a tension created in the reader who on the one hand might empathetically regard *characters* as "real," yet at the same time realize that they are "unreal" literary constructions.

tercet: a *stanza* or section of three lines of *verse*, often rhyming.

terza rima consists of *tercets* interlinked by a *rhyme scheme* whereby each second line rhymes with the succeeding first and third line (aba, bcb, cdc and so on). Used by Italian poets such as *Dante* and *Petrarch*, it was introduced by *Wyatt* into England. Among others *Chaucer, Milton, Byron*, and *T.S. Eliot* all used the *form*, as did *Percy Shelley*, notably in "Ode to the West Wind":

> O wild West Wind, thou breath of Autumn's being
> Thou, from whose unseen presence the leaves dead
> Are driven, like ghosts from an enchanter fleeing
> Yellow, and black, and pale, and hectic red,
> Pestilence-driven multitudes: O thou,
> Who chariotest to their dark wintery bed…

tetralogy: four related *novels* or plays, e.g. *Shakespeare's* RICHARD II (?1595), HENRY IV PART 1, HENRY IV PART 2, and HENRY V.

tetrameter: see *meter*.

tetrapody: a *verse* line containing four feet (see *meter*).

tetrastich: a section or *stanza* of *verse*, or complete *poem*, of four lines; another word for a *quatrain*.

text may mean:

- the words of a book
- the main body of a book, discounting such matter as *preface*, introduction, acknowledgments, list of contents, bibliography, appendices, and so forth
- a piece of *literature* prepared for critical analysis
- a passage taken from the *Bible* as a *theme* for a sermon.

textual criticism is the analysis of the various existing *text*s of a work in order to determine:

- the best possible (or definitive) text for publication
- authorship, if it is uncertain or in dispute.

texture refers to the surface qualities of a work rather than its *form*, *structure*, or *meaning*, e.g. its *diction* or *imagery*, which may create a particular *atmosphere*.

Thackeray, William Makepeace (1811–63): English novelist, journalist, and sketch and travel writer. His social awareness led to a *satirical* edge in much of his writing, but this is tempered by compassion for his *character*s and a fine comic energy. He was a great critical and popular success in his day, although his standing has since declined somewhat. Vanity Fair (1847–48), a title taken from *Bunyan*'s Pilgrim's Progress, is generally considered to be his masterpiece. Other notable works include The Yellowplush Papers (1837–38), The History of Pendennis (1848–50), The History of Henry Esmond (1852), The Newcomes (1853–55).

theater of the absurd: see *absurd, theater and literature of the*.

theater of cruelty originates from the theories of the French actor and director Antonin Artaud (1896–1948) who said that theater should disturb profoundly so as to release people's subconscious repressions, and that the director should be "a master of magic." For him, mime, gesture, scenery, and spectacular theatrical effects were all-important. The Marat/Sade (1964) by Peter Weiss is a good example of the *genre*.

theater in the round describes an auditorium where the audience are all around the actors, or at least in a horseshoe, rather than separated from the *action* by a *proscenium arch*. This *style* of presenting plays, probably common with medieval *mystery* and later *morality plays*, became increasingly popular again during the 20th century; and theater architecture in recent decades has often taken account of the need for a flexible stage in order to present plays within auditoria of various shapes.

theater of silence is a term applied to the principle in *drama* that silences are often as important as the *dialog*. Anton Chekhov (1860–1904) and *Pinter* are examples of playwrights who have used prolonged pauses to good effect, e.g. especially Pinter's Landscape (1970) and Silence (1970).

thematic imagery is *imagery* that runs through a work, helping to bring out a central *theme*. For instance, repeated clothing imagery in *Shakespeare*'s Macbeth underlies the idea that Macbeth has taken the clothing of kingship that does not belong to him, and images of imprisonment and darkness in *Webster*'s The Duchess of Malfi emphasize the claustrophobic world that closes in upon the Duchess.

theme: a central or essential idea in a *text*. The term is much abused, students sometimes using the word as an all-purpose term for other elements (see, for instance, *emblem, motif, setting*).

theories of criticism: see *literary/critical theory*.

Theroux, Paul (b.1941): American novelist, journalist, travel, and *short story* writer. He is a very versatile writer who is able to turn his hand to various subjects in different *genre*s and *style*s. Notable works include The Great Railway Bazaar (1975, one of three books about railway journeys), THE OLD PATAGONIAN EXPRESS (1978), RIDING THE IRON ROOSTER (1988), THE HAPPY ISLES OF OCEANIA (1992).

Thesiger, Wilfred (b.1910): British travel writer and autobiographer, born in Addis Ababa, Abyssinia (now Ethiopia). He writes of his experiences in energetic, direct *prose*, rejecting *modernist* concepts of technological progress. Notable works include ARABIAN SANDS (1959), THE MARSH ARABS (1964).

thesis: this can refer to:

- a long scholarly work presented to a university for a higher degree
- a main line of *argument* in a literary work (see *dissertation*)
- any proposition, against which is set its *antithesis*
- the unstressed syllable in an iambic or trochaic foot (see *meter*).

See *discourse, tract, treatise*.

thesis novel: sometimes called a sociological *novel*, this refers to a *didactic* novel that by means of its storyline advances a sociological, political, religious, or other moral point or *thesis*. Examples include *Stowe's* UNCLE TOM'S CABIN, *Dickens's* HARD TIMES (1854), *Samuel Butler's* THE WAY OF ALL FLESH, *Holtby's* SOUTH RIDING, *Steinbeck's* THE GRAPES OF WRATH, *Paton's* CRY, THE BELOVED COUNTRY. See also *documentary novel, proletarian novel*.

thesis play is another term for *drama of ideas*.

Thiong'o, Ngugi wa: see *Ngugi wa Thiong'o*.

third-person narrator: see *narrator/narrative voice*.

Thomas, Dylan (1914–53): Welsh poet, playwright, broadcaster, *short story* writer, and scriptwriter, who was famous for his extravagant behavior and hard-drinking lifestyle (which eventually killed him) as much as for his writing. His *poetry* was very popular in his lifetime, but some critics since have considered him overrated. His *verse* is variously exuberant, mystical, and psychologically complex, and the *imagery* of his later poetry is influenced by the Welsh coastal landscape. Notable works include PORTRAIT OF THE ARTIST AS A YOUNG DOG (1940), COLLECTED POEMS (1953), UNDER MILK WOOD (1953).

Thomas, Edward (1878–1917): English poet, critic, biographer, and *topographical* writer. Influenced and encouraged by *Frost*, he wrote *poetry* that included loving observations of the English countryside, and he attempted to use natural, and sometimes colloquial, language within a metrical *structure*. Notable works include THE WOODLAND LIFE (1897), AN ANNUAL OF NEW POETRY (1917, with others), LAST POEMS (1918).

Thomas, R.S. (1913–2000): Welsh poet and priest. His *poetry* gives a *realistic*, stark, uncompromising yet paradoxically beautiful picture of the harsh Welsh hill-farming life and a strong sense of the landscape. He also brings his sharp intellect to bear on personal and spiritual issues, and on Welsh cultural and linguistic matters. Notable works include THE STONES OF THE FIELD (1946), NOT THAT HE BROUGHT FLOWERS (1968), H'M (1972), SELECTED PROSE (1983), COMPLETE POEMS 1946–1990 (1993).

Thoreau, Henry David (1817–62): American essayist, travel writer, and poet. A friend of *Emerson*, he was much influenced by *transcendentalism*. He challenged authority, materialism, and the work ethic, and has been regarded as a pioneer ecologist. His most famous work is the enduring American *classic*, WALDEN, OR LIFE IN THE WOODS (1854), based on his two-year retreat to a cabin near Walden Pond in Concord, Massachusetts. Other notable works include A WEEK ON THE CONCORD AND MERRIMACK RIVERS (1849), "On the Duty of Civil Disobedience" (1849), EXCURSIONS (1863).

threnody nowadays refers to any work of lamentation, e.g. *Tennyson*'s IN MEMORIAM. See *complaint, dirge, elegy, monody.*

thriller: a loose term that covers many kinds of *fiction* written for sensational effect, but most often used as another word for the *crime novel.* See also *detective fiction, police procedural, spy story, whodunnit.*

Thurber, James (1894–1961): American essayist and *short story* writer. Through gentle, humorous *satire*, often illustrated by his own cartoons, he shows the innocent individual under threat in a bewildering world. Notable works include "The Secret Life of Walter Mitty" (1939), FABLES FOR OUR TIME (1940), MY WORLD – AND WELCOME TO IT (1942).

Tillyard, E.M.W. (1889–1962): English scholar and literary critic who specialized in the Elizabethan period. Notable works include THE ELIZABETHAN WORLD PICTURE (1943) in which he set out to consider the *viewpoint*s and assumptions, such as the *great chain of being*, of the Elizabethans who watched *Shakespeare*'s plays.

time novel is a term sometimes used to define *novel*s in which time is a major factor or of central thematic importance, and in which *stream of consciousness* is often employed, e.g. *Joyce*'s ULYSSES.

time play is a vague term for any kind of play in which time is an important factor. This could be through:

- a gap in the time sequence, as in *Shakespeare*'s THE WINTER'S TALE where there is a time gap of 16 years while Perdita grows up
- the sequence of the play not being strictly chronological, incorporating *flashback*s or *flashforward*s, as in *Priestley*'s TIME AND THE CONWAYS.

Writers in literary *genre*s other than *drama* have, of course, been preoccupied with time, especially writers of *science fiction.*

Tolstoy, Count Lev Nikolaevich (1828–1910): Russian novelist, playwright, *short story* writer, essayist, and philosopher who greatly influenced 19th and 20th century writing across Europe, especially the *novel.* Notable works include WAR AND PEACE (1863–69), ANNA KARENINA (1873–77).

tone: a term to describe the *attitude* taken by a writer toward both the reader and the *content* of the writing, and conveyed by such factors as language and syntax. For example, the tone may be *witty*, angry, compassionate, somber, detached, and so forth, as with a tone of *voice* in speech. See also *ambience, atmosphere, mood.*

topographical poetry: *poem*s written about specific places, usually rural landscapes but sometimes urban or other locations. Examples include *Gray*'s "Elegy Written in a Country Churchyard," *Wordsworth*'s "Tintern Abbey," *Ted Hughes*'s "River"

(1983), and much of the *poetry* of *Edward Thomas, MacCaig*, and *Nicholson*. See also *pastoral.*

touchstone: a hard stone used to test the purity of gold; in a literary sense, a standard or yardstick. In his *essay* THE STUDY OF POETRY (1880), *Arnold* uses the term to indicate passages of literary excellence against which other works may be judged. He regarded this as more objective than personal judgment or assessment by historical importance.

Tourneur, Cyril (?1575–1626): English playwright and poet. Little is known about him, and some critics think that THE REVENGER'S TRAGEDY (1607), an intense, bloody, *witty* piece with elements of *black comedy*, possibly a *parody* of the *revenge tragedy genre* and usually ascribed to him, was written by *Middleton*. Other notable works include THE ATHEIST'S TRAGEDY (1611).

tract: a *pamphlet* or *essay* on a contentious issue, usually religious or political. See *discourse, dissertation, thesis, treatise.*

tradition: in *literature* studies, a term to describe the great body of past writings that must necessarily influence later writers. However innovative or experimental a work may be, to a large degree its interest lies in a comparison with what has gone before. Writings which consider the impact of tradition include *T.S. Eliot*'s "Tradition and the Individual Talent" (1919) and *Leavis*'s THE GREAT TRADITION.

tragedy is a term that has come to describe a *drama* that ends disastrously, usually in the death of the *protagonist* and others. Broadly speaking there are two types:

- Greek tragedy, where fate brings about the downfall of the *character*(s) involved, e.g. in *Sophocles'* OEDIPUS REX, where it is fated by the gods that Oedipus will kill his father and marry his mother, and so he cannot escape this fate
- Shakespearean tragedy, where a character has free will but a *fatal flaw* causes the downfall, e.g. in *Shakespeare*'s OTHELLO, where it may be said that it is the protagonist's inability to control his jealousy that brings him down.

However, these are oversimplifications: there are also flaws in Oedipus' character, and unlucky circumstances of fate surrounding Othello's situation, that contribute to their respective falls. The *manner* of the unfolding of both kinds of tragedy involves a sense of inevitability. Usually a tragic protagonist should be of sufficient moral stature to make his or her fall worthy of *pathos*; however, not all central characters in tragedy are good – e.g. Shakespeare's Macbeth or Richard III. Tragic figures in modern plays sometimes come from humbler areas of society, and the *dénouement* does not necessarily result in death, e.g. in *Miller*'s THE PRICE (1968). Tragedy is a term that strictly speaking is restricted to plays, but the word has become extended to *poetry* and *prose*, e.g. some of *Hardy*'s *poems* and *novels*.

tragedy of blood is another term for *revenge tragedy*. After Bosola has carried out his revenge in *Webster*'s THE DUCHESS OF MALFI he is called "thou wretched thing of blood."

tragic flaw: a weakness of *character*, or *hamartia*, that brings about a person's downfall. The critic *Bradley* was foremost in advancing the theory of the "fatal flaw" in the character makeup of a tragic *protagonist*, pointing to Hamlet's speech in act I, scene 4 of *Shakespeare*'s HAMLET concerning men who carry "the stamp of one defect." See *hubris*, *tragedy*.

tragic irony is *dramatic irony* when it specifically relates to *tragedy*, with the *protagonist* moving toward the recognition (*anagnorisis*) of a truth of which the audience is already aware.

tragicomedy decribes plays (or sometimes other *literature*) that involve a mixture of *tragedy* and *comedy*. It may be used of plays that are "bitter-sweet" in their threat of tragedy, and in the presence of some unfortunate circumstances that are unresolved at the end, but that conclude more or less happily. *Shakespeare*'s THE MERCHANT OF VENICE (?1596) and THE WINTER'S TALE have been placed in this category. Plays such as Shakespeare's TWELFTH NIGHT or MUCH ADO ABOUT NOTHING, while classed as comedies, contain respectively dark *tones* and the potential for tragedy. The term may also be used of plays that contain elements of comedy but are ultimately grim – or at least bitter – such as Shakespeare's TROILUS AND CRESSIDA (?1602). Modern plays that have been placed in this *genre* include *Beckett*'s WAITING FOR GODOT and *Hare*'s SECRET RAPTURE (1989).

transcendentalism was an American intellectual movement active in New England between the 1830s and 1860s that stressed the importance of the individual's conscience and intuition as a basis for morality, creativity, and spiritual renewal. It was a continuation of many aspects of *Romanticism* in its reaction against *neoclassicism* and against modern materialism, advocating a return to nature for *inspiration*. *Emerson* was a foremost member, and others associated with it included *Hawthorne* and *Thoreau*.

transferred epithet: sometimes called "hypallage," a common *device* whereby an *epithet* is transferred from the noun to which it should apply (sometimes understood but not stated) and attached to another noun to which it does not apply. For instance, in the phrase "a sleepless night" the epithet "sleepless" has been transferred from the person who cannot sleep and attached to the night. The intended sense is easily understood.

travel literature is writing in which the *author* sets out to record experiences in a part of the world and culture that is different from her/his native place. It is usually *nonfiction*, but is sometimes *fiction* (or at least *faction*) or *poetry*. It may be written in a straightforward *narrative*, or in a *diary* or *epistolary form*. It may be some kind of literary or personal quest, a pilgrimage toward a spiritual goal, contain elements of *autobiography*, be a kind of escapism (for writer and reader) or wish for freedom from the restraints of a settled life, and/or an attempt to record a way of life about to be lost. The *genre* has a long history from classical times, through the writings of Elizabethan discoverers such as Walter Ralegh (*c.*1552–1618), the 18th and 19th century travelogues of *Boswell, Johnson, Smollett, Sterne,* and *Stevenson,* to notable modern travel writers including *Chatwin, Fermor,* Norman Lewis (b.1908), *Murphy,* Eric Newby (b.1919), *Theroux, Thesiger.*

treatise: a substantial and systematic written examination of every aspect of a subject, often on a philosophical, political, religious, scientific, or academic matter, e.g. *Sidney*'s THE DEFENCE OF POESY (1595). See *discourse, dissertation, thesis, tract.*

Trevor, William (b.1928): Irish novelist and *short story* writer. A technically very accomplished writer, he explores aspects of life in Ireland, and his *themes* include microcosmic worlds that are faded or in decay, loss of innocence, and the condition of old age. Notable works include THE OLD BOYS (1964), MRS. ECKDORF IN O'NEILL'S HOTEL (1969), THE CHILDREN OF DYNMOUTH (1976), FOOLS OF FORTUNE (1983), THE NEWS FROM IRELAND (1986), THE COLLECTED STORIES (1992), FELICIA'S JOURNEY (1994).

Trilling, Lionel (1905–75): American scholar and literary critic, whose wide-ranging writings concern the role of society and culture in *literature*, and show the value of psychological and philosophical approaches to intellectual history. Notable works include THE LIBERAL IMAGINATION (1950), THE OPPOSING SELF (1955), BEYOND CULTURE (1965), SINCERITY AND AUTHENTICITY (1972).

trilogy: three related *novels* or plays, e.g. *Golding*'s historical sea *stories* RITES OF PASSAGE (1980), CLOSE QUARTERS (1987), and FIRE DOWN BELOW (1989).

trimeter: see *meter.*

triple meter occurs when each foot (see *meter*) is made up of three syllables, as in *anapests* and *dactyls*. It is not as common in English *verse* as *double meter*, although used to effect in some 19th century verse by *Byron, Tennyson,* and others.

triple rhyme occurs when accented rhyming syllables are followed by two identical syllables (silvery/coppery, mothering/bothering, wittily/prettily), and is most often used for comic effect.

triplet: an alternative term for *tercet.*

trochaic: see *meter.*

trochee: a single trochaic foot. See *meter.*

Trollope, Anthony (1815–82): English novelist, biographer, autobiographer, travel and *short story* writer. His output was prolific. He modestly called himself a "grocer of words," but he was meticulously professional in his approach to his work. He shows a clear understanding of human motivation, and writes with low-key *irony* about Victorian life and institutions. THE BARSETSHIRE NOVELS (1855–67), of which THE WARDEN (1855) is the first in a series that developed *characters* and their lives within the same community, focused upon the clergy and represented a new kind of *regional novel.* THE PALLISER NOVELS (1864–80), including THE EUSTACE DIAMONDS (1872), deal with political life. Other notable works include THE WAY WE LIVE NOW (1874–75), which some consider to be his masterpiece.

Trollope, Frances (1780–1863): English novelist and travel writer, mother of *Anthony Trollope.* Much of her work, documentary and *fiction*, looks at social, religious, industrial, and other aspects of life in Victorian England. Notable works include DOMESTIC MANNERS OF THE AMERICANS (1832), THE VICAR OF WREXHILL (1837), THE LIFE AND ADVENTURES OF MICHAEL ARMSTRONG, THE FACTORY BOY (1840).

trope: in a general sense, any *rhetorical* or *figurative* use of language such as *metaphor, metonymy, personification, simile.*

truncation: see *catalexis.*

Tudor interludes: see *interlude.*

turning point: any kind of change (for instance of subject matter, *theme, mood,* or direction of a *story* or *drama*), e.g. in a *poem,* a shift between the *octave* and *sestet* in a *sonnet* (sometimes known as the "volta").

Twain, Mark (real name Samuel Clemens; 1835–1910): American novelist, *short story* writer, autobiographer, and journalist, working as the latter at some point with *Harte.* His most famous works, THE ADVENTURES OF TOM SAWYER (1876) and HUCKLEBERRY FINN (1884), draw greatly on his own Mississippi childhood. Much of his writing has a moral and/or humorously *satirical* quality. The energy and innovation of his earlier works, partly dissipated by personal troubles, converts to a somber but arresting pessimism in his later writings. Other notable works include THE CELEBRATED JUMPING FROG OF CALAVERAS COUNTY (1867), THE INNOCENTS ABROAD (1869), ROUGHING IT (1872), THE PRINCE AND THE PAUPER (1881), A CONNECTICUT YANKEE IN THE COURT OF KING ARTHUR (1889).

type is a term that may refer to:

- a stereotypical *character* (what *Forster* called a *flat character*)
- a *genre.*

ubi sunt is Latin for "Where are they now?" and denotes a frequent elegiac *motif* in *literature*, especially in *lyric poetry* where the writer laments a vanished past. Among notable examples are the *Old English poems* THE SEAFARER and THE WANDERER, and "Adieu, Farewell, Earth's Bliss" (1600) by Thomas Nashe (1567–1601). The motif is recurrent in *Tennyson's* work. Although strictly speaking the term relates to poetry, one can detect passages in *prose* works that may be described in the spirit of ubi sunt, e.g. in *Brittain's* TESTAMENT OF YOUTH.

Udall, Nicholas (1504–56): English playwright. His RALPH ROISTER DOISTER (?1553) is considered to be the first English *comedy*. Influenced by the Roman comedies of Plautus (?254–184BC) and Terence (?190–159BC), his play may in turn have influenced Elizabethan comedies such as *Shakespeare's* THE TAMING OF THE SHREW (?1592) and THE COMEDY OF ERRORS (?1594).

underground literature is a term used to describe any *literature* that is subversive or antiestablishment, and circulates in other than standard published *form* (e.g. in privately printed documents or through public readings). Under a suppressive political system it is necessary for writers to operate in this way, but in Western-style democracies such literature soon becomes a part of established studies, e.g. the *Beat movement*, the *Liverpool poets*. See *alternative literature*.

understatement: see *litotes*.

unities, dramatic: three guidelines for the construction of plays, which are:

- unity of *action*, which laid down that there should be one main action of a play and no *subplots*
- unity of place, which ruled that the action should occur in one place, and not keep shifting location
- unity of time, which ruled that the action of a play should not cover events exceeding a 24-hour period.

Unities of action and time were described by *Aristotle* in his POETICS as being features of Greek *tragedies*, to which later theorists added the unity of place. This formula for the construction of tragedies remained in use until *Shakespeare* and his contemporaries increasingly disregarded them (as did Spanish playwrights), often extending the action to multiple *plots* ranging over many years in different places. French and Italian playwrights tended to regard the unities as fixed rules until the 19th century. In his PREFACES TO SHAKESPEARE (1765) *Johnson* rejected the whole idea (upon which the supposed importance of the unities was based) that the stage presentation should necessarily give audiences the illusion of reality. See *rules, suspension of disbelief.*

unity, in literary terms, describes the concept that a work has complete structural coherence with nothing within it that is superfluous, and that the adding or taking away of anything will damage the whole.

universality in *literature* is the quality that gives a piece of literature appeal beyond the time and culture in which it is written. In general, modern critical thinking holds that this is impossible, all writing being culture-bound. However, writing that focuses upon the unchanging aspects of human nature is more likely to achieve universality. Among notable writers in English who are held to have achieved this are *Chaucer, Shakespeare, Jonson, Dryden, Jonathan Swift,* and *Pope,* often through satirizing the afore-mentioned human traits such as greed, hypocrisy, and lust for power.

university wits: a name given to a group of Elizabethan Oxford and Cambridge educated poets and playwrights who were active in London toward the end of the 16th century, including *Lyly, Marlowe,* Thomas Nashe (1567–1601). It is reputed that they met in the Mermaid Tavern off Cheapside. *Shakespeare* pokes gentle fun at this group in LOVE'S LABOURS LOST (?1594).

unreliable narrator: see *narrator/narrative voice.*

Unsworth, Barrie (b.1930): English novelist whose writing often has an historical dimension, empire featuring as a recurrent *theme.* Notable works include SUGAR AND RUM (1988), SACRED HUNGER (1992), MORALITY PLAY (1995), AFTER HANNIBAL (1996), THE PARTNERSHIP (2001).

untranslatableness, in the sense used by *Coleridge* in BIOGRAPHIA LITERARIA, is the quality of *literature* that makes it impossible to "translate" the words of *poetry* in the same language without damaging the *meaning.* Attempts to do this are normally done with the misguided intention of making the meaning clearer, and perhaps those who try to render *Shakespeare* into "plain English" should mark Coleridge's words.

Updike, John (b.1932): American novelist, journalist, *short story* and children's writer, and poet. His *novels* explore middle-class American life in a *witty,* urbane *style.* Notable works include THE POORHOUSE FAIR (1959), RABBIT RUN (1960), RABBIT IS RICH (1981), THE WITCHES OF EASTWICK (1984), RABBIT AT REST (1990), LICKS OF LOVE (2000).

urtext: a lost early version of a *text;* e.g. textual analysis suggests that *Shakespeare's* HAMLET is based on an urtext, possibly by *Kyd.*

utilitarianism is, in general terms, the doctrine that the value of things may only be weighed by their strict usefulness to the greatest number of people. Hence *literature* was considered of little practical use. Jeremy Bentham (1748–1832) and James Mill (1773–1836) were leading exponents of this philosophy, the emotionally crippling effects of which were attacked by *Dickens* in HARD TIMES (1845), where the *character* Gradgrind values facts and rejects *imagination.* The economist John Stuart Mill (1806–73), son of James, describes in his AUTOBIOGRAPHY (1873) such effects in his own upbringing, and goes on to record the spiritual awakening he experienced upon first reading the *poetry* of *Coleridge* and *Wordsworth. Wilde's* notion of one who "knows the price of everything and the value of nothing" may be taken as a cynic's definition of an utilitarian.

utopia: in *literature,* an ideal state where the inhabitants lead a completely well-governed life that approaches perfection on earth. The word is derived from *More's* 1516 *treatise,* UTOPIA (a conflation of the Greek words for "good place" and "no place") where, typical of subsequent literary utopias, an adventurous traveler discovers a distant fictional utopian state. The *genre* is a good vehicle for *satire,* as in *Jonathan Swift's* GULLIVER'S TRAVELS in which Gulliver visits various countries that display both utopian and *dystopian* characteristics. Modern *fiction* more often depicts dystopias than utopias.

V

valediction: a farewell speech, e.g. *Donne*'s *poem* "A Valediction: Forbidding Mourning" (1633).

Vanbrugh, John (1664–1726): English playwright of *Restoration comedy*, writer of *adaptations*, and architect. Notable works include THE RELAPSE, OR VIRTUE IN DANGER (1696, a *satirical* sequel to *Cibber*'s LOVE'S LAST SHIFT), THE PROVOK'D WIFE (1697).

vehicle: see *tenor*.

Venus and Adonis stanza: a six-line *stanza* rhyming ababcc, as used by *Shakespeare* in VENUS AND ADONIS (1593).

verisimilitude occurs when, to the mind of the reader, a writer has succeeded in depicting things with truth and *realism*, even when there are *fantastic* elements in a work. For example, it is claimed that *Jonathan Swift* achieves this in GULLIVER'S TRAVELS, notwithstanding Gulliver's travels into fantastic worlds.

verism: in *literature* and the arts, the use of elements to depict reality, however harsh or difficult that reality might be.

vernacular: the spoken, everyday language of one's native country. The term is often used to distinguish between "literary" English and writings in a local dialect – e.g. some of *Burns*'s *poem*s are written in Lowland Scots vernacular, William Barnes's (1801–86) in Dorset, *Walcott*'s in Caribbean Creole.

vers de société refers to *witty*, lightweight *verse* that deals with the trivial aspects of society. Much of *Betjeman*'s verse is considered to be of this type, and other notable exponents are *Pope, Belloc, Chesterton,* and *Auden. Larkin* produced an example actually called "Vers de Société" (in HIGH WINDOWS).

verse is a term used to refer to:

- a line written in *meter*
- a *stanza*
- a unit of writing in the *Bible*
- *poetry* in general as distinct from *prose* (although the term "verse" is sometimes used to suggest lightweight poetry).

verse drama describes any *drama* written in *verse*. *Elizabethan* and *Jacobean drama* was predominantly written in verse, but from the *Restoration period* onward *prose* was the main medium. In the mid-20th century an attempt was made to revive verse drama by *T.S. Eliot*, Christopher Fry (b.1907), and others, but its success was short-lived.

verse paragraph: is a defined section of (usually *blank verse*) lines that make up a distinct unit as found in *Milton*'s PARADISE LOST or *Wordsworth*'s THE PRELUDE.

verset: a flexible *form* of *verse* written in groups of long lines, often of irregular length, forming short *verse paragraph*s, as in *Lawrence*'s KANGAROO (1923). It is derived from the type of Old Testament biblical verse to be found in THE SONG OF SOLOMON.

versification can mean:

- the act of composing a *verse*
- studying verse *form*
- putting a *prose* work into verse.

Vice: a stock, buffoonish *character* who often appeared in *morality plays* and *interludes* as a tempter of mankind. *Shakespeare*'s Falstaff in HENRY IV PARTS 1 AND 2 is in many ways a re-creation of the Vice figure.

Victorian age: generally considered to cover *literature* written in England between approximately 1830 and 1901, comprising the reigns of William IV (1830–37) and Victoria (1838–1901).

viewpoint: see *narrator/narrative voice, showing and telling.*

vignette: originally a small decorative design on a blank page in a book at the beginning or end of a chapter (often of foliage and branches, or a small rural scene). In a literary sense the word has come to describe a part or whole of *prose* work that skillfully creates an image of something as though it were a small picture, as in *Woolf*'s short story KEW GARDENS (1919).

villain: the evil person in a story. The term often indicates a rather *flat character* type, although there are plenty of more complex villains such as Iago in *Shakespeare*'s OTHELLO. The villain is more often associated with *drama* than other *genres*. Sometimes the *antagonist*, the villain develops from the devils of medieval *mystery plays*, through the *Vices* of *morality plays*, into the megalomaniacs of *Elizabethan drama* such as Shakespeare's Richard III and *Marlowe*'s Tamburlaine. There are many villains in *revenge tragedy* and later in Victorian *melodrama*. Satan in *Milton*'s PARADISE LOST is sometimes regarded as the villain of all villains because he brings about the Fall of Man.

villanelle: a *poem* consisting of five *tercets* followed by a *quatrain*, with an interlinking *rhyme scheme* using only two *rhymes*: the first and third line of each tercet rhyme consistently throughout, as does each second line, the final quatrain using the same rhyme as *alternate rhyming couplets* (thus each tercet rhymes aba, and the concluding quatrain abab). This *form* originated in the Middle Ages, and experienced a revival in the mid-20th century, as in *Auden*'s "If I Could Tell You" (1940) and *Dylan Thomas*'s "Do Not Go Gentle into That Good Night" (1952).

virgule: a forward slash indicating foot divisions in a line of *verse*, e.g. "The cur/few tolls/ the knell/ of part/ing day" (the opening line of *Gray*'s "Elegy") indicates the divisions between the five iambic feet. See *meter.*

voice may refer to either:

- the *persona* created by the writer through which a *poem* or a *narrative* is communicated to the reader
- the authorial voice itself that emerges behind the *content.*

The two may sometimes be the same thing; that is, it is clear that the writer himself is speaking directly to the reader, not using a persona to give voice to the content. See *narrator/narrative voice, viewpoint.*

volta: see *turning point.*

vowel rhyme is another term for *assonance.*

Walcott, Derek (b.1930): St. Lucian-born British poet and playwright. He often uses a range of *verse forms* to explore the Caribbean experience, making use of both West Indian and European *traditions*. His plays draw on Creole language and use both *prose* and verse. Notable works include HENRI CHRISTOPHE (1950), IN A GREEN NIGHT (1962), THE CASTAWAY (1965, see *Robinson Crusoe myth*), THE DREAM ON MONEY MOUNTAIN AND OTHER PLAYS (1970), ANOTHER LIFE (1973), COLLECTED POEMS 1948–84 (1986), THE ODYSSEY (1993).

Walker, Alice (b.1944): American novelist, *short story* writer, and poet. She cites her mixed racial background and *Hurston* as important influences in her work. She writes with understanding and passion of women's struggles against racism and sexism, considering herself to be "womanist" rather than feminist. Notable works include IN LOVE AND TROUBLE (1973), REVOLUTIONARY PETUNIAS AND OTHER POEMS (1973), YOU CAN'T KEEP A GOOD WOMAN DOWN (1981), THE COLOR PURPLE (1982, a good example of an *epistolary novel*), HORSES MAKE A LANDSCAPE LOOK MORE BEAUTIFUL (1984), THE TEMPLE OF MY FAMILIAR (1989), POSSESSING THE SECRET OF JOY (1992), THE COMPLETE STORIES (1994), THE LIGHT OF MY FATHER'S SMILE (1998), THE WAY FORWARD IS WITH A BROKEN HEART (2001).

Walpole, Horace (1717–97): English novelist, editor, and writer of *verse drama*, whose literary fame rests largely on his detailed and fascinating letters. It is clear that his letters were written with an eye to publication and posterity, and over 4,000 of them have been gathered together in the 48-volume Yale edition (1939–83). He was a friend and editor of *Gray*. The rebuilding of his house in the gothic style encouraged the gothic revival, and his *gothic novel* THE CASTLE OF OTRANTO (1764) prefigures the *Romantic* interest in the *genre*. See *Mary Shelley, Beckford.*

Walsh, Jill Paton (b.1937): English novelist and children's writer. She often uses historical *settings*, and some of her books are *detective fiction*. Notable works include FAREWELL GREAT KING (1972), THE EMPEROR'S WINDING SHEET (1974), A CHANCE CHILD (1978), LAPSING (1986), THE WYNDHAM CASE (1993), A PIECE OF JUSTICE (1995).

war literature refers to *literature* whose chief subject is war, but the term has come to describe mainly *poetry* written as a result of World War I, some of which is patriotic (e.g. *Brooke*), but most of which expresses horror and can be classed as *protest literature* that deglamorizes war (e.g. *Owen, Sassoon*). Other notable writers include *Blunden, Rosenberg, Edward Thomas,* and *Jones,* whose IN PARENTHESIS, *epic* in scale, is a combination of poetry and *prose. Novels, short stories, autobiographies, memoirs, diaries,* escape stories, and many other kinds of literature came out of the war. Two notable memoirs are *Graves's* GOODBYE TO ALL THAT and Sassoon's MEMOIRS OF AN INFANTRY OFFICER, and a notable novel based on his experiences as an ambulance driver in Italy is *Hemingway's* A FAREWELL TO ARMS. Some minor literature came out of World War II, notably from *Alun Lewis, Fuller,* and *Causley.*

war poets: see *war literature.*

Warren, Robert Penn (1905–89): American poet, novelist, *short story* writer, and influential literary critic. His Southern background was a continued influence on his moral *themes*, and he achieved high literary acclaim in *poetry, fiction,* and literary *criticism.* Notable works include the critical works UNDERSTANDING POETRY (1938) and UNDERSTANDING FICTION (1943), the fiction works AT HEAVEN'S GATE (1943), ALL THE KING'S MEN (1946), THE CIRCUS IN THE ATTIC (1948, *stories*), BAND OF ANGELS (1950), and the poetry *collections* PROMISES (1957), SELECTED POEMS: NEW AND OLD (1966), OR ELSE (1974), RUMOR VERIFIED (1981).

Washington, Booker T. (1856–1915): American writer, campaigner, and auto-biographer. A freed slave, he came into conflict with *Du Bois* over his conciliatory approach with regard to his chief concern, the advancement of African-Americans. Notable works include THE FUTURE OF THE AMERICAN NEGRO (1899), his *autobiography* UP FROM SLAVERY (1901), FREDERICK DOUGLASS (1907, a *biography*), THE MAN FARTHEST DOWN (1912).

Wasserstein, Wendy (b.1950): American playwright and essayist. Her innovative plays have been produced off- and off-off-Broadway, and she is sometimes concerned with the world from a particular female perspective. Notable works include UNCOMMON WOMEN AND OTHERS (1975), THE HEIDI CHRONICLES (1989).

Waugh, Evelyn (1903–66): English novelist, *short story* and travel writer, and jour-nalist. His *style* is *witty* and his *satire* often reflects a cynical and trenchant view of his times. Notable works include DECLINE AND FALL (1928), A HANDFUL OF DUST (1934), SCOOP (1938), BRIDESHEAD REVISITED (1945), and the SWORD OF HONOUR *trilogy* (1952–61).

weak ending: in *poetry*, a term to describe an extra unstressed syllable added to the end of a *blank verse* line, sometimes known as "feminine ending." The most famous example is "To be, or not to be: that is the question" (from act III, scene 1 of *Shakepeare*'s HAMLET) where repeated weak endings in the lines that follow generate a sense of Hamlet's hesitancy as he tries to make sense of his situation. See also *meter.*

Webb, Mary (1881–1927): English novelist, *short story* writer, and poet, whose passionate rustic *romances* were famously parodied by *Gibbons* in COLD COMFORT FARM. Notable works include GONE TO EARTH (1917) and PRECIOUS BANE (1924), which has some emotional power and is evocative of the Shropshire landscape.

Webster, John (?1579–1632): English playwright. Some critics consider his two great *tragedies*, THE WHITE DEVIL (1612) and, especially, THE DUCHESS OF MALFI (?1614), to be the best plays of the period after those of *Shakespeare.* One of his hall-marks is the use of striking and often contrasting *imagery*, and a powerful sense of mortality. He collaborated with several other playwrights of the period.

Welch, James B. (b.1940): Native American novelist and poet. He sees himself as more in the general novelist *tradition* than as a Native American storyteller, but his work has highlighted the experience of Native Americans in modern American society. Notable works include RIDING THE EARTH BOY 40 (1971), WINTER IN THE BLOOD (1974), THE DEATH OF JIM LONEY (1979), FOOL'S CROW (1986).

well-made play: a neatly constructed play, e.g. by such as *Rattigan.* By the 1950s the term was used by the *angry young men* and others as an expression of contempt, implying that such plays were mechanical in *plot*, and superficial and bland in subject matter.

Wells, H.G. (1866–1946): English novelist, *short story* writer, and critic. His prolific output varies from comic *novels* inspired by his youth such as LOVE AND MR. LEWISHAM (1900), KIPPS (1905), TONO-BUNGAY (1908), and THE HISTORY OF MR. POLLY (1910) to *science fiction* (a *genre* upon which he had a considerable influence) such as THE INVISIBLE MAN (1897). His later writings, often socialist in *tone* and some of which may be classed as *novels of ideas*, become increasingly pessimistic with warnings of political and scientific doom. Other notable works include THE TIME MACHINE (1895), THE WAR OF THE WORLDS (1898).

Welty, Eudora (1909–2001): American *short story* writer and novelist with a particular interest in the past of the Southern states. Notable works include THE ROBBER BRIDEGROOM (1942), DELTA WEDDING (1946), LOSING BATTLES (1970), THE OPTIMIST'S DAUGHTER (1972), COLLECTED STORIES (1980).

Wendt, Albert (b.1939): West Samoan novelist, *short story* writer, literary critic, and poet whose works explore the diversity of Polynesian culture. Notable works include LEAVES OF THE BANYAN TREE (1979), BLACK RAINBOW (1992).

Wertenbaker, Timberlake (b.1951): British/American playwright and translator. Predominant *themes* in her work are a belief in the power of the creative *imagination* to enhance the lives of all people, not just artists; and concern for the position of women in male-dominated societies. Notable works include OUR COUNTRY'S GOOD (1988, adapted for the stage from *Keneally*'s *novel* THE PLAYMAKER).

Wesker, Arnold (b.1932): English playwright, essayist, and autobiographer. Much of his early work is committed to the idea of popularizing culture and the creation of a socialist *utopia*; more recent work, while retaining its leftwing *tone*, is broader in scope and less obviously *didactic*. Notable works include CHICKEN SOUP WITH BARLEY (1958), ROOTS (1959), I'M TALKING ABOUT JERUSALEM (1960), CHIPS WITH EVERYTHING (1962), THE FOUR SEASONS (1965), THE OLD ONES (1972), LOVE LETTERS ON BLUE PAPER (1974, *stories*), THE MERCHANT (1976, a reworking of aspects of *Shakespeare*'s THE MERCHANT OF VENICE).

West, Nathanael (1903–40): American novelist and screenwriter who focuses upon the illusions and emptiness of contemporary American life. Notable works include MISS LONELYHEARTS (1933), A COOL MILLION: THE DISMANTLING OF LEMUEL PITKIN (1934), THE DAY OF THE LOCUST (1939).

Wharton, Edith (1862–1937): American novelist, *short story* writer, poet, and travel writer. She was much influenced by her close friendship with *Henry James*, with whom she shared an interest in *witty* and *satiric* observation of the difference between American and European "tribal behavior," as she called social customs. She has been increasingly regarded as important in the development of the modern American *novel*. Notable works include THE HOUSE OF MIRTH (1905), ETHAN FROME (1911), THE CUSTOM OF THE COUNTRY (1913), XINGU AND OTHER STORIES (1916), THE AGE OF INNOCENCE (1920).

White, Antonia (1899–1979): English novelist, *short story* writer, essayist, diarist, and translator. Much of her writing is autobiographical, concerning such matters as her experiences of mental instability, relationships with men, and loss and regaining of her Catholic faith. Notable works include Frost in May (1933), The Lost Traveller (1950), The Sugar House (1952), Beyond the Glass (1954), As Once in May (1983), Diaries (1991, 1992).

White, E.B. (1899–1985): American essayist, journalist, literary critic, and children's writer who was associated with the New Yorker magazine for most of his working life. Notable works include Is Sex Necessary? (1929, in collaboration with *Thurber*), and the children's *classics* Stuart Little (1945) and Charlotte's Web (1952).

White, Gilbert (1720–93): English naturalist and diarist whose Natural History and Antiquities of Selbourne (1788–89), lovingly describing the nature and wildlife of his native place, is highly regarded for its combination of scientific content and *lyrical* literary charm.

White, Patrick (1912–90): Australian novelist, playwright, poet, *short story* writer, and essayist. Influenced by German *Romanticism* and showing a persistent interest in the Australian landscape, he is considered to be one of Australia's finest novelists and playwrights. Notable works include The Tree of Man (1955), Voss (1957), Riders in the Chariot (1961), A Season at Sarsaparilla (1962).

Whiting, John (1917–63): English playwright, *drama* critic, and essayist. His plays often powerfully portray spiritual struggles in a *style* that was ahead of its time and not always appreciated by critics or the theater-going public. Notable works include A Penny for a Song (1951), Saint's Day (1951), Marching Song (1954), The Devils (1961).

Whitman, Walt (1819–92): American poet, essayist, and journalist. He created a distinctively American *literature* through his *free verse*, written in everyday language and celebrating the extensiveness of his country, its landscape, and its people, while also considering the influences of the Civil War, and the importance of human sexuality. His masterpiece was the ongoing *verse collection*, Leaves of Grass, first published in 1855 and revised and expanded several times afterward until 1891–92. Other notable works include Drum-Taps (1865), Sequel to Drum-Taps (1865), Memoranda During the War (1876), November Boughs (1888).

Whittier, John Greenleaf (1807–92): American poet, essayist, and antislavery campaigner who was one of the most widely read and respected poets of his day. Although less popular now, he is still admired for his descriptive, evocative *verse*, his sensitive use of folk and *ballad themes*, and his consistent championing of social justice and basic moral values, much of which sprang from his Quaker faith. Notable works include "Ichabod" (1850), "Maud Muller" (1854), "Telling the Bees" (1858), Snow-Bound (1866).

whodunnit: ("who did it?") a *thriller* that depends upon *suspense* as regards who committed a crime.

Wilde, Oscar (1845–1900): Irish playwright, novelist, essayist, poet, and *short story* writer. He is associated with the aesthetic movement (see *aestheticism*) and was famous for his *wit*, which was often carefully studied and not as spontaneous as he pretended. His plays in the *comedy of manners tradition* were hugely successful and have remained popular. He died in poverty, having spent two years in jail after he was convicted of homosexuality in a notorious trial. Notable works include THE HAPPY PRINCE AND OTHER TALES (1888), THE PICTURE OF DORIAN GRAY (1890), LADY WINDERMERE'S FAN (1892), A WOMAN OF NO IMPORTANCE (1893), AN IDEAL HUSBAND (1895), THE IMPORTANCE OF BEING EARNEST (1895), THE BALLAD OF READING GAOL (1898).

Wilder, Thornton (1897–1975): American novelist and playwright. His plays sometimes blend *realism* with *expressionism*, and his priority is the depiction of psychological truth rather than *naturalistic* presentation. Notable works include THE BRIDGE OF SAN LUIS REY (1927), HEAVEN'S MY DESTINATION (1934), OUR TOWN (1938), THE SKIN OF OUR TEETH (1942), THE MATCHMAKER (a revised version of THE MERCHANT OF YONKERS, 1938, 1954, later adapted as the musical HELLO DOLLY).

Williams, Raymond (1921–88): Welsh critic and novelist. An influential figure in *Marxist criticism* of *literature*, he was concerned with literature's place alongside other media and means of communication within culture and society as a whole. Notable works include CULTURE AND SOCIETY, 1780–1950 (1958), THE ENGLISH NOVEL FROM DICKENS TO LAWRENCE (1970), MARXISM AND LITERATURE (1977).

Williams, Tennessee (1911–83): American playwright, novelist, and *short story* writer. He explores human feelings and desires with understanding and *sympathy*, often through *symbolism* and *expressionism*. Some of his writing examines the characteristics and prejudices of the deep South and its culture. Notable works include THE GLASS MENAGERIE (1944), A STREETCAR NAMED DESIRE (1947), THE ROSE TATTOO (1951), and CAT ON A HOT TIN ROOF (1955).

Williams, William Carlos (1883–1963): American poet, novelist, and *short story* writer. Always an experimenter, he wrote *poems* ranging from the minimalist to the long, from *imagist* through *objectivist* to *modernist* (he has been described as a master of *modernism*). However *free* his *verse* may appear, *rhythm* is always an important element. He is a great observer of ordinary everyday events and things. Notable works include SPRING AND ALL (1923), PATERSON (1946–63), PICTURES FROM BRUEGHEL AND OTHER POEMS (1962), COLLECTED POEMS (2001, edited by Litz and MacGowan).

Williamson, David (b.1942): Australian playwright and screenwriter. He is a *naturalistic* writer whose *witty*, observant, and often *satirical* plays of Australian life have contributed to Australia's "New Wave" of writers. Notable works include THE COMING OF THE STORK (1970), DON'S PARTY (1971), THE CLUB (1977), TRAVELLING NORTH (1979), COLLECTED PLAYS (1986 and 1994, in two volumes).

Wilmot, John (2nd Earl of Rochester, 1647–80): English poet. An intellectual libertine, described variously as *metaphysical* and one of the first *Augustans*, he wrote *poems* that are *witty*, *satirical*, scurrilous, skeptical, and/or bluntly *pornographic*. Notable works include A SATIRE AGAINST REASON AND MANKIND (1679).

Wilson, A.N. (b.1950): English novelist, biographer, and literary critic. His *tragicomic stories* often explore religious beliefs and human dilemmas, at times with slightly caustic *wit*, at others with gentle *satire*. Notable works include THE SWEETS OF PIMLICO (1977), THE HEALING ART (1980), WHO WAS OSWALD FISH? (1981), WISE VIRGIN (1982), PENFRIENDS FROM PORLOCK (1988), THE VICAR OF SORROWS (1993).

Wilson, Angus (1913–91): English novelist, *short story* writer, and critic. Through various *narrative techniques* he explores a range of human affairs with *wit* and sharp, sometimes *satiric*, observation. Notable works include THE WRONG SET (1949), SUCH DARLING DODOS (1950), HEMLOCK AND AFTER (1952), ANGLO-SAXON ATTITUDES (1956), NO LAUGHING MATTER (1967), AS IF BY MAGIC (1973), SETTING THE WORLD ON FIRE (1980).

Winterson, Jeanette (b.1959): English novelist. Among other *themes* she explores feminism and lesbianism, employing *magic realism* and various *narrative devices*. Notable works include BOATING FOR BEGINNERS (1985), ORANGES ARE NOT THE ONLY FRUIT (1985), SEXING THE CHERRY (1989), ART AND LIES (1994).

Winton, Tim (b.1960): Australian novelist, *short story* writer, and children's writer. He writes with compassion of ordinary people in small Western Australian communities, and of the land and sea by which they live. Notable works include AN OPEN SWIMMER (1982), SHALLOWS (1984), CLOUDSTREET (1991), THE RIDERS (1995).

wit has come to describe an intelligent, clever, neat, and usually humorous way of putting a point. Among poets, *Chaucer* and *Pope* have been noted for their wit, and *metaphysical* poets such as *Donne* and *Marvell* are noted for their ability to combine surprising verbal dexterity (that is, wit) with seriousness. *Hazlitt* rated wit as artificial and inferior to the naturalness of *imagination*. Broad, unsubtle verbal *humor* does not count as wit.

witty: see *wit*.

Wodehouse, P.G. (1881–1975): English novelist, *short story* writer, and playwright. His output was prolific. He characteristically uses light, genteel *humor* and *romance*, and he is now best known for the creation of the resourceful butler Jeeves and his master Bertie Wooster. Notable works include THE INIMITABLE JEEVES (1923), CARRY ON, JEEVES (1925), BLANDINGS CASTLE (1935), THE CODE OF THE WOOSTERS (1938).

Wolfe, Thomas (1900–38): American novelist, *short story* writer, and playwright. His greatest work is the autobiographical *novel* LOOK HOMEWARD, ANGEL (1929), which uses a highly personal, intensely lyrical, and frequently humorous *style* to chronicle the young life and aspirations of Eugene Grant, a thinly disguised version of the writer himself. Despite criticism for self-absorption, Wolfe's portrayal of an individual's search for the essence of the American ideal is reminiscent of *Whitman*. Other notable works include the sequels OF TIME AND THE RIVER (1935), THE WEB AND THE ROCK (1939), YOU CAN'T GO HOME AGAIN (1940).

Wolfe, Tom (b.1930): American novelist and journalist. He has been a foremost proponent of *new journalism*, which he once claimed "would wipe out the novel as literature's main event" – but this did not stop him writing novels. Notable works include the *essay collections* THE KANDY-KOLORED TANGERINE FLAKE STREAMLINE BABY (1965) and THE PUMPHOUSE GANG (1968), the account of the 1960s drug culture, THE ELECTRIC KOOL-AID ACID TEST (1968), and the *novel* THE BONFIRE OF THE VANITIES (1987).

Wolff, Tobias (b.1945): American *short story* writer identified with the so-called "*dirty realism*" style. Notable works include IN THE GARDEN OF THE NORTH AMERICAN MARTYRS (1981), THE BARRACKS THIEF (1984), BACK IN THE WORLD (1985).

Woolf, Virginia (1882–1941): English novelist, essayist, diarist, biographer, and literary critic. A leading member of the *Bloomsbury group,* she is identified with the development of the *stream of consciousness technique*. One of the 20th century's major experimental novelists, she is recognized as a leading exponent of *modernism* and an important figure in the advance of *feminist criticism*. Notable works include JACOB'S ROOM (1922), MRS. DALLOWAY (1925), TO THE LIGHTHOUSE (1927), ORLANDO (1928), A ROOM OF ONE'S OWN (1929), THE WAVES (1931).

Wordsworth, Dorothy (1771–1855) was a significant literary influence upon her brother William, with whom she lived most of her life. She did not write for her publication, but it is clear that *William Wordsworth* drew extensively on her *diaries* as a literary *source*, most famously in the composition of his *poem* "I Wandered Lonely as a Cloud" (1807). Notable works include her GRASMERE JOURNAL (1896, 1904, edited by W. Knight) which covers the period 1800–03.

Wordsworth, William (1770–1850): English poet and leading figure in the development of English *Romanticism*. The political radicalism of his youth (he thought it "very heaven to be alive" during the French Revolution) and the conservatism of his age are both reflected in his writings. He did much to change the course of English *poetry* in two crucial ways:

- he rejected the *poetic diction* of *neoclassicism* and aimed to write in "the ordinary language of ordinary men"
- he wrote about everyday things and people he saw around him.

He is closely associated with the topography and people of his native Lake District where he spent most of his life. Many critics believe that his best work was written before 1810, after which he reworked much of his early poetry, often to its disadvantage. Notable works include LYRICAL BALLADS (1798, in collaboration with *Coleridge*), including "Tintern Abbey," THE PRELUDE (written from 1798; published 1850), "Ode: Intimations of Immortality from Recollections of Early Childhood" (1807), "Resolution and Independence" (1807), THE EXCURSION (1814).

Wright, Judith (b.1915): Australian poet and essayist. Her passionate concern for wildlife, the environment, and the Aboriginal community is reflected in her *poetry*. Notable works include THE MOVING IMAGE (1946), ALIVE (1973), THE CRY FOR THE DEAD (1981).

Wright, Kit (b.1944): English poet and children's writer. A writer of light comic *verse*, he shows inventiveness and tenderness in his work. Notable works include THE BEAR LOOKED OVER THE MOUNTAIN (1977), BUMP-STARTING THE HEARSE (1983), GREAT SNAKES (1995).

Wright, Richard (1908–60): American novelist, social critic, *short story* writer, poet, and essayist. One of the most influential African-American writers of the 20th century, he explored the social causes of racism and oppression generally, especially in the Southern states. Notable works include NATIVE SON (1940), BLACK BOY (1945, an *autobiography*), THE OUTSIDER (1953), BLACK POWER (1954), WHITE MAN, LISTEN! (1957).

writerly: see *readerly/writerly*. See also *authorial intention/authorial attitude, intentional fallacy, poststructuralism*.

Wyatt, Thomas (1503–42): English poet, courtier, and diplomat who was much influenced by *Petrarch*, translating his *verse* and, with *Surrey*, adapting the *sonnet* to

English usage, developing the typical final *rhyming couplet.* He experimented with other new *form*s in English such as *terza rima.* Notable works include "They Flee from Me," "My Lute Awake!," "Stand Whoso List," "Whoso List to Hunt," all published after his death in SONGS AND SONNETS (1557), known as TOTTEL'S MISCELLANY, after the printer Richard Tottel.

Wycherley, William (1641–1715): English poet and playwright. His plays contain sharp observation of the manners of the period, especially sexual morality and marriage *convention*s. He is best known for THE COUNTRY-WIFE (1675). See also *comedy of manners* and *Restoration comedy.*

Wyndham, John (1903–69): English novelist and *short story* writer of *science fiction.* Influenced by *Wells* and Jules Verne (1828–1905), he writes what he called "logical *fantasy:*" that is, convincingly vivid stories about people's struggles with terrifying and bizarre situations. Notable works include THE DAY OF THE TRIFFIDS (1951), THE KRAKEN WAKES (1953), THE CHRYSALIDS (1955), THE MIDWICH CUCKOOS (1957), THE TROUBLE WITH LICHEN (1960), CONSIDER HER WAYS AND OTHERS (1961).